LIVERPOOL FC
THE OFFICIAL GUIDE
2009

Sport Media
A Trinity Mirror Business

HONOURS

LEAGUE CHAMPIONSHIP (18)
1900/01, 1905/06, 1921/22, 1922/23, 1946/47, 1963/64, 1965/66, 1972/73, 1975/76, 1976/77, 1978/79, 1979/80, 1981/82, 1982/83, 1983/84, 1985/86, 1987/88, 1989/90

DIVISION TWO WINNERS (4)
1893/94, 1895/96, 1904/05, 1961/62

FA CUP WINNERS (7)
1964/65, 1973/74, 1985/86, 1988/89, 1991/92, 2000/01, 2005/06

LEAGUE CUP WINNERS (7)
1980/81, 1981/82, 1982/83, 1983/84, 1994/95, 2000/01, 2002/03

EUROPEAN CUP/UEFA CHAMPIONS LEAGUE WINNERS (5)
1976/77, 1977/78, 1980/81, 1983/84, 2004/05

UEFA CUP WINNERS (3)
1972/73, 1975/76, 2000/01

EUROPEAN SUPER CUP WINNERS (3)
1977/78, 2001/02, 2005/06

FA CHARITY SHIELD WINNERS/FA COMMUNITY SHIELD WINNERS (10)
1966, 1974, 1976, 1979, 1980, 1982, 1988, 1989, 2001, 2006

FA CHARITY SHIELD WINNERS/FA COMMUNITY SHIELD SHARED (5)
1964, 1965, 1977, 1986, 1990

SCREEN SPORT SUPER CUP WINNERS (1)
1986/87

LANCASHIRE LEAGUE WINNERS (1)
1892/93

INTRODUCTION

Welcome to the fourth edition of Liverpool FC : The Official Guide, a publication that has continued to develop since its inception. A bible of club information for Liverpudlians, we strive to maintain the quality and variety of previous yearbooks, while also providing the essential club information for you, the fans.

As in previous years, we are fortunate to have the services of Liverpool experts Dave Ball and Ged Rea, who have generated fresh content which we hope you will find relevant and informative. With another successful campaign behind us, the duo take the opportunity to reflect on the achievements of 2007/08 with more club records broken by the Reds' squad - efforts which are reflected within these pages.

Again we hope you will find the order of contents to your liking, with club records and top flight landmarks presented in latter sections. Key elements are also retained, such as the review of the season, top 10 moments plus the club's continued success in European competition - presented within the 'European Progress' chapter.

Fresh content also includes 'Summer Diary 2008', a reminder of what has gone on at the club during the close season while the success of the Reds' Spanish contingent at Euro 2008 is recognised as we look back on Liverpool players who have appeared for their countries in the European Championships. There are also FA Cup and League Cup facts and statistics, which appear alongside the cup results of previous years - which have been slightly altered in this edition.

Our aim is to continue to produce this publication in order to act as a permanent record, a point of reference which can solve numerous pub quiz questions as well as providing the most accurate information possible - at the time of going to press. We hope you enjoy what is on offer.

WRITERS

Ged Rea and Dave Ball are Liverpool FC's official statisticians. Ged's Liverpool FC records are second-to-none, while Dave is a key researcher for long-running BBC TV show *A Question of Sport*. James Cleary has played a major role in writing and researching key information.

Executive Editor: KEN ROGERS Editor: STEVE HANRAHAN
Art Editor: RICK COOKE Production Editor: PAUL DOVE
Sub Editors: JAMES CLEARY, ROY GILFOYLE
Sales and Marketing Manager: ELIZABETH MORGAN
Design Team: BARRY PARKER, COLIN SUMPTER, GLEN HIND, LEE ASHUN, ALISON GILLILAND,
JAMIE DUNMORE, JAMES KENYON, LISA CRITCHLEY
Liverpool FC Writers: CHRIS McLOUGHLIN, DAVID RANDLES, GAVIN KIRK, JOHN HYNES

ISBN 978 1 9052 66654
Printed and finished by Scotprint, Haddington, Scotland

Sport Media
A Trinity Mirror Business

CLUB TELEPHONE NUMBERS

Main Switchboard	0151 263 2361
Customer Services	0844 844 2005
International callers	0044 870 220 2345
Ticket Office	0844 844 0844
Mail Order Hotline (UK)	0844 800 4239
International Mail Order Hotline	+ 44 1386 852035
Club Store (Anfield)	0151 263 1760
Club Store (Williamson Square - City Centre)	0151 330 3077
Club Store (Liverpool One - City Centre)	0151 709 4345
Club Store (Chester)	01244 344608
Conference and Banqueting (for your events at Anfield)	0151 263 7744
Corporate Sales	0151 263 9199
Development Association	0151 263 6391
Community Department	0151 264 2316
Museum & Tour Centre	0151 260 6677
Membership Department	0844 499 3000
Public Relations (including all charity requests)	0151 260 1433

BECOME A MEMBER OF THE **OFFICIAL LIVERPOOL FC MEMBERSHIP**
To join, please call: 0844 499 3000
International: +44 151 261 1444

SUBSCRIBE TO THE OFFICIAL **LFC PROGRAMME AND WEEKLY MAGAZINE**
To take out a subscription please call: 0845 1430001

LIVE AND BREATHE LFC 24/7
Official Club Media

The official club website **www.liverpoolfc.tv** - first for news, views, match reports, interviews, statistics, history and more. PLUS this season, watch every Premier League goal for FREE!

e-Season Ticket – Goals, highlights, video interviews, press conferences, every reserve match LIVE, Kop classics + LIVE commentary of every Reds' game...100% un-biased!

The Official Club TV Channel 'LFC TV' – Broadcast every day from the heart of your club. Sky channel 434, Virgin channel 544 and simulcast globally on e-Season Ticket at **www.liverpoolfc.tv**

LFC Mobile Site – wap.liverpoolfc.tv – Take us with you wherever you go!

Mobilezone – Official SMS Alerts (choose from goals, news, match, tickets), LFC downloads, player animations, videos, games, etc. Visit **www.liverpoolfc.tv/mobilezone**

LFC Save & Support Account with Britannia
For more information visit **britannia.co.uk/lfc**, call 0800 915 0503 or visit any Britannia branch.

Liverpool FC Credit Card in Association with MBNA
For more information call 0800 776 262.

CONTENTS

THE BOSS   16-25

A season-by-season analysis of Rafael Benitez's record as Liverpool manager, plus a look at the men in charge and their success after 150 games as boss, comparisions with Sir Alex Ferguson and Arsene Wenger plus Rafa's all-time European record.

THE PLAYERS 08/09   26-49

Includes the most accurate statistics of all first-team players (up to and including August 31 2008), plus analysis, fixtures, results and information related to the club's reserves, academy and ladies' teams. An added bonus is the addition of a Summer Diary 2008.

THE TOP 10 MOMENTS 07/08   50-57

The very best photos from the previous campaign highlighting the top moments of 07/08 - as voted for by our award-winning team of writers.

EUROPEAN PROGRESS   58-93

An in-depth look at the Reds' run to the UEFA Champions League semi-finals, plus the club's full record in European competition, club and player records.

THE 2007/08 SEASON   94-121

A month-by-month review of the campaign, including landmarks, quotes, facts and statistics - plus the club's man of the season.

THE TOP FLIGHT   122-141

Club records created in the Football League and Premier League including appearances, goals, sendings off - plus an A-Z of Liverpool's Premier League players.

THE CUPS   142-157

All the major and minor domestic cup competition records, including FA Cup and League Cup facts and statistics.

THE RECORDS   158-177

Including appearances, goals, oldest/youngest players, landmarks, clean sheets, internationals and a look at Liverpool players in the European Championship finals.

OPPOSITION   178-189

Liverpool's opponents in the top flight during 2008/09, including statistics and stadium guides.

CLUB ESSENTIALS   190-208

All the off-field information you need, from buying tickets, website information and stadium and museum tours, to the initiatives undertaken by LFC in the Community.

FOREWORD

Many books have been written about Liverpool Football Club which have charted the history and chronicled the records, but we hope to concentrate on the facts and statistics associated with the most successful club in England.

The purpose of this book, and the preceding three in the series, is not only to plug that gap, but possibly to help solve some arguments and provoke debate among Reds fans in homes, pubs and offices, as well as at the match. It is both for the average fan and the serious quiz buff. It is almost impossible to include all the trivia and statistics relating to the club in any one book. This is partly due to space and also to the fact that not all records are complete. Over the years we will attempt to include as much detail as possible.

Football, like cricket, is now very much statistics based and are the staple diet of many commentators and journalists. We are constantly asked to provide such material throughout the season. Naturally we are indebted to many organisations, especially the Association of Football Statisticians, which has grown out of all proportion over the last 20 years. There is now of course a whole plethora of material available on the internet. However, a lot of this has not been thoroughly researched. We are particularly grateful to the doyen of statisticians, Eric Doig, who has spent much of his life researching the early days of the club.

We are often asked, what is the relevance of such statistics? Well, they are of course helpful in placing both the club and players in context with others both in the past and the present. For older supporters there is always the question of comparing players of their generation with those of today – statistics can help in this respect. We can also use statistics for comparing managers – Shankly with Paisley, Houllier with Benitez, etc.

A lot of attention is paid to the Premier League, and rightly so, as there is a whole generation who have lived through nothing else. But despite what a lot of the media seem to intimate, football has been part and parcel of the social fabric of this country for more than 120 years. Liverpool's domination of England and Europe over a 30-year period saw records broken every season and deserves due respect. Therefore, as with the previous yearbooks, both eras are thoroughly covered, as well as everything you need to know about the club.

Ged Rea & Dave Ball

KEY DATES 2008/09

(Dates are subject to change)

August 2008

1	UEFA Champions League third qualifying round draw
12/13	UEFA Champions League third qualifying round, first leg
16	Barclays Premier League kick-off
26/27	UEFA Champions League third qualifying round, second leg
28	UEFA Champions League group stage draw
29	UEFA Cup first-round draw

September 2008

1	Transfer window closes
6	Andorra v England, World Cup qualifier (Barcelona)
10	Croatia v England, World Cup qualifier (Zagreb)
16/17	UEFA Champions League group stage matchday 1
18	UEFA Cup first round, first leg
23/24	Carling Cup third round
30	UEFA Champions League group stage matchday 2

October 2008

1	UEFA Champions League group stage matchday 2
2	UEFA Cup first round, second leg
7	UEFA Cup group stage draw
11	England v Kazakhstan, World Cup qualifier (Wembley Stadium, London)
15	Belarus v England, World Cup qualifier (Minsk)
21/22	UEFA Champions League group stage matchday 3
23	UEFA Cup group stage matchday 1

November 2008

4/5	UEFA Champions League group stage matchday 4
6	UEFA Cup group stage matchday 2
11/12	Carling Cup fourth round
19	Germany v England, international friendly (Berlin)
25/26	UEFA Champions League group stage matchday 5
27	UEFA Cup group stage matchday 3

December 2008

2/3	Carling Cup quarter-finals
3/4	UEFA Cup group stage matchday 4
9/10	UEFA Champions League group stage matchday 6
17/18	UEFA Cup group stage matchday 5
19	UEFA Champions League first knockout round draw
19	UEFA Cup round of 32 & round of 16 draw
31	Transfer window re-opens

KEY DATES 2008/09

(Dates are subject to change)

January 2009

3/4	FA Cup third round
6/7	Carling Cup semi-finals, first leg
20/21	Carling Cup semi-finals, second leg
24/25	FA Cup fourth round
31	Transfer window closes

February 2009

14/15	FA Cup fifth round
18/19	UEFA Cup round of 32, first leg
24/25	UEFA Champions League first knockout round, first leg
26	UEFA Cup round of 32, second leg

March 2009

1	Carling Cup Final (Wembley Stadium, London)
7/8	FA Cup quarter-finals
10/11	UEFA Champions League first knockout round, second leg
12	UEFA Cup round of 16, first leg
18/19	UEFA Cup round of 16, second leg
20	UEFA Champions League quarter-finals and semi-finals draw
20	UEFA Cup quarter-finals and semi-finals draw

April 2009

1	England v Ukraine, World Cup qualifier (Wembley Stadium, London)
7/8	UEFA Champions League quarter-finals, first leg
9	UEFA Cup quarter-finals, first leg
14/15	UEFA Champions League quarter-finals, second leg
16	UEFA Cup quarter-finals, second leg
18/19	FA Cup semi-finals
28/29	UEFA Champions League semi-finals, first leg
30	UEFA Cup semi-finals, first leg

May 2009

5/6	UEFA Champions League semi-finals, second leg
7	UEFA Cup semi-finals, second leg
20	UEFA Cup Final (Sukru Saracoglu Stadium, Istanbul, Turkey)
24	Barclays Premier League final day
27	UEFA Champions League Final (Stadio Olimpico, Rome, Italy)
30	FA Cup Final (Wembley Stadium, London)

June 2009

6	Kazakhstan v England, World Cup qualifier (Almaty)
10	England v Andorra, World Cup qualifier (Wembley Stadium, London)

FIXTURE LIST 2008/09

August 2008

13	Standard Liege C. LGE Q. 1	(A)	-	8.05pm
16	Sunderland	(A)	-	5.30pm
23	Middlesbrough	(H)	-	3pm
27	Standard Liege C. LGE Q. 2	(H)	-	8.05pm
31	Aston Villa	(A)	-	4pm

September 2008

13	Manchester United	(H)	-	12.45pm
16	Marseille C. LGE GROUP D	(A)	-	7.45pm
20	Stoke City	(H)	-	3pm
23	Crewe Alexandra C. CUP 3	(H)	-	8pm
27	Everton	(A)	-	12.45pm

October 2008

1	PSV Eindhoven C. LGE G. D	(H)	-	7.45pm
5	Manchester City	(A)	-	3pm
18	Wigan Athletic	(H)	-	3pm
22	Atletico Madrid C. LGE G. D	(A)	-	7.45pm
26	Chelsea	(A)	-	1.30pm
29	Portsmouth	(H)	-	8pm

November 2008

1	Tottenham Hotspur	(A)	-	5.30pm
4	Atletico Madrid C. LGE G. D	(H)	-	7.45pm
8	West Bromwich Albion	(H)	-	5.30pm
11/12	CARLING CUP FOURTH ROUND			
15	Bolton Wanderers	(A)	-	12.45pm
22	Fulham	(H)	-	3pm
26	Marseille C. LGE GROUP D	(H)	-	7.45pm

December 2008

1	West Ham United	(H)	-	8pm
2/3	CARLING CUP QUARTER-FINALS			
6	Blackburn Rovers	(A)	-	3pm
9	PSV Eindhoven C. LGE G. D	(A)	-	7.45pm
13	Hull City	(H)	-	3pm
20	Arsenal	(A)	-	3pm
26	Bolton Wanderers	(H)	-	3pm
28	Newcastle United	(A)	-	2pm

January 2009

3/4	FA CUP THIRD ROUND			
6/7	CARLING CUP SEMI-FINALS, FIRST LEG			
10	Stoke City	(A)	-	3pm

FIXTURE LIST 2008/09

January 2009

17	Everton	(H)	-	TBC
20/21	CARLING CUP SEMI-FINALS, SECOND LEG			
24/25	FA CUP FOURTH ROUND			
27	Wigan Athletic	(A)	-	TBC
31	Chelsea	(H)	-	TBC

February 2009

7	Portsmouth	(A)	-	TBC
14/15	FA CUP FIFTH ROUND			
21	Manchester City	(H)	-	TBC
24/25	UEFA CHAMPIONS LEAGUE FIRST KNOCKOUT ROUND, FIRST LEG			
28	Middlesbrough	(A)	-	TBC

March 2009

1	CARLING CUP FINAL			
4	Sunderland	(H)	-	TBC
7/8	FA CUP QUARTER-FINALS			
10/11	UEFA CHAMPIONS LEAGUE FIRST KNOCKOUT ROUND, SECOND LEG			
14	Manchester United	(A)	-	TBC
21	Aston Villa	(H)	-	TBC

April 2009

4	Fulham	(A)	-	TBC
7/8	UEFA CHAMPIONS LEAGUE QUARTER-FINALS, FIRST LEG			
11	Blackburn Rovers	(H)	-	TBC
14/15	UEFA CHAMPIONS LEAGUE QUARTER-FINALS, SECOND LEG			
18	Arsenal	(H)	-	TBC
18/19	FA CUP SEMI-FINALS			
25	Hull City	(A)	-	TBC
28/29	UEFA CHAMPIONS LEAGUE SEMI-FINALS, FIRST LEG			

May 2009

2	Newcastle United	(H)	-	TBC
5/6	UEFA CHAMPIONS LEAGUE SEMI-FINALS, SECOND LEG			
9	West Ham United	(A)	-	TBC
16	West Bromwich Albion	(A)	-	TBC
20	UEFA CUP FINAL			
24	Tottenham Hotspur	(H)	-	TBC
27	UEFA CHAMPIONS LEAGUE FINAL			
30	FA CUP FINAL			

Copyright © The FA Premier League Ltd and The Football League Ltd 2008.
Compiled in association with Atos Origin. All fixtures and kick off times subject to change.
Home UEFA Champions League matches kick off at 7.45pm.
FA Cup and Carling Cup kick off times to be confirmed.
All information correct at time of press - August 2008.

Please note all fixtures, kick-off times and dates are subject to change

ANFIELD PAST AND PRESENT

TOTAL CAPACITY - 45,522

First used in 1884 to house Everton Football Club, the Reds have called Anfield their home since 1892, when the Blues left to move to Goodison Park. Originally owned by John Orrell, fellow brewer and friend John Houlding purchased the ground in 1891, soon after Everton won their first league title. His proposed increase in rent to Everton (some records state a four-fold increase on their original agreement with Orrell) saw the club leave. With an empty ground and no football team, Houlding decided to form his own club - and so Liverpool Football Club were born.
Their first match at Anfield saw a 7-0 victory over Rotherham Town on September 1 1892, with the first Football League match played a year later, the Reds seeing off Lincoln City 4-0 on September 8 1893 in front of an estimated 5,000 spectators.
On its original inauguration in 1884 Anfield housed 20,000. Extensive redevelopment, has seen Anfield hold upwards of 60,000. The ground, which hosted European Championship games in 1996 and is rated a 4-star stadium by UEFA, holds 45,522 – with this figure taking into account the Press and disabled areas and all seating, some of which is not used due to segregation.

THE KOP GRANDSTAND

Built in 1906 after the Reds won the league championship for a second time. It was, of course, named 'The Spion Kop' after a South African hill in Natal which was the scene of a bloody Boer War battle. In 1928 it was rebuilt and a roof was added with the capacity reaching close to 30,000 - the largest covered terrace in the Football League at that time. It was rebuilt in summer 1994 to its current splendour after an emotional 'last stand' against Norwich City at the end of the 1993/94 campaign.

CENTENARY STAND

The original Kemlyn Road Stand incorporated a barrel roof and was fronted by an uncovered paddock. It was demolished in 1963 to make way for a new cantilever stand. In 1992 a second tier was added and the stand was renamed to mark the club's 100th anniversary.

MAIN STAND/PADDOCK

The original structure was erected in the late 19th century, a 3,000-capacity stand with a distinctive red and white tudor style with the club's name in the centre. In 1973 it was redeveloped with a new roof and officially opened by HRH the Duke of Kent. Seats were added to the Paddock in 1980.

ANFIELD ROAD STAND

In 1903 the first Anfield Road stand was built. Once a simple one-tier stand which contained a covered standing enclosure (the roof was first added in 1965), it was demolished to make way for a two-tier development in 1998 – the stand having been originally altered to accomodate multi-coloured seating in the early 1980s.

RECORD ANFIELD ATTENDANCES

HIGHS			LOWS		
Overall:	61,905 v Wolves,	2/2/1952	**Overall:**	1,000 v Loughborough,	07/12/1895
League:	58,757 v Chelsea,	27/12/1949	**FA Cup:**	4,000 v Newton,	29/10/1892
Lge Cup:	50,880 v Notts Forest,	12/2/1980	**Lge Cup:**	9,902 v Brentford,	25/10/1983
Europe:	55,104 v Barcelona,	14/4/1976	**Europe**:	12,021 v Dundalk,	28/09/1982

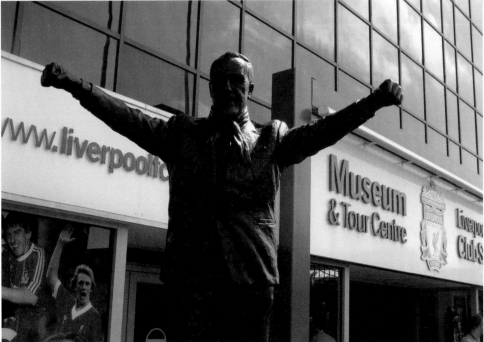

Anfield views - The corner of the Main Stand/Paddock and Kop (top),
and the statue of Bill Shankly outside the Kop

LIVERPOOL'S MANAGERS

The 2008/09 season sees Rafael Benitez enter his fifth full campaign at the Anfield helm, a period which has seen him become one of the most successful and most respected names in the modern era.

Having taken charge on June 16 2004, Benitez led the Reds to the League Cup final in his first season before helping the club secure an astonishing UEFA Champions League final triumph, seeing his side overcome a three-goal half-time deficit before overcoming AC Milan in a penalty shoot-out - arguably the greatest final in the history of the competition.

Subsequent seasons have brought further silverware in the form of the European Super Cup (2005), FA Cup (2006) and FA Community Shield (2006), a UEFA Champions League final and Club World Championship final appearance, plus continued improvement in the Premier League.

Benitez is Liverpool's 16th different full-time manager, the Reds being one of the first clubs in the country to employ a full-time boss when they were formed in 1892 - in the form of John McKenna, although his official title was secretary, not manager, being assisted by WE Barclay.

RAFAEL BENITEZ	**June 2004-Present**
PHIL THOMPSON (caretaker)	October 2001-March 2002
GERARD HOULLIER	November 1998-May 2004
ROY EVANS (joint manager with Gerard Houllier)	July 1998-November 1998
ROY EVANS	January 1994-November 1998
GRAEME SOUNESS	April 1991-January 1994
RONNIE MORAN (caretaker)	February 1991-April 1991
KENNY DALGLISH	May 1985-February 1991
JOE FAGAN	May 1983-May 1985
BOB PAISLEY	July 1974-May 1983
BILL SHANKLY	December 1959-July 1974
PHIL TAYLOR	May 1956-November 1959
DON WELSH	March 1951-May 1956
GEORGE KAY	May 1936-February 1951
GEORGE PATTERSON	February 1928-May 1936
MATT McQUEEN	February 1923-February 1928
DAVID ASHWORTH	December 1919-February 1923
TOM WATSON	August 1896-May 1915
JOHN McKENNA	August 1892-August 1896

RAFAEL BENITEZ'S RECORD

Although the 2007/08 campaign will go down as a trophyless season, the huge impact made by Fernando Torres can be reflected by the club's goals output - by far the Reds' most successful under the current manager. There was a second consecutive fourth-placed finish - improving statistically on the previous season, despite finishing in the same place.

The club also came close to a third UEFA Champions League final appearance in four seasons under Benitez, with memorable wins including defeats of Inter Milan and Arsenal before Chelsea made it third time lucky by winning through in the semi-final.

Unfortunately, domestic cup disappointment continued, with Barnsley shocking an under-strength Liverpool in round five of the FA Cup while Chelsea would go through in the League Cup quarter-finals at Stamford Bridge - the Reds' poor recent record at the ground being a statistic Benitez will be keen to amend in 2008/09.

The following statistics reflect Benitez's record in 2007/08, his season-by-season Liverpool record (including percentage of games won) and his overall record at the club.

BENITEZ RECORD SEASON 2007/2008

	Pld	W	D	L	F	A	Pts
LEAGUE	38	21	13	4	67	28	76
FA CUP	4	2	1	1	12	5	-
LEAGUE CUP	3	2	0	1	6	5	-
CHAMPIONS LEAGUE	14	8	3	3	34	12	-
TOTAL	**59**	**33**	**17**	**9**	**119**	**50**	**-**

BENITEZ AT LIVERPOOL - SEASON-BY-SEASON (ALL COMPETITIONS)

	Pld	W	D	L	F	A	%
SEASON 2004/2005	60	31	10	19	82	56	51.7
SEASON 2005/2006	62	41	10	11	104	44	66.1
SEASON 2006/2007	58	32	10	16	90	52	55.2
SEASON 2007/2008	59	33	17	9	119	50	55.9
TOTAL	**239**	**137**	**47**	**55**	**395**	**202**	**57.3**

BENITEZ'S OVERALL LIVERPOOL RECORD

	Pld	W	D	L	F	A	Pts
LEAGUE	152	83	35	34	233	121	284
FA CUP	12	8	1	3	33	17	-
LEAGUE CUP	13	9	0	4	25	20	-
FA CHARITY SHIELD	1	1	0	0	2	1	-
CHAMPIONS LEAGUE	58	34	11	13	96	41	-
EURO. SUPER CUP	1	1	0	0	3	1	-
CLUB WORLD C'SHIP	2	1	0	1	3	1	-
TOTAL	**239**	**137**	**47**	**55**	**395**	**202**	**-**

* Drawn games ending in a penalty shoot-out victory for Liverpool noted as matches won:
Tottenham Hotspur 1-1 Liverpool, League Cup quarter-final, 2004/05
AC Milan 3-3 Liverpool, UEFA Champions League final, 2005
Liverpool 3-3 West Ham, FA Cup final 2006

LIVERPOOL MANAGER'S LEAGUE RECORD

The 2007/08 saw Rafael Benitez pass the 150 league game mark as Liverpool boss, and the following tables suggest a record comparable with the club's most successful managers - note only the managers who have taken charge of 150 or more league matches are included.

LIVERPOOL MANAGERS - FIRST 150 LEAGUE GAMES							
(First 150 league games only - all divisions, listed chronologically. Note 3 points for a win)							
MANAGER	**Played**	**W**	**D**	**L**	**F**	**A**	**Points**
Tom Watson	150	66	29	55	232	192	227
Matt McQueen	150	58	43	49	214	193	217
George Patterson	150	56	39	55	281	276	207
George Kay	150	54	40	56	243	254	202
Don Welsh	150	44	42	64	226	282	174
Bill Shankly	150	77	33	40	307	195	264
Bob Paisley	150	79	42	29	220	119	279
Kenny Dalglish	150	87	39	24	289	123	300
Roy Evans	150	72	39	39	239	148	255
Gerard Houllier	150	81	35	34	258	142	278
Rafael Benitez	150	81	35	34	230	121	278

HIGHEST-RANKED LIVERPOOL MANAGERS - AFTER 150 LEAGUE GAMES							
(First 150 league games only - all divisions, listed best to worst)							
MANAGER	**Pld**	**W**	**D**	**L**	**F**	**A**	**Points**
Kenny Dalglish	150	87	39	24	289	123	300
Bob Paisley	150	79	42	29	220	119	279
Gerard Houllier	150	81	35	34	258	142	278
Rafael Benitez	150	81	35	34	230	121	278
Bill Shankly	150	77	33	40	307	195	264
Roy Evans	150	72	39	39	239	148	255
Tom Watson	150	66	29	55	232	192	227
Matt McQueen	150	58	43	49	214	193	217
George Patterson	150	56	39	55	281	276	207
George Kay	150	54	40	56	243	254	202
Don Welsh	150	44	42	64	226	282	174

In at number four - Rafael Benitez

LIVERPOOL MANAGER'S LEAGUE RECORD

The comparison can also be made for Liverpool managers who have overseen the club's fortunes in the top division of English football. Again, there are similarities in the fortunes of the respective men, although Don Welsh misses out on a rating, having failed to meet the 150-game criteria in the top flight.

Manager	Played	W	D	L	F	A	Points
LIVERPOOL MANAGERS - FIRST 150 LEAGUE GAMES (First 150 league games in top flight, listed chronologically)							
Tom Watson	150	66	29	55	232	192	227
Matt McQueen	150	58	43	49	214	193	217
George Patterson	150	56	39	55	281	276	207
George Kay	150	54	40	56	243	254	202
Don Welsh	[NEVER REACHED 150 GAMES IN TOP FLIGHT]						
Bill Shankly	150	75	29	46	279	198	254
Bob Paisley	150	79	42	29	220	119	279
Kenny Dalglish	150	87	39	24	289	123	300
Roy Evans	150	72	39	39	239	148	255
Gerard Houllier	150	81	35	34	258	142	278
Rafael Benitez	150	81	35	34	230	121	278

Manager	Played	W	D	L	F	A	Points
HIGHEST-RANKED LIVERPOOL MANAGERS - AFTER 150 LEAGUE GAMES (First 150 league games in top flight, listed best to worst)							
Kenny Dalglish	150	87	39	24	289	123	300
Bob Paisley	150	79	42	29	220	119	279
Gerard Houllier	150	81	35	34	258	142	278
Rafael Benitez	150	81	35	34	230	121	278
Roy Evans	150	72	39	39	239	148	255
Bill Shankly	150	75	29	46	279	198	254
Tom Watson	150	66	29	55	232	192	227
Matt McQueen	150	58	43	49	214	193	217
George Patterson	150	56	39	55	281	276	207
George Kay	150	54	40	56	243	254	202
Don Welsh	[NEVER REACHED 150 GAMES IN TOP FLIGHT]						

Kenny Dalglish - Top of the 150 club

LIVERPOOL MANAGER'S LEAGUE RECORD

Extending the idea of rating Liverpool's managers after 150 top-flight games in charge, the following table ranks two of the most successful bosses of the modern era, Sir Alex Ferguson and Arsene Wenger, against Liverpool managers - with Kenny Dalglish again coming out at the head of the pack.

HIGHEST-RANKED MANAGERS - AFTER 150 LEAGUE GAMES							
(First 150 league games in top flight, listed best to worst - including Ferguson and Wenger)							
Manager	Played	W	D	L	F	A	Points
Kenny Dalglish	150	87	39	24	289	123	300
Arsene Wenger	150	84	39	27	257	125	291
Bob Paisley	150	79	42	29	220	119	279
Gerard Houllier	150	81	35	34	258	142	278
Rafael Benitez	150	81	35	34	230	121	278
Roy Evans	150	72	39	39	239	148	255
Bill Shankly	150	75	29	46	279	198	254
Sir Alex Ferguson	150	63	44	43	205	152	233
Tom Watson	150	66	29	55	232	192	227
Matt McQueen	150	58	43	49	214	193	217
George Patterson	150	56	39	55	281	276	207
George Kay	150	54	40	56	243	254	202
Don Welsh	(NEVER REACHED 150 GAMES IN TOP FLIGHT)						

Paisley and Shankly (opposite) - Above Ferguson in the 150 club

RAFA'S MANAGERIAL RECORD IN EUROPE

Rafael Benitez's most impressive results have often come in European competition, and the following statistics, taking in his time at Valencia and Liverpool, reflect this as he closes in on 100 European games as manager.

VALENCIA - 2001/02 UEFA CUP					
Pld	**W**	**D**	**L**	**F**	**A**
10	5	3	2	20	7

PERFORMANCE Quarter-final stage (beaten 2-1 on aggregate by Inter Milan)
TEAMS BEATEN FC Chernomorets Novorossiysk, Legia Warsaw, Celtic, Servette
WINNERS Feyenoord

VALENCIA - 2002/03 UEFA CHAMPIONS LEAGUE					
Pld	**W**	**D**	**L**	**F**	**A**
14	8	4	2	24	12

PERFORMANCE Quarter-final stage (beaten on away goals by Inter Milan)
OTHER TEAMS FACED Liverpool, Spartak Moscow, FC Basel, Ajax, Arsenal, AS Roma, Inter Milan
WINNERS AC Milan

VALENCIA - 2003/04 UEFA CUP					
Pld	**W**	**D**	**L**	**F**	**A**
13	10	2	1	20	5

PERFORMANCE Winners (beat Marseille 2-0 in Gothenburg)
TEAMS BEATEN AIK, Maccabi Haifa, Besiktas, Genclerbirligi, Bordeaux, Villarreal

LIVERPOOL - 2004/05 UEFA CHAMPIONS LEAGUE					
Pld	**W**	**D**	**L**	**F**	**A**
15	9	3	3	20	10

PERFORMANCE Winners (beat AC Milan 3-2 on penalties after 3-3 draw, in Istanbul)
OTHER TEAMS FACED Grazer AK, AS Monaco, Olympiakos, Deportivo La Coruna, Bayer Leverkusen, Juventus, Chelsea

LIVERPOOL - 2005/06 UEFA CHAMPIONS LEAGUE					
Pld	**W**	**D**	**L**	**F**	**A**
14	8	3	3	20	7

PERFORMANCE Last 16 stage (beaten 3-0 on aggregate by Benfica)
OTHER TEAMS FACED TNS, FBK Kaunas, CSKA Sofia, Real Betis, Chelsea, Anderlecht
WINNERS Barcelona

RAFA'S MANAGERIAL RECORD IN EUROPE

LIVERPOOL - 2005/06 UEFA SUPER CUP					
Pld	**W**	**D**	**L**	**F**	**A**
1	1	0	0	3	1

PERFORMANCE   Winners (beat CSKA Moscow 3-1 in Monaco)

LIVERPOOL - 2006/07 UEFA CHAMPIONS LEAGUE					
Pld	**W**	**D**	**L**	**F**	**A**
15	9	2	4	22	12

PERFORMANCE   Runners-up (beaten 2-1 by AC Milan in Athens)
OTHER TEAMS FACED   Maccabi Haifa, Bordeaux, Galatasaray, PSV Eindhoven, Barcelona, Chelsea

LIVERPOOL - 2007/08 UEFA CHAMPIONS LEAGUE					
Pld	**W**	**D**	**L**	**F**	**A**
14	8	3	3	34	12

PERFORMANCE   Semi-final stage (beaten 4-3 on aggregate by Chelsea)
OTHER TEAMS FACED   Toulouse, FC Porto, Marseille, Besiktas, Inter Milan, Arsenal
WINNERS   Manchester United

RAFAEL BENITEZ CAREER RECORD IN EUROPEAN COMPETITION					
Pld	**W**	**D**	**L**	**F**	**A**
VALENCIA	37	23	9	5	64	24
LIVERPOOL	59	35	11	13	99	42
TOTAL	**96**	**58**	**20**	**18**	**163**	**66**

Rafa lifts the 'big one' with skipper Steven Gerrard in 2005

adidas
adidas
Carlsberg
Carlsberg
Carlsberg
Carlsberg
Carlsberg

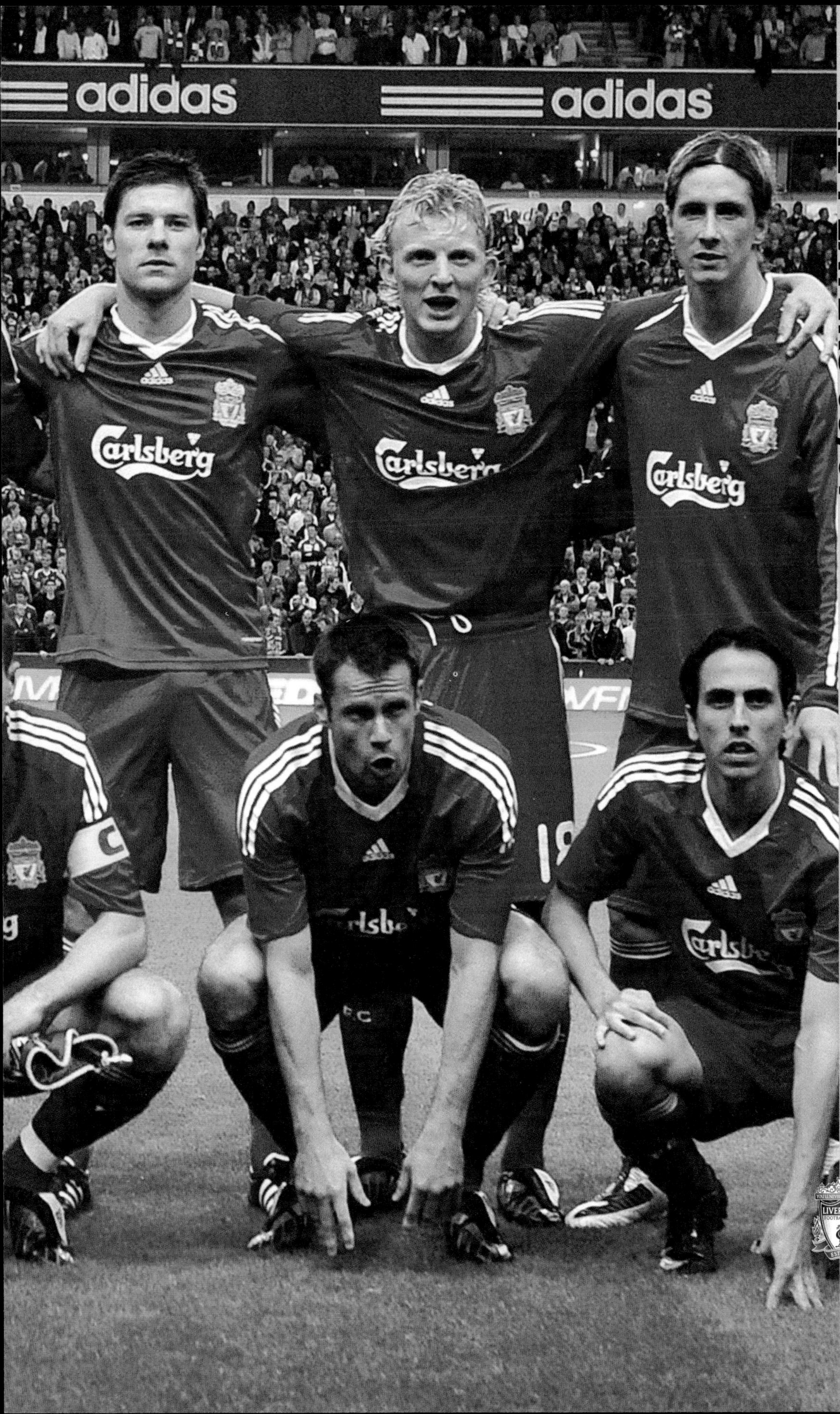
adidas
adidas
Carlsberg
Carlsberg
Carlsberg

THE SQUAD 2008/09

Diego Cavalieri - Squad number 1

Position	Goalkeeper
Born	Sao Paulo, Brazil
Age (at start of 08/09)	25
Birth date	01/12/82
Height	6ft 2ins
Other club	Palmeiras
Honours	2003 Brazilian Serie B, 2008 Sao Paulo State Championship
Liverpool debut	-
Liverpool appearances	-
Liverpool goals	-

Charles Itandje - Squad number 30

Position	Goalkeeper
Born	Bobigny, France
Age (at start of 08/09)	25
Birth date	02/11/82
Height	6ft 4ins
Other clubs	Red Star 93, Lens
Honours	-
Liverpool debut	25/09/07 v Reading
Liverpool appearances	7
Liverpool goals	0

David Martin (on loan to Leicester City)

Position	Goalkeeper
Born	Romford
Age (at start of 08/09)	22
Birth date	22/01/86
Height	6ft 1ins
Other clubs	Milton Keynes Dons, Accrington Stanley
Honours	2006, 2007 FA Youth Cup
Liverpool debut	-
Liverpool appearances	-
Liverpool goals	-

Pepe Reina - Squad number 25

Position	Goalkeeper
Born	Madrid, Spain
Age (at start of 08/09)	25
Birth date	31/08/82
Height	6ft 2ins
Other clubs	Barcelona, Villarreal
Honours	2004, 2005 UEFA Intertoto Cup, 2005 European Super Cup, 2006 FA Cup, 2006 FA Community Shield
Liverpool debut	13/07/05 v TNS
Liverpool appearances	156
Liverpool goals	0
International caps	10 (0 goals)
International honours	2008 Euro C'ships

Daniel Agger - Squad number 5

Position	Central Defence
Born	Hvidovre, Denmark
Age (at start of 08/09)	23
Birth date	12/12/84
Height	6ft 3ins
Other clubs	Rosenhoj, Brondby
Honours	2005 Danish League, 2005 Danish Cup, 2006 FA Comm. Shield
Liverpool debut	01/02/06 v Birmingham
Liverpool appearances	48 + 5 as substitute
Liverpool goals	4
International caps	18 (2 goals)

Godwin Antwi (on loan at Tranmere Rovers)

Positions	Central Defence
Born	Kumasi, Ghana
Age (at start of 08/09)	20
Birth date	07/06/88
Height	6ft 1ins
Other clubs	Asante Kotoko, Real Zaragoza, Accrington Stanley, Hartlepool United
Honours	2006 FA Youth Cup
Liverpool debut	-
Liverpool appearances	-
Liverpool goals	-

Alvaro Arbeloa - Squad number 17

Positions	Right/Central Defence
Born	Salamanca, Spain
Age (at start of 08/09)	25
Birth date	17/01/83
Height	6ft 0ins
Other clubs	Real Madrid, Deportivo La Coruna
Liverpool debut	10/02/07 v Newcastle
Liverpool appearances	50 + 5 as substitute
Liverpool goals	1
International caps	3 (0 goals)
International honours	2008 Euro C'ships

Fabio Aurelio - Squad number 12

Position	Left Defence
Born	Sao Carlos, Brazil
Age (at start of 08/09)	28
Birth date	24/09/79
Height	5ft 8ins
Other clubs	Sao Paulo, Valencia
Honours	1998, 2000 Sao Paulo State C'ship, 2002, 2004 Spanish League, 2004 European Super Cup, 2006 FA Community Shield
Liverpool debut	13/08/06 v Chelsea
Liverpool appearances	37 + 17 as substitute
Liverpool goals	1

Jamie Carragher - Squad number 23

Position	Central Defence
Born	Bootle, Liverpool
Age (at start of 08/09)	30
Birth date	28/01/78
Height	6ft 1ins
Honours	2001, 2006 FA Cup, 2001, 2003 Lge Cup, 2001 UEFA Cup, 2001, 2005 European Super Cup, 2001, 2006 FA Comm. Shield, 2005 Champions Lge
Liverpool debut	08/01/97 v M'boro
Liverpool appearances	503 + 20 as sub.
Liverpool goals	4
International caps	34 (0 goals)

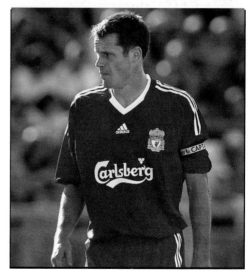

Stephen Darby - Squad number 32

Position	Right Defence
Born	Liverpool
Age (at start of 08/09)	19
Birth date	06/10/88
Height	5ft 8ins
Other clubs	-
Honours	FA Youth Cup 2006, 2007, 2008 FA Premier Reserve League
Liverpool debut	-
Liverpool appearances	-
Liverpool goals	-

Philipp Degen - Squad number 27

Position	Right Defence
Born	Holstein, Switzerland
Age (at start of 08/09)	25
Birth date	15/02/83
Height	6ft 1ins
Other club	FC Basel, FC Aarau Borussia Dortmund
Honours	2002, 2004, 2005 Swiss League, 2003 Swiss Cup
Liverpool debut	-
Liverpool appearances	-
Liverpool goals	-
International caps	30 (0 goals)

Andrea Dossena - Squad number 2

Position	Left Defence
Born	Lodi, Italy
Age (at start of 08/09)	26
Birth date	11/09/81
Height	5ft 11ins
Other clubs	Verona, Treviso, Udinese
Honours	-
Liverpool debut	-
Liverpool appearances	-
Liverpool goals	-
International caps	1 (0 goals)

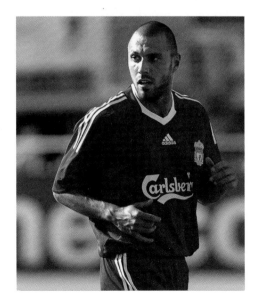

Jack Hobbs (on loan to Leicester City)

Position	Central Defence
Born	Portsmouth
Age (at start of 08/09)	19
Birth date	18/08/88
Height	6ft 3ins
Other club	Lincoln City
Honours	2006 FA Youth Cup
Liverpool debut	25/09/07 v Reading
Liverpool appearances	3 + 2 as substitute
Liverpool goals	0

Sami Hyypia - Squad number 4

Position	Central Defence
Born	Porvoo, Finland
Age (at start of 08/09)	34
Birth date	07/10/73
Height	6ft 4ins
Other clubs	Pallo-Pelkot, Ku Mu My Pa Anjalankoski, Willem II Tilburg
Honours	1992, 1995 Finnish Cup, 2001, 2006 FA Cup, 2001, 2003 League Cup, 2001 UEFA Cup, 2001, 2005 European Super Cup, 2001, 2006 FA Community Shield, 2005 Champions League
Liverpool debut	07/08/99 at Sheff Wed
Liverpool appearances	440 + 5 as sub.
Liverpool goals	33
International caps	90 (5 goals)

Emiliano Insua - Squad number 22

Position	Left Defence
Born	Buenos Aires, Argentina
Age (at start of 08/09)	19
Birth date	07/01/89
Height	5ft 8ins
Other club	Boca Juniors
Honours	2008 FA Premier Reserve League
Liverpool debut	28/04/07 v Portsmouth
Liverpool appearances	4 + 1 as substitute
Liverpool goals	0

Martin Kelly - Squad number 34

Positions	Central Defence
Born	Bolton
Age (at start of 08/09)	18
Birth date	27/04/90
Height	6ft 3ins
Other clubs	-
Honours	2008 FA Premier Reserve League
Liverpool debut	-
Liverpool appearances	-
Liverpool goals	-

Martin Skrtel - Squad number 37

Position	Central Defence
Born	Handlova, Slovakia
Age (at start of 08/09)	23
Birth date	15/12/84
Height	6ft 1ins
Other clubs	FK AS Trencin, Zenit St. Petersburg
Honours	2007 Russian Premier League
Liverpool debut	21/01/08 v Aston Villa
Liverpool appearances	19 + 1 as substitute
Liverpool goals	0
International caps	18 (1 goals)

Robbie Threlfall (on loan at Hereford United)

Position	Defence
Born	Liverpool
Age (at start of 08/09)	19
Birth date	25/11/88
Height	6ft 0ins
Other clubs	Hereford United
Honours	2006, 2007 FA Youth Cup
Liverpool debut	-
Liverpool appearances	-
Liverpool goals	-

Xabi Alonso - Squad number 14

Position	Central Midfield
Born	Tolosa, Spain
Age (at start of 08/09)	26
Birth date	25/11/81
Height	6ft 0ins
Other clubs	Eibar, Real Sociedad
Honours	2005 Champions Lge, 2005 European Super Cup, 2006 FA Cup, 2006 FA Comm. Shield
Liverpool debut	29/08/04 v Bolton W.
Liverpool appearances	141 + 22 as substitute
Liverpool goals	14
International caps	47 (1 goal)

Paul Anderson (on loan to Nottingham Forest)

Position	Right Midfield
Born	Leicester
Age (at start of 08/09)	20
Birth date	23/07/88
Height	5ft 9ins
Other clubs	Hull City, Swansea City
Honours	2006 FA Youth Cup, 2008 League One
Liverpool debut	-
Liverpool appearances	-
Liverpool goals	-

Yossi Benayoun - Squad number 15

Position	Midfield
Born	Dimona, Israel
Age (at start of 08/09)	28
Birth date	05/05/80
Height	5ft 8ins
Other clubs	Hapoel Be'er Sheva, Maccabi Haifa, Racing Santander, West Ham
Honours	2001, 2002 Israeli League
Liverpool debut	15/08/07 v Toulouse
Liverpool appearances	26 + 21 as substitute
Liverpool goals	11
International caps	63 (15 goals)

Ryan Flynn - Squad number 35

Position	Central Midfield
Born	Falkirk, Scotland
Age (at start of 08/09)	19
Birth date	04/09/88
Height	5ft 10ins
Other club	Falkirk
Honours	2006, 2007 FA Youth Cup, 2008 FA Premier Reserve League
Liverpool debut	-
Liverpool appearances	-
Liverpool goals	-

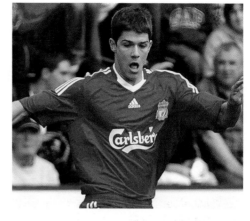

Steven Gerrard MBE - Squad number 8

Positions	Central/Right Midfield
Born	Whiston, Merseyside
Age (at start of 08/09)	28
Birth date	30/05/80
Height	6ft 0ins
Honours	2001, 2006 FA Cup, 2001, 2003 Lge Cup, 2001 UEFA Cup, 2001 European Super Cup, 2001, 2006 FA Community Shield, 2005 Champions League
Liverpool debut	29/11/98 v Blackburn Rovers
Liverpool appearances	400 + 39 as substitute
Liverpool goals	96
International caps	67 (13 goals)

Adam Hammill (on loan to Blackpool)

Positions	Midfield/Forward
Born	Liverpool
Age (at start of 08/09)	20
Birth date	25/01/88
Height	5ft 8ins
Other clubs	Dunfermline Athletic, Southampton
Honours	2006 FA Youth Cup
Liverpool debut	-
Liverpool appearances	-
Liverpool goals	-

Steven Irwin - Squad number 36

Positions	Defence/Midfield
Born	Liverpool
Age (at start of 08/09)	17
Birth date	29/09/90
Height	5ft 8ins
Other clubs	-
Honours	2007 FA Youth Cup
Liverpool debut	-
Liverpool appearances	-
Liverpool goals	-

Lucas Leiva - Squad number 21

Position	Central Midfield
Born	Dourados, Brazil
Age (at start of 08/09)	21
Birth date	09/01/87
Height	5ft 10ins
Other club	Gremio
Honours	2005 Brazilian Serie B, 2006, 2007 Rio Grande do Sul State Championship, 2008 FA Prem Res. Lge
Liverpool debut	28/08/07 v Toulouse
Liverpool appearances	20 + 12 as substitute
Liverpool goals	1
International caps	2 (0 goals)
International honours	2008 Olympics Bronze Medal

Javier Mascherano - Squad number 20

Position	Central Midfield
Born	San Lorenzo, Argentina
Age (at start of 08/09)	24
Birth date	08/06/84
Height	5ft 9ins
Other clubs	River Plate, Corinthians, West Ham
Honours	2004 Argentine Lge (Closing C'ship), 2005 Brazilian Lge
Liverpool debut	24/02/07 v Sheff Utd
Liverpool appearances	50 + 2 as substitute
Liverpool goals	1
International caps	41 (2 goals)
International honours	2004, 2008 Olympics Gold Medal

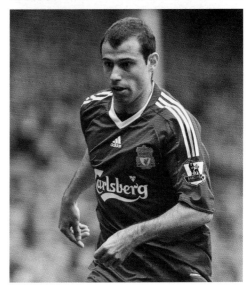

Jermaine Pennant - Squad number 16

Position	Right Midfield
Born	Nottingham
Age (at start of 08/09)	25
Birth date	15/01/83
Height	5ft 9ins
Other clubs	Notts County, Arsenal, Watford, Leeds United, Birmingham City
Honours	2004, 2006 FA Community Shield
Liverpool debut	09/08/06 v Macc. Haifa
Liverpool appearances	51 + 26 as substitute
Liverpool goals	3

Damien Plessis - Squad number 28

Position	Central Midfield
Born	Neuville-aux-Bois, France
Age (at start of 08/09)	20
Birth date	05/03/88
Height	6ft 4ins
Other club	Lyon
Honours	2008 FA Premier Reserve League
Liverpool debut	05/04/08 v Arsenal
Liverpool appearances	2 + 0 as substitute
Liverpool goals	0

Albert Riera - Squad number 11

Position	Left Midfield
Born	Manacor, Spain
Age (at start of 08/09)	26
Birth date	15/04/82
Height	6ft 2ins
Other clubs	Real Mallorca, Bordeaux, Espanyol, Manchester City
Honours	2003 Spanish Cup
Liverpool debut	-
Liverpool appearances	-
Liverpool goals	-
International caps	5 (1 goal)

Jay Spearing - Squad number 26

Position	Central Midfield
Born	Wirral
Age (at start of 08/09)	19
Birth date	25/11/88
Height	5ft 6ins
Other clubs	-
Honours	2006, 2007 FA Youth Cup, 2008 FA Premier Reserve League
Liverpool debut	-
Liverpool appearances	-
Liverpool goals	-

Ryan Babel - Squad number 19

Position	Forward
Born	Amsterdam, Holland
Age (at start of 08/09)	21
Birth date	19/12/86
Height	6ft 0ins
Other club	Ajax
Honours	2005, 2006 Dutch Super Cup, 2006, 2007 Dutch Cup, 2007 UEFA U21 Championship
Liverpool debut	11/08/07 v Aston Villa
Liverpool appearances	29 + 20 as substitute
Liverpool goals	10
International caps	25 (5 goals)

Nathan Eccleston - Squad number 39

Positions	Forward
Born	Manchester
Age (at start of 08/09)	17
Birth date	30/12/90
Height	N/A
Other clubs	-
Honours	2007 FA Youth Cup
Liverpool debut	-
Liverpool appearances	-
Liverpool goals	-

Nabil El Zhar - Squad number 31

Position	Forward
Born	Ales, France
Age (at start of 08/09)	21
Birth date	27/08/86
Height	5ft 9ins
Other clubs	Olympique Ales, Nimes Olympique, AS Saint-Etienne
Honours	2008 FA Premier Reserve League
Liverpool debut	29/11/06 v Portsmouth
Liverpool appearances	1 + 5 as substitute
Liverpool goals	1
International caps	5 (2 goals)

Robbie Keane - Squad number 7

Position	Forward
Born	Dublin, Republic of Ireland
Age (at start of 08/09)	28
Birth date	08/07/80
Height	5ft 9ins
Other clubs	Wolves, Coventry City, Inter Milan, Leeds Utd, Tottenham Hotspur
Honours	2008 League Cup
Liverpool debut	-
Liverpool appearances	-
Liverpool goals	-
International caps	81 (33 goals)

Dirk Kuyt - Squad number 18

Position	Forward
Born	Katwijk, Holland
Age (at start of 08/09)	28
Birth date	22/07/80
Height	6ft 0ins
Other clubs	FC Utrecht, Feyenoord
Honours	2003 Dutch Cup
Liverpool debut	26/08/06 v West Ham
Liverpool appearances	74 + 22 as substitute
Liverpool goals	25
International caps	41 (8 goals)

Craig Lindfield (on loan to Bournemouth)

Position	Centre Forward
Born	Wirral
Age (at start of 08/09)	19
Birth date	07/09/88
Height	6ft 0ins
Other clubs	Notts County, Chester City
Honours	2006, 2007 FA Youth Cup, 2008 FA Premier Reserve League
Liverpool debut	-
Liverpool appearances	-
Liverpool goals	-

Krisztian Nemeth - Squad number 29

Position	Centre Forward
Born	Gyor, Hungary
Age (at start of 08/09)	19
Birth date	05/01/89
Height	5ft 10ins
Other clubs	MTK Hungaria
Honours	2008 FA Premier Reserve League
Liverpool debut	-
Liverpool appearances	-
Liverpool goals	-

David Ngog - Squad number 24

Position	Centre Forward
Born	Gennevilliers, France
Age (at start of 08/09)	19
Birth date	01/04/89
Height	6ft 3ins
Other clubs	Paris Saint-Germain
Honours	2008 French League Cup
Liverpool debut	-
Liverpool appearances	-
Liverpool goals	-

Fernando Torres - Squad number 9

Position	Centre Forward
Born	Madrid, Spain
Age (at start of 08/09)	24
Birth date	20/03/84
Height	6ft 1ins
Other club	Atletico Madrid
Honours	2002 Spanish Second Division, 2002 UEFA U19 Championship
Liverpool debut	11/08/07 v Aston Villa
Liverpool appearances	40 + 6
Liverpool goals	33
International caps	53 (17 goals)
International honours	2008 Euro C'ships

Andriy Voronin (on loan to Hertha Berlin)

Position	Centre Forward
Born	Odessa, Ukraine
Age (at start of 08/09)	29
Birth date	21/07/79
Height	5ft 10ins
Other clubs	Borussia Moenchengladbach, Mainz, Cologne, Bayer Leverkusen
Honours	-
Liverpool debut	11/08/07 v Aston Villa
Liverpool appearances	18 + 10 as substitute
Liverpool goals	6
International caps	53 (6 goals)

OTHER PLAYERS ON LOAN 2008/09

Miki Roque

Position	Defence
Born	Tremp, Spain
Age	20
Birth date	08/07/88
Height	6ft 1ins
Club	FC Cartagena
Loan spell	One year
Honours	2006 FA Youth Cup

Charlie Barnett

Position	Midfield
Born	Liverpool
Age	19
Birth date	19/09/88
Height	5ft 7ins
Club	Tranmere Rovers
Loan spell	One year
Honours	2006, 2007 FA Youth Cup

Sebastian Leto

Position	Left Midfield
Born	Buenos Aires, Argentina
Age	21
Birth date	30/08/86
Height	6ft 2ins
Club	Olympiakos
Loan spell	One year

SUMMER DIARY 2008

A reminder of what went on and when during the summer months involving Liverpool FC.

JUNE

1	Steven Gerrard plays the full 90 minutes and Peter Crouch makes a substitute apperance during England's 3-0 defeat of Trinidad & Tobago.
	Dirk Kuyt features in Holland's 2-0 stroll over Wales in Rotterdam.
	Ryan Babel is on target to be fit for the start of the new season, having been forced to miss Holland's Euro 2008 campaign due to torn ankle ligaments.
4	Udinese left-back Andrea Dossena undergoes a medical ahead of a proposed switch.
	Fernando Torres, Xabi Alonso and Alvaro Arbeloa feature in Spain's 1-0 defeat of USA.
	Javier Mascherano is in the Argentina side who impress during a 4-1 defeat of Mexico.
9	Dirk Kuyt impresses during Holland's 3-0 win over world champions Italy at Euro 2008.
10	Spain ease to a 4-1 success over Russia at Euro 2008, Fernando Torres and Xabi Alonso both being involved.
13	Dirk Kuyt heads Holland into the lead in their 4-1 Euro 2008 demolition of France.
14	Fernando Torres is on target in Spain's 2-1 defeat of Sweden at Euro 2008.
15	Javier Mascherano plays an hour as Argentina are held to a 1-1 draw by Ecuador in a World Cup qualifier.
16	The Premier League fixtures pair Liverpool with Sunderland on the opening day.
17	Dirk Kuyt comes off the bench in Holland's 2-0 defeat of Romania at Euro 2008, the Liverpool forward being one of nine players rested ahead of their quarter-final.
18	John Arne Riise completes his move to AS Roma.
	Xabi Alonso captains a much-changed Spain side, also featuring Jose Reina and Alvaro Arbeloa, to a 2-1 win over Euro 2004 champions Greece.
21	Dirk Kuyt' Holland bow out of Euro 2008 after going down 3-1 to Russia.
	Nabil El Zhar scores in Morocco's 2-0 victory over Rwanda in a World Cup qualifer.
22	Spain, with Fernando Torres in the team, reach the last four of a major tournament for the first time in 24 years thanks to a penalty shoot-out triumph over Italy.
27	Winger Paul Anderson joins Nottingham Forest on a season-long loan deal.
29	Fernando Torres is the toast of Spain after his first-half goal earns his country a first European Championship crown in 44 years, at the expense of Germany in Vienna.
30	The majority of the club's first-team squad return to pre-season training.
	Former defender Mauricio Pellegrino returns to the club as first-team coach.

JULY

2	Anthony Le Tallec officially leaves Anfield, joining Le Mans on a permanent deal.
	Fernando Torres is named in UEFA's squad of Euro 2008.
	Paul Anderson extends his Liverpool deal until 2011.
3	Defender Emiliano Insua pens a new three-year contract.
4	Philipp Degen officially signs for the club on a Bosman free transfer.
5	Andrea Dossena completes his move from Udinese.
	Javier Mascherano is named in Argentina's Olympic squad.
6	Harry Kewell agrees to join Galatasaray on a three-year deal.
8	Nikola Saric, 17, agrees a three-year contract.
	Lucas Leiva is included in Brazil's 18-man Olympic squad.
9	Hungarian prospect Zslot Poloskei signs on a season-long loan deal.
10	Andrea Dossena (No. 2) and Philipp Degen (No. 27) are handed their squad numbers.
11	Dutchman Vincent Lucas Weijl becomes the latest youngster to sign, from AZ Alkmaar.
12	Peter Crouch completes his move to Portsmouth.
	Brazilian goalkeeper Diego Cavalieri is signed, coming in from Palmeiras.
	The club's first pre-season run-out sees a 1-0 win for the Reds at Tranmere Rovers.
14	Danny Guthrie completes his switch to Newcastle United.
16	Ryan Babel, returning to full fitness, is included in Holland's Olympic squad.

SUMMER DIARY 2008

A reminder of what went on and when during the summer months involving Liverpool FC.

JULY

16   The Reds defeat FC Lucerne 2-1 in their latest pre-season outing, in Switzerland.

19   Youth Cup-winner Adam Hammill joins Blackpool on a six-month loan deal soon after agreeing to extend his Liverpool contract.
Scott Carson completes his move to newly-promoted West Bromwich Albion.
The Reds draw 1-1 with Polish side Wisla Krakow.

22   Liverpool draw 0-0 at Hertha Berlin.

23   Full-back Emmanuel Mendy completes his move from Spanish side Murcia Deportivo.

24   David Ngog agrees to join from Paris St Germain.

25   Defenders Jack Hobbs (season) and Godwin Antwi (six months) agree loan deals with Leicester City and Tranmere Rovers respectively.

28   Republic of Ireland skipper Robbie Keane joins his boyhood idols from Tottenham Hotspur - he will wear the legendary No. 7 shirt.

30   Robbie Keane impresses on his Liverpool bow as the Reds draw 0-0 at Villarreal.

AUGUST

1   Belgian champions Standard Liege are drawn against the Reds in the third qualifying round of the UEFA Champions League.

2   A rampant Liverpool ease to a 4-0 friendly success at Rangers.

5   Argentine winger Sebastian Leto is again denied a work permit - it is subsequently revealed that he will join Olympiakos on loan.
Goalkeeper David Martin joins Leicester City on a six-month loan.
Liverpool stroll to a 4-1 friendly win in Norway against Valerenga.

7   Liverpool's Olympics trio of Javier Mascherano, Lucas Leiva and Ryan Babel are unbeaten as they all play 90 minutes in their countries' first game of the tournament.

8   The final pre-season game sees a 1-0 win over Lazio in front of a bumper Anfield gate.

10   Ryan Babel is on target for Holland in their 2-2 draw with the USA at the Olympics, while Mascherano and Lucas are through to the quarter-finals after second wins.

12   Defender Miki Roque joins Spanish third-tier side Cartagena on a season-long loan.

13   Ryan Babel's Holland will meet Javier Mascherano's Argentina in the last eight of the Olympics following their 1-0 defeat of Japan.
Liverpool earn a 0-0 draw at Standard Liege in the first leg of the UEFA Champions League third qualfying round, with Pepe Reina saving a penalty.

16   The Barclaycard Premiership kick-off sees the Reds earn a 1-0 win at Sunderland thanks to a late Fernando Torres strike.
Argentina defeat Holland 2-1 at the Olympics, with Ryan Babel now set to return to Anfield. It will be Mascherano against Lucas and Brazil in the semis.

19   Javier Mascherano's Argentina reach the Olympic final after defeating nine-man Brazil 3-0 in the semi-final - Lucas Leiva being one of the men dismissed, ironically for a foul on his Liverpool team-mate.

20   Eleven players are on international duty, with Xabi Alonso (2) and Robbie Keane in scoring form for Spain and the Republic of Ireland respectively.

22   Craig Lindfield joins Bournemouth on loan until the end of 2008.

23   Javier Mascherano wins Olympic gold as Argentina beat Nigeria 1-0 in the final.
Two goals in the last five minutes see the Reds defeat Middlesbrough 2-1.
Four Liverpool players are nominated for the European Footballer of the Year award.

27   Liverpool reach the UEFA Champions League group stages after edging past Standard Liege 1-0, courtesy of Dirk Kuyt's extra-time winner.

28   Marseille, PSV Eindhoven and Atletico Madrid are paired with the Reds in Group D.

30   The third-round draw for the Carling Cup sees Liverpool face Crewe at Anfield.

31   A 0-0 draw at Aston Villa means the club end the month second in the Premier League.

RESERVES

SEASON REVIEW

Gary Ablett helped oversee one of the most successful seasons in recent memory, guiding the reserves to Play-Off Final glory - the Reds qualified by easing to the FA Premier League Reserve League North title (their first league crown for eight years). The 3-0 victory over Aston Villa in front of a 7,580 crowd at Anfield completed a memorable hat-trick of trophies for the 2007/08 season, Ablett's side having also won the prestigious Dallas Cup.

Jordy Brouwer and Krisztian Nemeth topped the goalscoring charts for the side (Nemeth topped the goalscoring charts for the Reserve League North with nine goals), while the only disappointments came in the Liverpool Senior Cup and the Lancashire Senior Cup, with final defeats coming at the hands of Marine and Manchester United respectively.

Liverpool's home matches will again be played at Warrington Wolves' 13,024-capacity Halliwell Jones Stadium, with matches kicking off at 7pm.

2007/08 STATISTICS

RES. LGE & CUP APPS. & GOALS 2007/08

	Appearances	Goals
Daniel Agger	2	0
Astrit Ajdarevic	1	0
Xabi Alonso	1	1
Daniel Ayala	11	0
Dean Bouzanis	4	0
Jordy Brouwer	28	13
Gerardo Bruna	16	3
Ryan Crowther	12	0
Stephen Darby	27	0
Francisco Duran	2	0
Nathan Eccleston	1	1
Nabil El Zhar	7	1
Ryan Flynn	25	0
Peter Gulacsi	10	0
Martin Hansen	2	0
Jack Hobbs	4	0
Ronald Huth	25	1
Emiliano Insua	26	0
Steven Irwin	7	0
Charles Itandje	2	0
Martin Kelly	17	0
Harry Kewell	2	2
Sebastian Leto	7	0
Craig Lindfield	16	2
Lucas Leiva	3	1
David Martin	12	0
Gary Mackay-Steven	2	0
Krisztian Nemeth	18	11
Daniel Pacheco	17	5
Jermaine Pennant	1	0
Damien Plessis	26	0
Marvin Pourie	1	0
Ray Putterill	13	3
Mikel San Jose	28	0
Andras Simon	8	4
Martin Skrtel	1	0
Jay Spearing	28	4

RESERVES LEAGUE RESULTS 2007/08

Date	Opponent		Result
04.09.07	Middlesbrough	A	1-1
19.09.07	Wigan Athletic	A	3-0
02.10.07	Sunderland	H	0-1
11.10.07	Manchester United	A	1-1
25.10.07	Newcastle United	H	2-1
13.11.07	Blackburn Rovers	H	0-0
27.11.07	Manchester City	A	3-2
04.12.07	Everton	H	3-0
10.12.07	Middlesbrough	H	4-0
04.02.08	Bolton Wanderers	A	3-0
12.02.08	Sunderland	A	1-0
18.02.08	Newcastle United	A	0-0
26.02.08	Manchester United	H	2-0
04.03.08	Bolton Wanderers	H	1-0
01.04.08	Everton	A	1-0
07.04.08	Blackburn Rovers	A	1-0
10.04.08	Manchester City	H	2-1
21.04.08	Wigan Athletic	H	3-1
07.05.08	Aston Villa (P-OF)	H	3-0

BARCLAYS PREMIERSHIP RESERVE LEAGUE NORTH — RESERVES LEAGUE NORTH TABLE 2007/08

	Pld	W	D	L	F	A	Pts
1 Liverpool	18	13	4	1	31	8	43
2 Man City	18	8	6	4	34	29	30
3 Man Utd	18	8	5	5	25	19	29
4 Sunderland	18	9	2	7	28	24	29
5 Blackburn R.	18	8	4	6	32	25	28
6 Newcastle U.	18	5	7	6	31	27	22
7 Middlesboro	18	5	7	6	23	26	22
8 Everton	18	4	4	10	21	31	16
9 Wigan Ath.	18	4	3	11	19	36	15
10 Bolton Wan.	18	3	4	11	13	32	13

FA PREMIER RESERVE LEAGUE NORTHERN SECTION FIXTURES 2008/09

SEPTEMBER

02 Middlesbrough	(A)
17 Sunderland	(A)

OCTOBER

07 Manchester City	(A)
14 Everton	(H) - 7.30pm KO

NOVEMBER

06 Manchester United	(A)
18 Wigan Athletic	(H)
24 Newcastle United	(A)

DECEMBER

02 Blackburn Rovers	(H)
10 Bolton Wanderers	(A)
16 Hull City	(H)

All fixtures 7pm,
subject to change.

JANUARY

06 Sunderland	(H)
20 Middlesbrough	(H)

FEBRUARY

10 Manchester City	(H)
17 Everton	(A)

MARCH

10 Manchester United	(H)
17 Wigan Athletic	(A)
24 Newcastle United	(H)

APRIL

06 Blackburn Rovers	(A)
14 Hull City	(A)
21 Bolton Wanderers	(H)

Please note reserve play-off final is scheduled
for Wednesday 20th May.

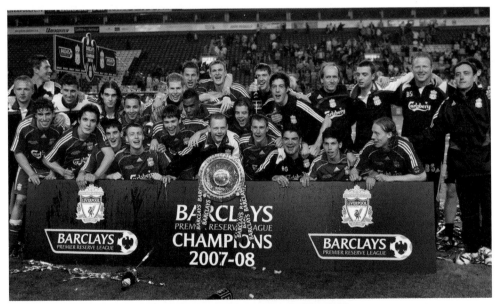

Play-off glory for the Reds in May 2008

THE ACADEMY

SEASON REVIEW

Although John Owen's youngsters failed in their bid for a hat-trick of FA Youth Cup successes following defeat at Sunderland in round five, there was much to be proud of involving players who have come through the youth set-up during 2007/08.

Prospects such as Astrit Ajdarevic, Nathan Eccleston and Marvin Pourie were all given experience with the reserves during the campaign, while a mix of reserve and Academy prospects combined to secure the Reds silverware in the Dallas Cup tournament held in the USA.

2007/08 STATISTICS

U18s APPEARANCES & GOALS 2007/08

	Appearances	Goals
Astrit Ajdarevic	30	3
David Amoo	31	9
Mattone Awang	15	0
Daniel Ayala	7	0
Charlie Barnett	1	0
Dean Bouzanis	12	0
Gerardo Bruna	3	0
Button	1	0
Michael Collins	16	3
Ryan Crowther	2	1
Lauri Dalla Valle	1	0
Nathan Eccleston	30	18
Martin Hansen	13	0
Sean Highdale	28	0
Steven Irwin	28	2
Alexander Kacaniklic	20	0
Pajtim Kasami	1	0
Martin Kelly	9	1

U18s APPEARANCES & GOALS 2007/08

	Appearances	Goals
Joe Kennedy	31	2
Gary Mackay-Steven	20	4
Matty McGiveron	1	0
Jack Metcalf	5	0
Krisztian Nemeth	1	0
Shane O'Connor	26	0
Chris Oldfield	6	0
Daniel Pacheco	2	1
Ben Parsonage	6	0
Adam Pepper	7	1
Marvin Pourie	26	12
Michael Roberts	2	0
Michael Scott	13	0
Andras Simon	1	0
Robbie Threlfall	1	0
Adam Wilson	1	0
Scott Wooton	3	0

U18s LEAGUE & YOUTH CUP RESULTS 07/08

			Result
18.08.07	Aston Villa	A	0-5
08.09.07	Nottingham Forest	A	3-0
15.09.07	Sheffield Wednesday	H	2-0
22.09.07	Middlesbrough	A	2-4
29.09.07	Stoke City	A	3-2
06.10.07	Blackburn Rovers	H	2-0
13.10.07	Wolves	A	4-1
20.10.07	Crewe Alexandra	H	2-2
24.10.07	Sunderland	H	3-0
27.10.07	West Bromwich Albion	A	0-0
03.11.07	Everton	H	1-1
10.11.07	Bolton Wanderers	H	5-2
17.11.07	Manchester City	H	0-3
01.12.07	Manchester United	A	2-2
08.12.07	Crewe Alexandra	A	3-1
12.12.07	Wycombe (FAYC3)	A	5-0
15.12.07	West Bromwich Albion	H	5-0
05.01.08	Bolton Wanderers	A	1-1
11.01.08	Everton	A	3-3
19.01.08	Manchester United	H	0-1
29.01.08	Arsenal (FAYC4)	H	1-0
02.02.08	Huddersfield Town	H	0-1
09.02.08	Stoke City	H	1-1
13.02.08	Sunderland (FAYC5)	A	3-5

U18s LEAGUE & YOUTH CUP RESULTS 07/08

			Result
16.02.08	Blackburn Rovers	A	2-0
23.02.08	Newcastle United	A	0-0
01.03.08	Wolves	H	1-1
15.03.08	Barnsley	H	3-0
05.04.08	Derby County	H	0-1
09.04.08	Manchester City	A	1-1
12.04.08	Leeds United	A	0-1

FA PREMIER ACADEMY 2007/08 GROUP C

	P	W	D	L	F	A	Pts
1 Man City	28	21	4	3	75	22	67
2 Everton	28	17	7	4	56	24	58
3 Man Utd	28	14	6	8	47	44	48
4 Crewe Alex.	28	14	6	8	50	51	48
5 Liverpool	**28**	**11**	**10**	**7**	**49**	**34**	**43**
6 Blackburn	28	10	5	13	36	38	35
7 West Brom	28	8	7	13	44	66	31
8 Wolves	28	7	8	13	29	37	29
9 Bolton W.	28	6	9	13	42	47	27
10 Stoke C.	28	5	7	15	26	41	22

ACADEMY/RESERVE CUP RESULTS

LIVERPOOL IN THE LANCASHIRE SENIOR CUP 2007/08

Quarter-final

17th April 2008
Liverpool 3-0 Wigan Athletic

Liverpool goalscorers: Lindfield, Brouwer, Bruna

Team: Hansen, Kelly, Darby (Irwin 45), San Jose (Spearing 45), Huth, Ayala, Flynn, Pacheco, Brouwer, (Plessis 74), Lindfield, Bruna.

Semi-final

28th April 2008
Accrington Stanley 0-3 Liverpool

Liverpool goalscorers: Nemeth, Simon, Pacheco

Team: Bouzanis, Darby, Irwin, San Jose, Huth (Insua 24), Kelly, Lindfield, Spearing (Pacheco 33), Brouwer (Nemeth 77), Simon, Flynn.

Final

30th July 2008
Liverpool 2-3 Manchester United   (The County Ground, Leyland)

Liverpool goalscorers: Eccleston, Brouwer

Team: Bouzanis, Scott, Irwin, San Jose, Huth, Kelly, Lindfield, Eccleston (Amoo 03), Brouwer, Simon, Bruna (Kacaniklic 70).

LIVERPOOL IN THE LIVERPOOL SENIOR CUP 2007/08

Quarter-final

7th February 2008
Everton 0-1 Liverpool   (Finch Farm, Halewood)

Liverpool goalscorer: Bruna

Team: Martin, Irwin, Insua, San Jose, Ayala, Plessis, Flynn (Darby 27), Spearing (Ajdarevic 54), Pacheco, Bruna (Brouwer 58).

Semi-final

14th April 2008
Prescot Cables 0-1 Liverpool (aet)   (Valerie Park, Prescot)

Liverpool goalscorer: Pacheco

Team: Martin, Kelly, Insua, San Jose, Ayala (Darby 100), Plessis, Flynn (Pacheco 45), Spearing, Brouwer, Lindfield, Bruna (Huth 45).

Final

24th April 2008
Marine 1-0 Liverpool   (The Arriva Stadium, Crosby)

Team: Gulacsi, Kelly, Darby, San Jose, Huth, Ayala (Irwin 70), Flynn, Spearing, Brouwer (Lindfield 74), Nemeth, Bruna.

LIVERPOOL IN THE FA YOUTH CUP 2007/08

Round 3

12th December 2007
Wycombe Wanderers 0-5 Liverpool   (Adams Park)

Liverpool goalscorers: David Amoo, Nathan Eccleston (2), Gary MacKay-Steven, Marvin Pourie

Round 4

29th January 2008
Liverpool 1-0 Arsenal   (Anfield)

Liverpool goalscorer: Irwin

Round 5

13th February 2008
Sunderland 5-3 Liverpool (aet)   (Stadium of Light)

Liverpool goalscorers: Eccleston (pen), Pourie, Pacheco

47

FA PREMIER ACADEMY LEAGUE
FIXTURES 2008/09

AUGUST
23 Crystal Palace (H)
30 Coventry City (A) - 11.30am KO

SEPTEMBER
06 Nottingham Forest (H) - 12.00pm KO
13 Newcastle United (H) - 1.00pm KO
20 Sheffield Wednesday (A) - 12.00pm KO
27 Crewe Alexandra (A)

OCTOBER
04 Wolverhampton W. (H) - 11.30am KO
11 Blackburn Rovers (A)
18 Manchester United (A)

NOVEMBER
01 Bolton Wanderers (H)
08 Manchester City (A)
15 Everton (H)
22 Stoke City (A)

DECEMBER
06 West Bromwich Albion (H)
13 Manchester United (H)

FA YOUTH CUP DATES
RND 3   To be played by December 13
RND 4   To be played by January 17
RND 5   To be played by January 31
Q-F   To be played by February 14

JANUARY
17 Bolton Wanderers (A)
24 Manchester City (H)
31 Everton (A)

FEBRUARY
07 Stoke City (H)
14 West Bromwich Albion (A) -11.30am KO
21 Crewe Alexandra (H)

MARCH
07 Wolverhampton W. (A) - 11.30am KO
14 Blackburn Rovers (H)
21 Leeds United (A)
28 Huddersfield Town (A)

APRIL
18 Sunderland (A) - 1.00pm KO
25 Sheffield Wednesday (H)

MAY
02 Barnsley (A) - 11.30am KO

All fixtures 11am unless stated, subject to change.

FA YOUTH CUP DATES
S-F L. 1 To be played by March 7
S-F L. 2 To be played by March 21
F L. 1   To be confirmed
F L. 2   To be confirmed

Liverpool reserves line-up before the play-off final with Aston Villa

LIVERPOOL LADIES

SEASON REVIEW

After a memorable promotion campaign in 2006/07, the ladies team were brought back down to earth. Although the Reds survived in their first season back in the FA Women's Premier League, a finish of 10th out of 12 teams meant that manager David Bradley lost his job less than 12 months after taking over. New boss Robbie Johnson, who holds a UEFA A licence and possesses a wealth of coaching experience in the USA, has been given the task of improving on last term.

Season highlights included a run to the semi-final of the FA Premier League Cup and the final of the Liverpool Senior Cup, while their biggest league win was a 4-0 defeat of Cardiff City.

The club have also lost key members of coaching staff, with midfielder Tammy Byrne, star forward Chantelle Parry and England U19 striker Faye McCoy all leaving for Blackburn Rovers.

The team will continue to play home games at Skelmersdale United FC's Ashley Travel Stadium this term, with Sunday games kicking off at 2pm.

SQUAD LIST

GOALKEEPERS

Nicky Davies, Kim Griffiths, Hannah Williams

DEFENDERS

Carmel Bennett, Emma Catterall, Sam Chappell, Caroline Charlton, Lauren Clinton Gayle Formiston (captain),

Natalie Holt, Vicky Jones, Jess King, Lesley McGowan, Jackie McLaughlin, Katy Nocton, Elizabeth Old, Jo Traynor, Kali Whitbread

MIDFIELDERS

Micha Deane, Georgie Donnelly, Jo Edwards, Amie Flemming, Cheryl Foster, Kelly Jones, Sophie Jones, Linda Mathisen,

Stacey McMahon, Sophia Riccio, Natalie Sage, Rachel Snellgrove, Jennifer Toole, Lisa Topping, Hannah Twigg

FORWARDS

Steph Daley, Gill Hart, Ally Hastie, Shelley James, Molly McCann, Danielle Sheen

FA WOMEN'S PREMIER LEAGUE FIXTURES 2008/09

AUGUST

17	Chelsea	(A)
24	Arsenal	(H)
26	Everton	(H)
31	Bristol Academy	(A)

SEPTEMBER

07	Fulham	(H)
14	Nottingham F. (FAPLC1)	(A)
17	Blackburn Rovers	(H)
21	Nottingham Forest	(A)
28	Doncaster Rovers Belles	(H)

OCTOBER

05	FA PREM. LGE CUP R2	
12	Leeds Carnegie	(A)
19	Birmingham City	(A)
22	Everton	(A)
26	Bristol Academy	(H)

NOVEMBER

02	FA PREM. LGE CUP R3	
05	Blackburn Rovers	(A)
09	Watford	(A)

NOVEMBER

23	Arsenal	(A)
30	Nottingham Forest	(H)

DECEMBER

07	Fulham	(A)
07	FA PREM. LGE CUP S-F	
14	Birmingham City	(H)
21	Doncaster Rovers Belles	(A)

JANUARY

04	FA CUP ROUND 4	
11	Watford	(H)
18	Chelsea	(H)
25	FA CUP ROUND 5	

FEBRUARY

22	FA CUP ROUND 6	

MARCH

22	FA CUP SEMI-FINAL	

MAY

04	FA CUP FINAL	

Fixtures subject to change. Home fixtures kick-off at 2pm subject to change.

10

Rams to the slaughter

Although Derby County have been proven to be the worst side in Premier League history, a 6-0 victory against any side is not to be sniffed at. The September win was also the first time the Reds had been top of the table since 2002/03.

9

Inter late show

Dirk Kuyt and Steven Gerrard goals in the last five minutes gave the Reds the ideal first-leg platform to see off Champions League favourites Inter Milan at Anfield in February.

8 The perfect start

With Fernando Torres making his Premier League debut, the Reds produced an accomplished display at Aston Villa. It was Steven Gerrard's late free-kick that gave the Reds a 2-1 win, their first opening-day victory for five years.

7 Rough ride for Royals

Reading were treated to a Fernando Torres masterclass in the League Cup - the Spanish star netting his first hat-trick for the club. His performance was reminiscent of Ian Rush in his pomp, according to Steven Gerrard.

6 Dirk holds his nerve

Wins at Goodison Park are always sweet, and with memories of the previous season's defeat still fresh, Dirk Kuyt's penalty double, the second in the last minute, made this an even greater occasion to relish.

5 Eight wonders

The biggest Champions League win in history, 8-0 against Besiktas, was even more staggering considering the defeat in Turkey two weeks before - and that anything other than victory could have seen the Reds exit the competition.

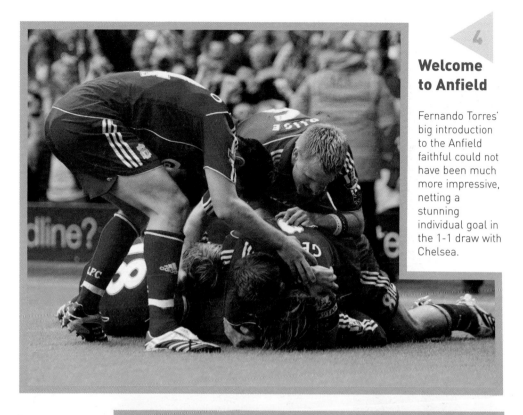

4

Welcome to Anfield

Fernando Torres' big introduction to the Anfield faithful could not have been much more impressive, netting a stunning individual goal in the 1-1 draw with Chelsea.

3

French fancies

An impressive 4-0 win at Marseille secured the Reds' passage into the knockout phase of the Champions League, while Steven Gerrard's goal saw him become Liverpool's record goalscorer in European competition.

43 years of hurt

The 1-0 Champions League win in the San Siro was some revenge for 1965, when the Reds lost over two legs to Inter. This match was also Jamie Carragher's 100th European appearance.

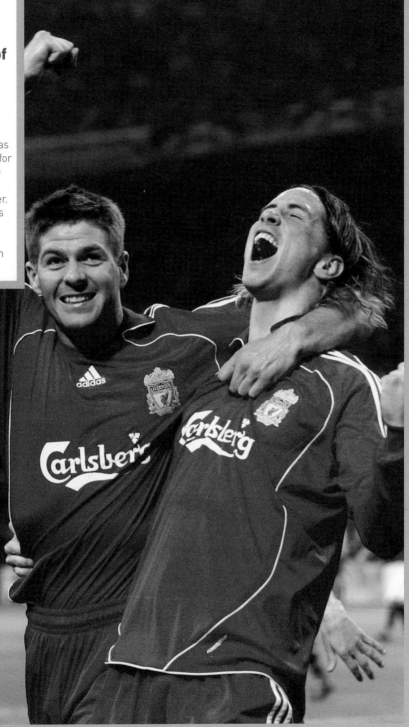

Gunners downed

1

Arsenal at Anfield, Champions League QF, second leg. Behind early on, the Reds turned it around to lead only to be pegged back, the Gunners now ahead on away goals. Enter Ryan Babel to win a penalty, converted by Steven Gerrard, before hitting No. 4 - cue pandemonium.

Team line-ups

Toulouse (4-1-4-1):

Bergougnoux

Elmander

Dieuze   Cesar   Sirieix

Emana

Mathieu   Ebondo
      Fofano   Cetto

Douchez

Subs: Mansare (Bergougnoux) 46, Gignac
(Cesar) 69, Moussa Sissoko (Ebondo) 83
Subs not used: Riou, Batlles, Jonsson, Fabinho

Liverpool (4-4-2):

Crouch   Voronin

Babel   Mascherano   Gerrard   Benayoun

Arbeloa   Hyypia   Carragher   Finnan

Reina

Subs: Riise (Benayoun) 58, Sissoko (Gerrard)
64, Torres (Voronin) 78
Subs not used: Itandje, Agger, Alonso, Kuyt

TOULOUSE 0
LIVERPOOL 1

UEFA Champions League
Third Qualifying Round, 1st Leg
Wednesday August 15, 2007.
Attendance: 30,380

Goal: Voronin (43)
Bookings: Elmander, Cetto, Moussa Sissoko
(Toulouse)
Referee: Kyros Vassaras (Greece)

Team line-ups

Liverpool (4-4-2):

Crouch   Kuyt

Leto   Mascherano   Sissoko   Benayoun

Riise   Hyypia   Agger   Arbeloa

Reina

Subs: Lucas (Sissoko) 68, Babel (Leto) 74,
Finnan (Agger) 81
Subs not used: Itandje, Torres, Alonso, Pennant

Toulouse (4-4-1-1)

Elmander

Emana

Gignac   Dieuze   Fofano   Sirieix

Mathieu   Ilunga   Cetto   Cesar

Douchez

Subs: Bergougnoux (Gignac) 53, Fabinho
(Emana) 76, Moussa Sissoko (Mathieu) 81
Subs not used: Riou, Jonsson, Mansare,
Batlles

LIVERPOOL   4
TOULOUSE   0

UEFA Champions League
Third Qualifying Round, 2nd Leg
Tuesday August 28, 2007.
Attendance: 43,118

Goals: Crouch (19), Hyypia (49), Kuyt (87, 90)
Bookings: None
Referee: Wolfgang Stark (Germany)

Team line-ups

FC Porto (4-3-3):

Lisandro
Quaresma   Sektioui

Meireles   Assuncao   Lucho Gonzalez

Fucile   Alves   Paulo   Bosingwa

Nuno

Subs: Mariano Gonzalez (Meireles) 64, Farias (Sektioui) 64
Subs not used: Ventura, Stepanov, Cech, Bolatti, Kazmierczak

Liverpool (4-4-2):

Torres   Kuyt

Babel   Mascherano   Gerrard   Pennant

Arbeloa   Hyypia   Carragher   Finnan

Reina

Subs: Voronin (Torres) 76, Aurelio (Babel) 85
Subs not used: Itandje, Agger, Benayoun, Crouch, Lucas

FC PORTO   1
LIVERPOOL   1

**UEFA Champions League
Group A game 1**
Tuesday September 18, 2007.
Attendance: 41,208

Goals: Lucho Gonzalez (8, pen), Kuyt (17)
Bookings: Bosingwa (FC Porto), Pennant, Torres, Kuyt, Mascherano (Liverpool)
Sent off: Pennant (Liverpool)
Referee: Lubos Michel (Slovakia)

Team line-ups

Liverpool (4-4-2):

Torres Voronin

Babel Mascherano Gerrard Benayoun

Arbeloa Hyypia Carragher Finnan

Reina

Subs: Kewell (Voronin) 63, Crouch (Benayoun) 71, Kuyt (Babel) 85
Subs not used: Itandje, Riise, Lucas, Sissoko

FC Porto (4-4-1-1):

Lisandro

Quaresma

Kazmierczak L. Gonzalez M. Gonzalez
Assuncao

Cech Alves Stepanov Bosingwa

Helton

Subs: Meireles (Kazmierczak) 65, Sektioui (M. Gonzalez) 77, Postiga (Assuncao) 81
Subs not used: Nuno, Emanuel, Fucile, Bolatti

LIVERPOOL 4
FC PORTO 1

UEFA Champions League
Group A game 5
Wednesday November 28, 2007.
Attendance: 41,095

Goals: Torres (19, 78), Lisandro (33), Gerrard (84, pen) Crouch (87)
Bookings: Hyypia (Liverpool), Assuncao, Stepanov, Quaresma (Porto)
Referee: Roberto Rosetti (Italy)

Team line-ups

Liverpool (4-4-2):

Torres   Crouch

Leto   Sissoko   Gerrard   Benayoun

Aurelio   Hyypia   Carragher   Finnan

Reina

Subs: Riise (Leto) 52, Voronin (Aurelio) 70, Kuyt (Crouch) 76
Subs not used: Itandje, Arbeloa, Babel, Mascherano

Marseille (4-2-3-1):

Niang

Zenden   Ziani   Valbuena

Cheyrou   Cana

Taiwo   Givet   Rodriguez   Bonnart

Mandanda

Subs: Cisse (Niang) 70, Oruma (Valbuena) 84, Arrache (Zenden) 88
Subs not used: Hamel, Zubar, M'Bami, Moussilou

LIVERPOOL   0
MARSEILLE   1

**UEFA Champions League
Group A game 2**
Wednesday October 3, 2007.
Attendance: 41,355

Goal: Valbuena (77)
Bookings: Gerrard, Sissoko, Carragher (Liverpool)
Referee: Konrad Plautz (Austria)

MARSEILLE 0
LIVERPOOL 4

Team line-ups

Niang

Zenden   Valbuena   Ziani

Cheyrou   Cana

Taiwo   Bonnart
Rodriguez   Givet

Mandanda

Nasri (Cheyrou) 34, Faty (Givet) 45,
Cisse (Zenden) 46
        Mate, Oruma, Zubar, M'Bami

Liverpool (4-4-2):

Torres   Kuyt

Kewell   Mascherano   Gerrard   Benayoun

Riise   Hyypia   Carragher   Arbeloa

Reina

Subs: Aurelio (Kewell) 67, Babel (Torres) 77,
Lucas (Kuyt) 86
Subs not used: Itandje, Finnan, Crouch, Hobbs

UEFA Champions League
Group A game 6
Tuesday December 11, 2007.
Attendance: 53,000

Goals: Gerrard (4), Torres (11), Kuyt (48),
Babel (90)
Bookings: Cana (Marseille),
Carragher, Aurelio (Liverpool)
Referee: Terje Hauge (Norway)

90:00
0-4

90'+1 BABEL
48' KUYT
11' TORRES
4' GERRARD

Team line-ups

☪ Besiktas (4-3-3)

Delgado
Bobo
Ozkan

Tello
Cisse
Kurtulus

Uzulun
Toraman
Zan
Tandogan

Arikan

Subs: Avci (Kurtulus) 42, Higuain (Delgado) 62,
Diatta (Bobo) 86
Subs not used: Ozmen, Yozgati, Nobre,
Ricardinho

Liverpool (4-4-2)

Kuyt
Voronin

Babel
Mascherano
Gerrard
Pennant

Riise
Hyypia
Carragher
Finnan

Reina

Subs: Benayoun (Pennant) 59, Lucas
(Mascherano) 76, Crouch (Hyypia) 83
Subs not used: Itandje, Alonso, Sissoko, Hobbs

BESIKTAS 2
LIVERPOOL 1

**UEFA Champions League
Group A game 3**
Wednesday October 24, 2007.
Attendance: 32,500

Goals: Hyypia (13, o.g.), Bobo (82), Gerrard (85)
Bookings: None
Referee: Claus Bo Larsen (Denmark)

Team line-ups

Liverpool (4-4-2):

Crouch Voronin

Riise Mascherano Gerrard Benayoun

Aurelio Hyypia Carragher Arbeloa

Reina

Subs: Babel (Aurelio) 63, Kewell (Voronin) 72, Lucas (Gerrard) 73
Subs not used: Martin, Finnan, Torres, Kuyt

Besiktas (4-3-1-2):

Bobo

Ozkan Delgado

Sedef Cisse Avci

Uzulun Toraman Diatta Kurtulus

Arikan

Subs: Tandogan (Ozkan) 46, Higuain (Kurtulus) 62, Ricardinho (Sedef) 78
Subs not used: Recber, Yozgatli, Kas, Karadeniz

LIVERPOOL 8
BESIKTAS 0

**UEFA Champions League
Group A game 4**
Tuesday November 6, 2007.
Attendance: 41,143

Goals: Crouch (19, 89), Benayoun (32, 53, 56), Gerrard (69), Babel (78, 81)
Booking: Ozkan (Besiktas)
Referee: Markus Merk (Germany)

LIVERPOOL 2
INTER MILAN 0

UEFA Champions League
First knockout round, 1st Leg
Tuesday February 19, 2008.
Attendance: 41,999

Goals: Kuyt (85), Gerrard (90)
Bookings: Chivu, Materazzi
Sending-off: Materazzi
Referee: Frank De Bleeckere (Belgium)

Team line-ups

Liverpool (4-4-2)

Torres
Kuyt

Babel   Lucas   Gerrard
Mascherano

Aurelio   Finnan
Hyypia   Carragher

Reina

Subs: Crouch (Lucas) 64, Pennant (Babel) 72
Subs not used: Itandje, Riise, Arbeloa, Benayoun, Alonso

Inter Milan (4-4-2)

Ibrahimovic
Cruz

Maxwell   Stankovic   Zanetti
Cambiasso

Chivu   Materazzi   Cordoba   Maicon

Cesar

Subs: Vieira (Cruz) 55, Burdisso (Cordoba) 76
Subs not used: Toldo, Maniche, Figo, Suazo, Crespo

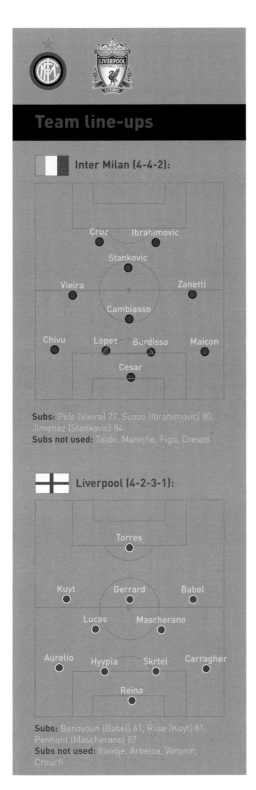

Team line-ups

Inter Milan (4-4-2):

Cruz, Ibrahimovic
Stankovic
Vieira, Zanetti
Cambiasso
Chivu, Lopez, Burdisso, Maicon
Cesar

Subs: Pele (Vieira) 77, Suazo (Ibrahimovic) 80, Jimenez (Stankovic) 84
Subs not used: Toldo, Maniche, Figo, Crespo

Liverpool (4-2-3-1):

Torres
Kuyt, Gerrard, Babel
Lucas, Mascherano
Aurelio, Hyypia, Skrtel, Carragher
Reina

Subs: Benayoun (Babel) 61, Riise (Kuyt) 81, Pennant (Mascherano) 87
Subs not used: Itandje, Arbeloa, Voronin, Crouch

INTER MILAN 0
LIVERPOOL 1

UEFA Champions League
First knockout round, 2nd Leg
Tuesday March 11, 2008.
Attendance: 80,000

Goal: Torres (64)
Bookings: Burdisso, Lopez, Stankovic, Chivu (Inter Milan), Babel, Gerrard, Aurelio, Benayoun (Liverpool)
Referee: Tom Henning Ovrebo (Norway)

Team line-ups

Arsenal (4-4-2)

Adebayor
Van Persie

Hleb
Flamini
Fabregas
Eboue

Clichy
Senderos
Gallas
Toure

Almunia

Subs: Walcott (Van Persie) 46, Bendtner (Eboue) 67
Subs not used: Lehmann, Hoyte, Diaby, Song, Gilberto

Liverpool (4-2-3-1)

Torres

Gerrard
Babel
Kuyt

Alonso
Mascherano

Aurelio
Skrtel
Hyypia
Carragher

Reina

Subs: Benayoun (Babel) 58, Lucas (Alonso) 77, Voronin (Torres) 86
Subs not used: Itandje, Arbeloa, Riise, Crouch

ARSENAL 1
LIVERPOOL 1

**UEFA Champions League
Quarter-final, 1st Leg**
Wednesday April 2, 2008.
Attendance: 60,041

Goals: Adebayor (23), Kuyt (26)
Bookings: None
Referee: Pieter Vink (Holland)

Team line-ups

Liverpool (4-4-2)

Crouch
Torres

Gerrard
Alonso
Mascherano
Kuyt

Aurelio
Skrtel
Hyypia
Carragher

Reina

Subs: Babel (Crouch) 78, Riise (Torres) 87, Arbeloa (Kuyt) 90
Subs not used: Itandje, Lucas, Benayoun, Voronin

Arsenal (4-4-1-1)

Adebayor

Hleb

Diaby
Flamini
Fabregas
Eboue

Clichy
Senderos
Gallas
Toure

Almunia

Subs: Gilberto (Flamini) 42, Van Persie (Diaby) 72, Walcott (Eboue) 72
Subs not used: Lehmann, Hoyte, Song, Bendtner

LIVERPOOL 4
ARSENAL 2

**UEFA Champions League
Quarter-final, 2nd Leg**
Tuesday April 8, 2008.
Attendance: 41,985

Goals: Diaby (13), Hyypia (30), Torres (69), Adebayor (84), Gerrard (86, pen), Babel (90)
Bookings: Senderos, Toure (Arsenal)
Referee: Peter Frojdfeldt (Sweden)

Team line-ups

Liverpool (4-2-3-1)

Torres

Gerrard

Babel Kuyt

Alonso Mascherano

Aurelio Carragher Skrtel Arbeloa

Reina

Subs: Riise (Aurelio) 62, Benayoun (Babel) 76
Subs not used: Itandje, Hyypia, Lucas,
Pennant, Crouch

Chelsea (4-1-4-1)

Drogba

Malouda J. Cole

Lampard Ballack

Makelele

A. Cole Terry Carvalho Ferreira

Cech

Subs: Kalou (J. Cole) 63, Anelka (Ballack) 86
Subs not used: Hilario, Alex, Belletti, Mikel,
Shevchenko

LIVERPOOL 1
CHELSEA 1

**UEFA Champions League
Semi-final, 1st Leg**
Tuesday April 22, 2008
Attendance: 42,180

Goals: Kuyt (43), Riise (90, o.g.)
Booking: Terry (Chelsea)
Referee: Konrad Plautz (Austria)

CHELSEA 3
LIVERPOOL 2
(AET)

UEFA Champions League
Semi-final, 2nd Leg
Wednesday April 30, 2008
Attendance: 38,900

Goals: Drogba (33, 105), Torres (64), Lampard (98, pen), Babel (117)
Bookings: Arbeloa, Alonso (Liverpool)
Referee: Roberto Rosetti (Italy)

Team line-ups

Chelsea (4-1-4-1)

Drogba

J. Cole   Lampard   Ballack   Kalou

Makelele

A. Cole   Terry   Carvalho   Essien

Cech

Subs: Malouda (Kalou) 70, Anelka (J. Cole) 91, Shevchenko (Lampard) 119
Subs not used: Cudicini, Belletti, Alex, Mikel

Liverpool (4-2-3-1)

Torres

Benayoun   Gerrard   Kuyt

Alonso   Mascherano

Riise   Skrtel   Carragher   Arbeloa

Reina

Subs: Hyypia (Skrtel) 22, Pennant (Benayoun) 78, Babel (Torres) 98
Subs not used: Itandje, Finnan, Lucas, Crouch

EUROPEAN/WORLD ROLL OF HONOUR

EUROPEAN CHAMPIONS CUP/UEFA CHAMPIONS LEAGUE

WINNERS
1976/1977, 1977/1978, 1980/1981, 1983/1984, 2004/2005

RUNNERS-UP
1984/1985, 2006/2007

UEFA CUP

WINNERS
1972/1973, 1975/1976, 2000/2001

EUROPEAN CUP WINNERS' CUP

RUNNERS-UP
1965/1966

UEFA SUPER CUP

WINNERS
1977, 2001, 2005

RUNNERS-UP
1978, 1985

INTERCONTINENTAL CUP/FIFA CLUB WORLD CUP

RUNNERS-UP
1981, 1984, 2005

EUROPEAN RESULTS

The 2007/08 campaign again saw Liverpool excel in European competition, the Reds' run to the semi-final of the UEFA Champions League confirming the club's reputation as one of the most successful clubs in Europe - now, as well as historically. Indeed, UEFA's Team Ranking list currently sees the club standing as 2nd in Europe, with only Chelsea above them (ranking based on five-year performance in European competition - correct at August 2008).

The following pages document every Liverpool season in European competition, updated to take into account last season's statistics. In addition, European Player Records, a list of European opponents and Liverpool's club-by-club record will also be noted.

Incidentally, the 2008/09 season will be the club's 35th in European competition.

LIVERPOOL'S RESULTS IN EUROPEAN COMPETITION

Season	Round	Venue	Opponents	Opponent Country	Score	Scorers	Att
1964/65	**EUROPEAN CUP**						
17th Aug	1 Leg 1	(a)	Reykjavik	Ice	5-0	Wallace 2, Hunt 2, Chisnall	10,000
14th Sept	1 Leg 2	(h)	Reykjavik	"	6-1	Byrne, St John 2, Hunt, Graham, Stevenson	32,957
25th Nov	2 Leg 1	(h)	Anderlecht	Bel	3-0	St John, Hunt, Yeats	44,516
16th Dec	2 Leg 2	(a)	Anderlecht	"	1-0	Hunt	60,000
10th Feb	3 Leg 1	(a)	FC Cologne	W.Ger	0-0		40,000
17th Mar	3 Leg 2	(h)	FC Cologne	"	0-0		48,432
24th Mar	Replay	Rotterdam	FC Cologne	"	2-2	St John, Hunt	45,000
			(Liverpool won on toss of a coin)				
4th May	SF Leg 1	(h)	Inter Milan	Ita	3-1	Hunt, Callaghan, St John	54,082
12th May	SF Leg 1	(a)	Inter Milan	"	0-3		90,000
1965/66	**EUROPEAN CUP WINNERS' CUP**						
29th Sept	Pr Leg 1	(a)	Juventus	Ita	0-1		12,000
13th Oct	Pr Leg 2	(h)	Juventus	"	2-0	Lawler, Strong	51,055
1st Dec	1 Leg 1	(h)	Standard Liege	Bel	3-1	Lawler 2, Thompson	46,112
15th Dec	1 Leg 2	(a)	Standard Liege	"	2-1	Hunt, St John	35,000
1st Mar	2 Leg 1	(a)	Honved	Hun	0-0		20,000
8th Mar	2 Leg 2	(h)	Honved	"	2-0	Lawler, St John	54,631
14th Apr	SF Leg 1	(a)	Celtic	Sco	0-1		80,000
19th Apr	SF Leg 2	(h)	Celtic	"	2-0	Smith, Strong	54,208
5th May	Final	Glasgow	B. Dortmund	W.Ger	1-2 aet	Hunt	41,657
1966/67	**EUROPEAN CUP**						
28th Sept	Pr Leg 1	(h)	Petrolul Ploesti	Rom	2-0	St John, Callaghan	44,463
12th Oct	Pr Leg 2	(a)	Petrolul Ploesti	"	1-3	Hunt	20,000
19th Oct	Replay	Brussels	Petrolul Ploesti	"	2-0	St John, Thompson	15,000
7th Dec	1 Leg 1	(a)	Ajax Amsterdam	Hol	1-5	Lawler	65,000
14th Dec	1 Leg 2	(h)	Ajax Amsterdam	"	2-2	Hunt 2	53,846
1967/68	**INTER-CITIES FAIRS CUP**						
19th Sept	1 Leg 1	(a)	Malmo	Swe	2-0	Hateley 2	14,314
4th Oct	1 Leg 2	(h)	Malmo	"	2-1	Yeats, Hunt	39,795
7th Nov	2 Leg 1	(h)	TSV Munich 1860	W.Ger	8-0	St John, Hateley, Smith (pen) Hunt 2, Thompson, Callaghan 2	44,812
14th Nov	2 Leg 2	(a)	TSV Munich 1860	"	1-2	Callaghan	10,000
28th Nov	3 Leg 1	(a)	Ferencvaros	Hun	0-1		30,000
9th Jan	3 Leg 2	(h)	Ferencvaros	"	0-1		46,892
1968/69	**INTER-CITIES FAIRS CUP**						
18th Sept	1 Leg 1	(a)	Athletic Bilbao	Spa	1-2	Hunt	35,000
2nd Oct	1 Leg 2	(h)	Athletic Bilbao	"	2-1 aet	Lawler, Hughes	49,567
			(Liverpool lost on toss of coin)				
1969/70	**INTER-CITIES FAIRS CUP**						
16th Sept	1 Leg 1	(h)	Dundalk	Rep. Ire	10-0	Evans 2, Lawler, Smith 2, Graham 2, Lindsay, Thompson, Callaghan	32,562
30th Sept	1 Leg 2	(a)	Dundalk	"	4-0	Thompson 2, Graham, Callaghan	6,000
12th Nov	2 Leg 1	(a)	Vitoria Setubal	Por	0-1		16,000
26th Nov	2 Leg 2	(h)	Vitoria Setubal	"	3-2	Smith (pen), Evans, Hunt	41,633

LIVERPOOL'S RESULTS IN EUROPEAN COMPETITION

Season	Round	Venue	Opponents	Opponent Country	Score	Scorers	Att
1970/71	**INTER-CITIES FAIRS CUP**						
15th Sept	1 Leg 1	(h)	Ferencvaros	Hun	1-0	Graham	37,531
29th Sept	1 Leg 2	(a)	Ferencvaros	"	1-1	Hughes	25,000
21st Oct	2 Leg 1	(h)	D. Bucharest	Rom	3-0	Lindsay, Lawler, Hughes	36,525
4th Nov	2 Leg 2	(a)	D. Bucharest	"	1-1	Boersma	45,000
9th Dec	3 Leg 1	(a)	Hibernian	Sco	1-0	Toshack	30,296
22nd Dec	3 Leg 2	(h)	Hibernian	"	2-0	Heighway, Boersma	37,815
10th Mar	4 Leg 1	(h)	Bayern Munich	W.Ger	3-0	Evans 3	45,616
24th Mar	4 Leg 2	(a)	Bayern Munich	"	1-1	Ross	23,000
14th Apr	SF Leg 1	(h)	Leeds United	Eng	0-1		52,577
28th Apr	SF Leg 2	(a)	Leeds United	"	0-0		40,462
1971/72	**EUROPEAN CUP WINNERS' CUP**						
15th Sept	1 Leg 1	(a)	Servette Geneva	Swi	1-2	Lawler	16,000
29th Sept	1 Leg 2	(h)	Servette Geneva	"	2-0	Hughes, Heighway	38,591
20th Oct	2 Leg 1	(h)	Bayern Munich	W.Ger	0-0		42,949
3rd Nov	2 Leg 2	(a)	Bayern Munich	"	1-3	Evans	40,000
1972/73	**UEFA CUP**						
12th Sept	1 Leg 1	(h)	E. Frankfurt	W.Ger	2-0	Keegan, Hughes	33,380
26th Sept	1 Leg 2	(a)	E. Frankfurt	"	0-0		20,000
24th Oct	2 Leg 1	(h)	AEK Athens	Gre	3-0	Boersma, Cormack, Smith (pen)	31,906
7th Nov	2 Leg 2	(a)	AEK Athens	"	3-1	Hughes 2, Boersma	25,000
29th Nov	3 Leg 1	(a)	Dynamo Berlin	E.Ger	0-0		19,000
13th Dec	3 Leg 2	(h)	Dynamo Berlin	"	3-1	Boersma, Heighway, Toshack	34,140
7th Mar	4 Leg 1	(h)	Dynamo Dresden	E.Ger	2-0	Hall, Boersma	33,270
21st Mar	4 Leg 2	(a)	Dynamo Dresden	"	1-0	Keegan	35,000
10th Apr	SF Leg 1	(h)	Tottenham H.	Eng	1-0	Lindsay	42,174
25th Apr	SF Leg 2	(a)	Tottenham H.	"	1-2	Heighway	46,919
10th May	F Leg 1	(h)	B. Moench'bach	W.Ger	3-0	Keegan 2, Lloyd	41,169
23rd May	F Leg 2	(a)	B. Moench'bach	"	0-2		35,000
1973/74	**EUROPEAN CUP**						
19th Sept	1 Leg 1	(a)	Jeunesse D'Esch	Lux	1-1	Hall	5,000
3rd Oct	1 Leg 2	(h)	Jeunesse D'Esch	"	2-0	Mond o.g., Toshack	28,714
24th Oct	2 Leg 1	(a)	R.S. Belgrade	Yug	1-2	Lawler	40,000
6th Nov	2 Leg 2	(h)	R.S. Belgrade"		1-2	Lawler	41,774
1974/75	**EUROPEAN CUP WINNERS' CUP**						
17th Sept	1 Leg 1	(h)	Stromsgodset	Nor	11-0	Lindsay (pen), Boersma 2, Thompson 2, Heighway, Cormack, Hughes, Smith Callaghan, Kennedy	24,743
1st Oct	1 Leg 2	(a)	Stromsgodset	"	1-0	Kennedy	17,000
23rd Oct	2 Leg 1	(h)	Ferencvaros	Hun	1-1	Keegan	35,027
5th Nov	2 Leg 2	(a)	Ferencvaros	"	0-0		30,000
1975/76	**UEFA CUP**						
17th Sept	1 Leg 1	(a)	Hibernian	Sco	0-1		19,219
30th Sept	1 Leg 2	(h)	Hibernian	"	3-1	Toshack 3	29,963
22nd Oct	2 Leg 1	(a)	Real Sociedad	Spa	3-1	Heighway, Callaghan, Thompson	20,000
4th Nov	2 Leg 2	(h)	Real Sociedad	"	6-0	Toshack, Kennedy 2, Fairclough, Heighway, Neal	23,796

LIVERPOOL'S RESULTS IN EUROPEAN COMPETITION

Season	Round	Venue	Opponents	Opponent Country	Score	Scorers	Att
1975/76	**UEFA CUP (cont)**						
26th Nov	3 Leg 1	(a)	Slask Wroclaw	Pol	2-1	Kennedy, Toshack	46,000
10th Dec	3 Leg 2	(h)	Slask Wroclaw	"	3-0	Case 3	17,886
3rd Mar	4 Leg 1	(a)	Dynamo Dresden	E.Ger	0-0		33,000
17th Mar	4 Leg 2	(h)	Dynamo Dresden	"	2-1	Case, Keegan	39,300
30th Mar	SF Leg 1	(a)	Barcelona	Spa	1-0	Toshack	70,000
14th Apr	SF Leg 2	(h)	Barcelona	"	1-1	Thompson	55,104
28th Apr	F Leg 1	(h)	FC Bruges	Bel	3-2	Kennedy, Case, Keegan (pen)	49,981
19th May	F Leg 2	(a)	FC Bruges	"	1-1	Keegan	33,000
1976/77	**EUROPEAN CUP**						
14th Sept	1 Leg 1	(h)	Crusaders	N.Ire	2-0	Neal (pen), Toshack	22,442
28th Sept	1 Leg 2	(a)	Crusaders	"	5-0	Keegan, Johnson 2, McDermott Heighway	10,500
20th Oct	2 Leg 1	(a)	Trabzonspor	Tur	0-1		25,000
3rd Nov	2 Leg 2	(h)	Trabzonspor	"	3-0	Heighway, Johnson, Keegan	42,275
2nd Mar	3 Leg 1	(a)	St Etienne	Fra	0-1		38,000
16th Mar	3 Leg 2	(h)	St Etienne	"	3-1	Keegan, Kennedy, Fairclough	55,043
6th Apr	SF Leg 1	(a)	FC Zurich	Swi	3-1	Neal 2 (1 pen), Heighway	30,500
20th Apr	SF Leg 2	(h)	FC Zurich	"	3-0	Case 2, Keegan	50,611
25th May	Final	Rome	B. Moench'bach	W.Ger	3-1	McDermott, Smith, Neal (pen)	57,000
1977/78	**EUROPEAN CUP**						
19th Oct	2 Leg 1	(h)	Dynamo Dresden	E.Ger	5-1	Hansen, Case 2, Neal (pen) Kennedy	39,835
2nd Nov	2 Leg 2	(a)	Dynamo Dresden	"	1-2	Heighway	33,000
1st Mar	3 Leg 1	(a)	Benfica	Por	2-1	Case, Hughes	70,000
15th Mar	3 Leg 2	(h)	Benfica	"	4-1	Callaghan, Dalglish, McDermott, Neal	48,364
29th Mar	SF Leg 1	(a)	B. Moench'bach	W.Ger	1-2	Johnson	66,000
12th Apr	SF Leg 2	(h)	B. Moench'bach	"	3-0	Kennedy, Dalglish, Case	51,500
10th May	Final	Wembley	FC Bruges	Bel	1-0	Dalglish	92,000
1977/78	**EUROPEAN SUPER CUP**						
22nd Nov	Leg 1	(a)	SV Hamburg	W.Ger	1-1	Fairclough	16,000
6th Dec	Leg 2	(h)	SV Hamburg	"	6-0	Thompson, McDermott 3 Fairclough, Dalglish	34,931
1978/79	**EUROPEAN CUP**						
13th Sept	1 Leg 1	(a)	Nottingham Forest	Eng	0-2		38,316
27th Sept	1 Leg 2	(h)	Nottingham Forest	"	0-0		51,679
1978/79	**EUROPEAN SUPER CUP**						
4th Dec	1 Leg 1	(a)	Anderlecht	Bel	1-3	Case	35,000
19th Dec	1 Leg 2	(h)	Anderlecht	"	2-1	Hughes, Fairclough	23,598

LIVERPOOL'S RESULTS IN EUROPEAN COMPETITION

Season	Round	Venue	Opponents	Opponent Country	Score	Scorers	Att
1979/80	**EUROPEAN CUP**						
19th Sept	1 Leg 1	(h)	Dynamo Tblisi	Rus	2-1	Johnson, Case	35,270
3rd Oct	1 Leg 2	(a)	Dynamo Tblisi	"	0-3		80,000
1980/81	**EUROPEAN CUP**						
17th Sept	1 Leg 1	(a)	Oulu Palloseura	Fin	1-1	McDermott	14,000
1st Oct	1 Leg 2	(h)	Oulu Palloseura	"	10-1	Souness 3 (1pen), McDermott 3, Lee, R.Kennedy, Fairclough 2	21,013
22nd Oct	2 Leg 1	(a)	Aberdeen	Sco	1-0	McDermott	24,000
5th Nov	2 Leg 2	(h)	Aberdeen	"	4-0	Miller o.g., Neal, Dalglish, Hansen	36,182
4th Mar	3 Leg 1	(h)	CSKA Sofia	Bul	5-1	Souness 3, Lee, McDermott	37,255
18th Mar	3 Leg 2	(a)	CSKA Sofia	"	1-0	Johnson	65,000
8th Apr	SF Leg 1	(h)	Bayern Munich	W.Ger	0-0		44,543
22nd Apr	SF Leg 2	(a)	Bayern Munich	"	1-1	R.Kennedy	77,600
27th May	Final	Paris	Real Madrid	Spa	1-0	A.Kennedy	48,360
1981/82	**EUROPEAN CUP**						
16th Sept	1 Leg 1	(a)	Oulu Palloseura	Fin	1-0	Dalglish	8,400
30th Sept	1 Leg 2	(h)	Oulu Palloseura	"	7-0	Dalglish, McDermott 2, R.Kennedy, Johnson, Rush, Lawrenson	20,789
21st Oct	2 Leg 1	(a)	AZ '67 Alkmaar	Hol	2-2	Johnson, Lee	15,000
4th Nov	2 Leg 2	(h)	AZ '67 Alkmaar	"	3-2	McDermott (pen), Rush, Hansen	29,703
3rd Mar	3 Leg 1	(h)	CSKA Sofia	Bul	1-0	Whelan	27,388
17th Mar	3 Leg 2	(a)	CSKA Sofia	"	0-2 aet		60,000
1982/83	**EUROPEAN CUP**						
14th Sept	1 Leg 1	(a)	Dundalk	Rep. Ire	4-1	Whelan 2, Rush, Hodgson	16,500
28th Sept	1 Leg 2	(h)	Dundalk	"	1-0	Whelan	12,021
19th Oct	2 Leg 1	(a)	JK Helsinki	Fin	0-1		5,722
2nd Nov	2 Leg 2	(h)	JK Helsinki	"	5-0	Dalglish, Johnson, Neal, A.Kennedy 2	16,434
2nd Mar	3 Leg 1	(a)	Widzew Lodz	Pol	0-2		45,531
16th Mar	3 Leg 2	(h)	Widzew Lodz	"	3-2	Neal (pen), Rush, Hodgson	44,494
1983/84	**EUROPEAN CUP**						
14th Sept	1 Leg 1	(a)	BK Odense	Den	1-0	Dalglish	30,000
28th Sept	1 Leg 2	(h)	BK Odense	"	5-0	Robinson 2, Dalglish 2, Clausen o.g.	14,985
19th Oct	2 Leg 1	(h)	Athletic Bilbao	Spa	0-0		33,063
2nd Nov	2 Leg 2	(a)	Athletic Bilbao	"	1-0	Rush	47,500
7th Mar	3 Leg 1	(h)	Benfica	Por	1-0	Rush	39,096
21st Mar	3 Leg 2	(a)	Benfica	"	4-1	Whelan 2, Johnston, Rush	70,000
11th Apr	SF Leg 1	(h)	D. Bucharest	Rom	1-0	Lee	36,941
25th Apr	SF Leg 2	(a)	D. Bucharest	"	2-1	Rush 2	60,000
30th May	Final	Rome	AS Roma	Ita	1-1 aet	Neal	69,693
			(Liverpool won 4-2 on penalties)				

LIVERPOOL'S RESULTS IN EUROPEAN COMPETITION

Season	Round	Venue	Opponents	Opponent Country	Score	Scorers	Att
1984/85	**EUROPEAN CUP**						
19th Sept	1 Leg 1	(a)	Lech Poznan	Pol	1-0	Wark	35,000
3rd Oct	1 Leg 2	(h)	Lech Poznan	"	4-0	Wark 3, Walsh	22,143
24th Oct	2 Leg 1	(h)	Benfica	Por	3-1	Rush 3	27,733
7th Nov	2 Leg 2	(a)	Benfica	"	0-1		50,000
6th Mar	3 Leg 1	(a)	Austria Vienna	Aut	1-1	Nicol	21,000
20th Mar	3 Leg 2	(h)	Austria Vienna	"	4-1	Walsh 2, Nicol, Obermayer o.g.	32,761
10th Apr	SF Leg 1	(h)	Panathinaikos	Gre	4-0	Wark, Rush 2, Beglin	39,488
24th Apr	SF Leg 2	(a)	Panathinaikos	"	1-0	Lawrenson	60,000
29th May	Final	Brussels	Juventus	Ita	0-1		60,000
1984/85	**EUROPEAN SUPER CUP**						
16th Jan		(a)	Juventus	Ita	0-2		60,000
1991/92	**UEFA CUP**						
18th Sept	1 Leg 1	(h)	Kuusysi Lahti	Fin	6-1	Saunders 4, Houghton 2	17,131
2nd Oct	1 Leg 2	(a)	Kuusysi Lahti	"	0-1		8,435
23rd Oct	2 Leg 1	(a)	Auxerre	Fra	0-2		16,500
6th Nov	2 Leg 2	(h)	Auxerre	"	3-0	Molby (pen), Marsh, Walters	23,094
27th Nov	3 Leg 1	(a)	Swarovski Tirol	Aut	2-0	Saunders 2	12,500
11th Dec	3 Leg 2	(h)	Swarovski Tirol	"	4-0	Saunders 3, Venison	16,007
4th Mar	4 Leg 1	(a)	Genoa	Ita	0-2		40,000
18th Mar	4 Leg 2	(h)	Genoa	"	1-2	Rush	38,840
1992/93	**EUROPEAN CUP WINNERS' CUP**						
16th Sept	1 Leg 1	(h)	Apollon Limassol	Cyp	6-1	Stewart 2, Rush 4	12,769
29th Sept	1 Leg 2	(a)	Apollon Limassol	"	2-1	Rush, Hutchison	8,000
22nd Oct	2 Leg 1	(a)	Spartak Moscow	Rus	2-4	Wright, McManaman	60,000
4th Nov	2 Leg 2	(h)	Spartak Moscow	"	0-2		37,993
1995/96	**UEFA CUP**						
12th Sept	1 Leg 1	(a)	S. Vladikavkaz	Rus	2-1	McManaman, Redknapp	43,000
26th Sept	1 Leg 2	(h)	S. Vladikavkaz	"	0-0		35,042
17th Oct	2 Leg 1	(a)	Brondby	Den	0-0		37,648
31st Oct	2 Leg 2	(h)	Brondby	"	0-1		35,878
1996/97	**EUROPEAN CUP WINNERS' CUP**						
12th Sept	1 Leg 1	(a)	MyPa 47	Fin	1-0	Bjornebye	5,500
26th Sept	1 Leg 2	(h)	MyPa 47	"	3-1	Berger, Collymore, Barnes	39,013
17th Oct	2 Leg 1	(a)	Sion	Swi	2-1	Fowler, Barnes	16,500
31st Oct	2 Leg 2	(h)	Sion	"	6-3	McManaman, Bjornebye Barnes, Fowler 2, Berger	38,514
6th Mar	3 Leg 1	(a)	Brann Bergen	Nor	1-1	Fowler	12,700
20th Mar	3 Leg 2	(h)	Brann Bergen	"	3-0	Fowler 2 (1 pen), Collymore	40,326
10th Apr	SF Leg 1	(a)	Paris St Germain	Fra	0-3		35,142
24th Apr	SF Leg 2	(h)	Paris St Germain	"	2-0	Fowler, Wright	38,984

LIVERPOOL'S RESULTS IN EUROPEAN COMPETITION

Season	Round	Venue	Opponents	Opponent Country	Score	Scorers	Att
1997/98	**UEFA CUP**						
16th Sept	1 Leg 1	(a)	Celtic	Sco	2-2	Owen, McManaman	48,526
30th Sept	1 Leg 2	(h)	Celtic	"	0-0		38,205
21st Oct	2 Leg 1	(a)	RC Strasbourg	Fra	0-3		18,813
4th Nov	2 Leg 2	(h)	RC Strasbourg	"	2-0	Fowler (pen), Riedle	32,426
1998/99	**UEFA CUP**						
15th Sept	1 Leg 1	(a)	FC Kosice	Slovakia	3-0	Berger, Riedle, Owen	4,500
29th Sept	1 Leg 2	(h)	FC Kosice	"	5-0	Redknapp 2, Ince, Fowler 2	23,792
20th Oct	2 Leg 1	(h)	Valencia	Spa	0-0		36,004
3rd Nov	2 Leg 2	(a)	Valencia	"	2-2	McManaman, Berger	49,000
24th Nov	3 Leg 1	(a)	Celta Vigo	Spa	1-3	Owen	32,000
8th Dec	3 Leg 2	(h)	Celta Vigo	"	0-1		30,289
2000/01	**UEFA CUP**						
14th Sept	1 Leg 1	(a)	Rapid Bucharest	Rom	1-0	Barmby	12,000
28th Sept	1 Leg 2	(h)	Rapid Bucharest	"	0-0		37,954
26th Oct	2 Leg 1	(h)	Slovan Liberec	Cz Rep	1-0	Heskey	29,662
9th Nov	2 Leg 2	(a)	Slovan Liberec	"	3-2	Barmby, Heskey, Owen	6,808
23rd Nov	3 Leg 1	(a)	Olympiakos	Gre	2-2	Barmby, Gerrard	43,855
7th Dec	3 Leg 2	(h)	Olympiakos	"	2-0	Heskey, Barmby	35,484
15th Feb	4 Leg 1	(a)	AS Roma	Ita	2-0	Owen 2	59,718
22nd Feb	4 Leg 2	(h)	AS Roma	"	0-1		43,688
8th Mar	5 Leg 1	(a)	FC Porto	Por	0-0		21,150
15th Mar	5 Leg 2	(h)	FC Porto	"	2-0	Murphy, Owen	40,502
5th Apr	SF Leg 1	(a)	Barcelona	Spa	0-0		90,000
19th Apr	SF Leg 2	(h)	Barcelona	"	1-0	McAllister	44,203
16th May	Final	Dortmund	Alaves	Spa	5-4 aet	Babbel, Gerrard, McAllister (pen), Fowler, Geli o.g.	65,000

(Liverpool won on golden goal)

Season	Round	Venue	Opponents	Opponent Country	Score	Scorers	Att
2001/02	**EUROPEAN CUP**						
8th Aug	Q. Leg 1	(a)	FC Haka	Fin	5-0	Heskey, Owen 3, Hyypia	33,217
21st Aug	Q. Leg 2	(h)	FC Haka	"	4-1	Fowler, Redknapp, Heskey, Wilson o.g.	31,602
	First Group Stage						
11th Sept	Group B	(h)	Boavista	Por	1-1	Owen	30,015
19th Sept	Group B	(a)	B. Dortmund	Ger	0-0		50,000
26th Sept	Group B	(h)	Dynamo Kiev	Ukr	1-0	Litmanen	33,513
16th Oct	Group B	(a)	Dynamo Kiev	"	2-1	Murphy, Gerrard	55,000
24th Oct	Group B	(a)	Boavista	Por	1-1	Murphy	6,000
30th Oct	Group B	(h)	B. Dortmund	Ger	2-0	Smicer, Wright	41,507
	Second Group Stage						
20th Nov	Group B	(h)	Barcelona	Spa	1-3	Owen	41,521
5th Dec	Group B	(a)	AS Roma	Ita	0-0		57,819
20th Feb	Group B	(h)	Galatasaray	Tur	0-0		41,605
26th Feb	Group B	(a)	Galatasaray	"	1-1	Heskey	22,100
13th Mar	Group B	(a)	Barcelona	Spa	0-0		75,362
19th Mar	Group B	(h)	AS Roma	Ita	2-0	Litmanen (pen), Heskey	41,794
3rd Apr	QF Leg 1	(h)	B. Leverkusen	Ger	1-0	Hyypia	42,454
9th Apr	QF Leg 2	(a)	B. Leverkusen	"	2-4	Xavier, Litmanen	22,500

LIVERPOOL'S RESULTS IN EUROPEAN COMPETITION

Season	Round	Venue	Opponents	Opponent Country	Score	Scorers	Att
2001/02	**EUROPEAN SUPER CUP**						
24th Aug		Monaco	Bayern Munich	Ger	3-2	Riise, Heskey, Owen	15,000
2002/03	**EUROPEAN CUP**						
			First Group Stage				
17th Sept	Group B (a)		Valencia	Spa	0-2		43,000
25th Sept	Group B (h)		FC Basel	Swi	1-1	Baros	37,634
2nd Oct	Group B (h)		Spartak Moscow	Rus	5-0	Heskey 2, Cheyrou, Hyypia, Diao	40,812
22nd Oct	Group B (a)		Spartak Moscow	"	3-1	Owen 3	15,000
30th Oct	Group B (h)		Valencia	Spa	0-1		41,831
12th Nov	Group B (a)		FC Basel	Swi	3-3	Murphy, Smicer, Owen	35,000
2002/03	**UEFA CUP**						
28th Nov	3 Leg 1 (a)		Vitesse Arnhem	Hol	1-0	Owen	28,000
12th Dec	3 Leg 2 (h)		Vitesse Arnhem	"	1-0	Owen	23,576
20th Feb	4 Leg 1 (a)		Auxerre	Fra	1-0	Hyypia	20,452
27th Feb	4 Leg 2 (h)		Auxerre	"	2-0	Owen, Murphy	34,252
13th Mar	5 Leg 1 (a)		Celtic	Sco	1-1	Heskey	59,759
20th Mar	5 Leg 2 (h)		Celtic	"	0-2		44,238
2003/04	**UEFA CUP**						
24th Sept	1 Leg 1 (a)		Olimpija Ljubljana	Slovenia	1-1	Owen	10,000
15th Oct	1 Leg 2 (h)		Olimpija Ljubljana	"	3-0	LeTallec, Heskey, Kewell	42,880
6th Nov	2 Leg 1 (a)		Steaua Bucharest	Rom	1-1	Traore	25,000
27th Nov	2 Leg 2 (h)		Steaua Bucharest	"	1-0	Kewell	42,837
26th Feb	3 Leg 1 (h)		Levski Sofia	Bul	2-0	Gerrard, Kewell	39,149
3rd Mar	3 Leg 2 (a)		Levski Sofia	"	4-2	Gerrard, Owen, Hamann, Hyypia	40,281
11th Mar	4 Leg 1 (h)		O. Marseille	Fra	1-1	Baros	41,270
25th Mar	4 Leg 2 (a)		O. Marseille	"	1-2	Heskey	50,000
2004/05	**EUROPEAN CUP**						
10th Aug	Q. Leg 1 (a)		AK Graz	Aut	2-0	Gerrard 2	15,000
24th Aug	Q. Leg 2 (h)		AK Graz	"	0-1		42,950
			Group Stage				
15th Sept	Group A (h)		AS Monaco	Fra	2-0	Cisse, Baros	33,517
28th Sept	Group A (a)		Olympiakos	Gre	0-1		33,000
19th Oct	Group A (h)		D. La Coruna	Spa	0-0		40,236
3rd Nov	Group A (a)		D. La Coruna	"	1-0	Andrade o.g.	32,000
23rd Nov	Group A (a)		AS Monaco	Fra	0-1		15,000
8th Dec	Group A (h)		Olympiakos	Gre	3-1	Sinama-Pongolle, Mellor, Gerrard	42,045
22nd Feb	L. 16 L1 (h)		B. Leverkusen	Ger	3-1	Garcia, Riise, Hamann	40,942
9th Mar	L. 16 L2 (a)		B. Leverkusen	"	3-1	Garcia 2, Baros	23,000
5th Apr	QF Leg 1 (h)		Juventus	Ita	2-1	Hyypia, Garcia	41,216
13th Apr	QF Leg 2 (a)		Juventus	"	0-0		55,464
27th Apr	SF Leg 1 (a)		Chelsea	Eng	0-0		40,497
3rd May	SF Leg 2 (h)		Chelsea	"	1-0	Garcia	42,529
25th May	Final	Istanbul	AC Milan	Ita	3-3 aet	Gerrard, Smicer, Alonso	65,000
			(Liverpool won 3-2 on penalties)				

LIVERPOOL'S RESULTS IN EUROPEAN COMPETITION

Season	Round	Venue	Opponents	Opponent Country	Score	Scorers	Att
2005/06	**EUROPEAN CUP**						
13th July	Q.1 Leg 1	(h)	TNS	Wal	3-0	Gerrard 3	44,760
19th July	Q.1 Leg 2	(a)	TNS	"	3-0	Cisse, Gerrard 2	8,009
26th July	Q.2 Leg 1	(a)	FBK Kaunas	Lith	3-1	Cisse, Carragher, Gerrard (pen)	8,300
2nd Aug	Q.2 Leg 2	(h)	FBK Kaunas	"	2-0	Gerrard, Cisse	43,717
10th Aug	Q.3 Leg 1	(a)	CSKA Sofia	Bul	3-1	Cisse, Morientes 2	16,512
23rd Aug	Q.3 Leg 2	(h)	CSKA Sofia	"	0-1		42,175
	Group Stage						
13th Sept	Group G	(a)	Real Betis	Spa	2-1	Sinama-Pongolle, Garcia	45,000
28th Sept	Group G	(h)	Chelsea	Eng	0-0		42,743
19th Oct	Group G	(a)	Anderlecht	Bel	1-0	Cisse	25,000
1st Nov	Group G	(h)	Anderlecht	Bel	3-0	Morientes, Garcia, Cisse	42,607
23rd Nov	Group G	(h)	Real Betis	Spa	0-0		42,077
6th Dec	Group G	(a)	Chelsea	Eng	0-0		41,598
21st Feb	L. 16 L1	(a)	Benfica	Por	0-1		65,000
8th Mar	L. 16 L2	(h)	Benfica	Por	0-2		42,745
2005/06	**EUROPEAN SUPER CUP**						
26th Aug		Monaco	CSKA Moscow	Rus	3-1 aet	Cisse 2, Garcia	18,000
2006/07	**EUROPEAN CUP**						
9th Aug	Q.3 Leg 1	(h)	Maccabi Haifa	Isr	2-1	Bellamy, Gonzalez	40,058
22nd Aug	Q.3 Leg 2	(a)	Maccabi Haifa	"	1-1	Crouch	12,500
	Group Stage						
12th Sept	Group C	(a)	PSV Eindhoven	Hol	0-0		35,000
27th Sept	Group C	(h)	Galatasaray	Tur	3-2	Crouch 2, Garcia	41,976
18th Oct	Group C	(a)	Bordeaux	Fra	1-0	Crouch	33,000
31st Oct	Group C	(h)	Bordeaux	Fra	3-0	Garcia 2, Gerrard	41,978
22nd Nov	Group C	(h)	PSV Eindhoven	Hol	2-0	Gerrard, Crouch	41,948
5th Dec	Group C	(a)	Galatasaray	Tur	2-3	Fowler 2	23,000
21st Feb	L. 16 L1	(a)	Barcelona	Spa	2-1	Bellamy, Riise	88,000
6th Mar	L. 16 L2	(h)	Barcelona	Spa	0-1		42,579
3rd Apr	QF L1	(a)	PSV Eindhoven	Hol	3-0	Gerrard, Riise, Crouch	36,500
11th Apr	QF L2	(h)	PSV Eindhoven	Hol	1-0	Crouch	41,447
25th Apr	SF L1	(a)	Chelsea	Eng	0-1		39,483
1st May	SF L2	(h)	Chelsea	Eng aet	1-0	Agger	42,554
			(Liverpool won 4-1 on penalties)				
23rd May	Final	Athens	AC Milan	Ita	1-2	Kuyt	74,000
2007/08	**EUROPEAN CUP**						
15th Aug	Q. Leg 1	(a)	Toulouse	Fra	1-0	Voronin	30,380
28th Aug	Q. Leg 2	(h)	Toulouse	"	4-0	Crouch, Hyypia, Kuyt 2	43,118
	Group Stage						
18th Sept	Group A	(a)	FC Porto	Por	1-1	Kuyt	41,208
3rd Oct	Group A	(h)	Marseille	Fra	0-1		41,355
24th Oct	Group A	(a)	Besiktas	Tur	1-2	Gerrard	32,500
6th Nov	Group A	(h)	Besiktas	"	8-0	Crouch 2, Benayoun 3, Gerrard, Babel 2	41,143

LIVERPOOL'S RESULTS IN EUROPEAN COMPETITION

Season	Round	Venue	Opponents	Opponent Country	Score	Scorers	Att
2007/08	**EUROPEAN CUP (cont)**						
28th Nov	Group A	(h)	FC Porto	Por	4-1	Torres 2, Gerrard (pen), Crouch	41,095
11th Dec	Group A	(a)	Marseille	Fra	4-0	Gerrard, Torres, Kuyt, Babel	53,000
19th Feb	L. 16 L1	(h)	Inter Milan	Ita	2-0	Kuyt, Gerrard	41,999
11th Mar	L. 16 L2	(a)	Inter Milan	"	1-0	Torres	80,000
2nd Apr	QF Leg 1	(a)	Arsenal	Eng	1-1	Kuyt	60,041
8th Apr	QF Leg 2	(h)	Arsenal	"	4-2	Hyypia, Torres, Gerrard (pen), Babel	41,985
22nd Apr	SF Leg 1	(h)	Chelsea	Eng	1-1	Kuyt	42,180
30th Apr	SF Leg 2	(a)	Chelsea	"	2-3 aet	Torres, Babel	38,900

The captains greet before Liverpool's 8-0 victory over Besiktas - a Champions League record

EUROPEAN PLAYER RECORDS

CORRECT AT END OF 2007/2008 SEASON - Games played includes substitute appearances

EUROPEAN APPEARANCES - ALL COMPETITIONS (45+ GAMES)

		FIRST-TEAM CAREER	GAMES
1	Jamie Carragher	1997-	104
2	Sami Hyypia	1999-	94
3	Steven Gerrard	1998-	91
4	Ian Callaghan	1960-1978	89
5	Tommy Smith	1963-1978	85
6	Ray Clemence	1968-1981	80
7	Emlyn Hughes	1967-1979	79
=	John Arne Riise	2001-2008	79
9	Phil Neal	1974-1985	74
10	Steve Heighway	1970-1981	67
11	Chris Lawler	1963-1975	66
12	Dietmar Hamann	1999-2006	61
13	Kenny Dalglish	1977-1990	51
=	Steve Finnan	2003-2008	51
15	Ray Kennedy	1974-1981	50
=	Michael Owen	1997-2004	50
=	Phil Thompson	1972-1983	50
18	Alan Hansen	1977-1990	46
=	Danny Murphy	1997-2004	46
20	Emile Heskey	2000-2004	45

EUROPEAN CUP/CHAMPIONS LEAGUE APPEARANCES (30+ GAMES)

		FIRST-TEAM CAREER	GAMES
1	Jamie Carragher	1997-	74
2	John Arne Riise	2001-2008	68
3	Sami Hyypia	1999-	67
4	Steven Gerrard	1998-	66
5	Phil Neal	1974-1985	57
6	Kenny Dalglish	1977-1990	47
7	Steve Finnan	2003-	44
8	Alan Hansen	1977-1990	43
9	Pepe Reina	2005-	40
10	Xabi Alonso	2004-	37
=	Dietmar Hamann	1999-2006	37
12	Graeme Souness	1978-1984	36
13	Alan Kennedy	1978-1985	34
14	Ray Clemence	1968-1981	33
=	Sammy Lee	1978-1986	33
16	Ray Kennedy	1974-1981	32
=	Phil Thompson	1972-1983	32
18	Luis Garcia	2004-2007	31
=	Terry McDermott	1974-1982	31
20	Peter Crouch	2005-2008	30
=	Ian Callaghan	1960-1978	30
=	Bruce Grobbelaar	1981-1994	30

EUROPEAN PLAYER RECORDS

INTER-CITIES FAIRS CUP/UEFA CUP APPEARANCES (20+ GAMES)

		FIRST-TEAM CAREER	GAMES
1	Emlyn Hughes	1967-1979	45
2	Ian Callaghan	1960-1978	41
=	Tommy Smith	1963-1978	41
4	Ray Clemence	1968-1981	36
5	Chris Lawler	1963-1975	35
6	Michael Owen	1997-2004	33
7	Steve Heighway	1970-1981	30
8	Jamie Carragher	1997-	28
9	Brian Hall	1969-1976	25
=	Sami Hyypia	1999-	25
11	Robbie Fowler	1993-2001 & 2006-2007	24
=	Steven Gerrard	1998-	24
=	Danny Murphy	1997-2004	24
=	John Toshack	1970-1977	24
15	Larry Lloyd	1969-1974	23
16	Dietmar Hamann	1999-2006	22
=	Emile Heskey	2000-2004	22
=	Kevin Keegan	1971-1977	22
=	Alec Lindsay	1969-1977	22
20	Peter Thompson	1963-1972	20

EUROPEAN CUP WINNERS' CUP APPEARANCES (8+ GAMES)

		FIRST-TEAM CAREER	GAMES
1	Ian Callaghan	1960-1978	17
2	Tommy Smith	1963-1978	16
3	Chris Lawler	1963-1975	15
4	Steve McManaman	1990-1999	11
=	Jamie Redknapp	1991-2001	11
=	Peter Thompson	1963-1972	11
7	Gerry Byrne	1957-1969	9
=	David James	1992-1999	9
=	Tommy Lawrence	1962-1971	9
=	Willie Stevenson	1962-1967	9
=	Ian St John	1961-1971	9
=	Ron Yeats	1961-1971	9
13	Stig Inge Bjornebye	1992-1999	8
=	Ray Clemence	1968-1981	8
=	Steve Heighway	1970-1981	8
=	Emlyn Hughes	1967-1979	8
=	Jason McAteer	1995-1999	8
=	Michael Thomas	1991-1998	8
=	Mark Wright	1991-1998	8

EUROPEAN PLAYER RECORDS

CORRECT AT END OF 2007/08 SEASON- Games played includes substitute appearances

EUROPEAN GOALS

		FIRST-TEAM CAREER	GAMES	GOALS
1	Steven Gerrard	1998-	91	25
2	Michael Owen	1997-2004	50	22
3	Ian Rush	1980-87 & 1988-96	38	20
4	Roger Hunt	1959-1969	31	17
5	Terry McDermott	1974-1982	34	15
6	Robbie Fowler	1993-2001 & 2006-07	44	14
7	Jimmy Case	1975-1981	35	13
=	Emile Heskey	2000-2004	45	13
9	Kevin Keegan	1971-1977	40	12
=	Ray Kennedy	1974-1981	50	12
11	Peter Crouch	2005-2008	30	11
=	Luis Garcia	2004-2007	32	11
=	Kenny Dalglish	1977-1990	51	11
=	Chris Lawler	1963-1975	66	11
=	Steve Heighway	1970-1981	67	11
=	Phil Neal	1974-1985	74	11

EUROPEAN CUP/CHAMPIONS LEAGUE GOALS

		FIRST-TEAM CAREER	GAMES	GOALS
1	Steven Gerrard	1998-	66	21
2	Ian Rush	1980-87 & 1988-96	25	14
3	Terry McDermott	1974-1982	31	12
4	Peter Crouch	2005-2008	30	11
5	Roger Hunt	1959-1969	14	10
=	Luis Garcia	2004-2007	31	10
=	Kenny Dalglish	1977-1990	47	10
=	Phil Neal	1974-1985	57	10
9	Michael Owen	1997-2004	16	9
10	David Johnson	1976-1982	20	8
=	Dirk Kuyt	2006-	23	8
12	Ian St John	1961-1971	13	7
=	Jimmy Case	1975-1981	22	7
=	Djibril Cisse	2004-2006	22	7
15	Fernando Torres	2007-	11	6
=	Emile Heskey	2000-2004	22	6
=	Ronnie Whelan	1981-1994	23	6
=	Ray Kennedy	1974-1981	32	6
=	Graeme Souness	1978-1984	36	6
=	Sami Hyypia	1999-	67	6
21	John Wark	1984-1987	9	5
=	Ryan Babel	2007-	13	5

*First-team career noted as the year a player made his first appearance for the first team, and the year they made their last appearance

EUROPEAN PLAYER RECORDS

CORRECT AT END OF MAY 2008 – Games played includes substitute appearances

INTER-CITIES FAIRS CUP/UEFA CUP GOALS

		FIRST-TEAM CAREER	GAMES	GOALS
1	Michael Owen	1997-2004	33	12
2	Dean Saunders	1991-1992	5	9
3	John Toshack	1970-1977	24	8
4	Kevin Keegan	1971-1977	22	7
5	Phil Boersma	1969-1975	13	6
=	Ian Callaghan	1960-1978	41	6
=	Alun Evans	1968-1972	10	6
=	Emile Heskey	2000-2004	22	6
=	Emlyn Hughes	1967-1979	45	6
10	Jimmy Case	1975-1981	9	5
=	Steve Heighway	1970-1981	30	5
=	Roger Hunt	1959-1969	10	5
=	Tommy Smith	1963-1978	41	5

EUROPEAN CUP WINNERS' CUP GOALS

		FIRST-TEAM CAREER	GAMES	GOALS
1	Robbie Fowler	1993-2001 & 2006-2007	7	7
2	Chris Lawler	1963-1975	15	5
=	Ian Rush	1980-1987 & 1988-1996	4	5
4	John Barnes	1987-1997	7	3

Sami Hyypia - In the Liverpool record books for appearances and goals

LIVERPOOL'S EUROPEAN OPPONENTS

Another three clubs were added to Liverpool's past opposition in European competition following the 2007/2008 season - namely Toulouse, Besiktas and Arsenal. Standard Liege were the 2008/09 opposition in the third qualifying round of the UEFA Champions League, the Reds having last faced the Belgians in 1965/66.

Spain (9) and France (8) are the countries that have provided the biggest variety of clubs that the Reds have faced, with Atletico Madrid set to become the 10th Spanish club in the list following the draw for the 2008/09 UEFA Champions League group stage.

UEFA co-efficients decreed that the Reds again missed out on competing against one of the 19 remaining countries that they have yet to visit in European competition. They are (with qualifiers for the 2008/09 competition in brackets):

Albania (Dinamo Tirana), Andorra (Santa Coloma), Armenia (Pyunik Yerevan), Azerbaijan (Inter Baku), Belarus (BATE Borisov), Bosnia-Herzegovina (FK Modrica), Croatia (Dinamo Zagreb), Estonia (FC Levadia Tallinn), FYR Macedonia (FK Rabotnicki), Faroe Islands (NSI Runavik), Georgia (Dinamo Tbilisi), Kazakhstan (FC Aktobe), Latvia (Ventspils), Liechtenstein, Malta (Valletta), Moldova (Sheriff Tiraspol), Montenegro (Buducnost Podgorica), San Marino (S.S. Murata), Serbia (Partizan Belgrade).

The countries, and the clubs, that Liverpool have faced (up to and including the 2007/2008 season) are listed below and opposite:

AUSTRIA (3)
AK Graz, Austria Vienna, Swarovski Tirol.

BELGIUM (3)
FC Bruges, Anderlecht, Standard Liege.

BULGARIA (2)
CSKA Sofia, Levski Sofia.

CYPRUS (1)
Apollon Limassol.

CZECH REPUBLIC (1)
Slovan Liberec.

DENMARK (2)
Brondby, Odense.

ENGLAND (5)
Arsenal, Chelsea, Leeds United, Nottingham Forest, Tottenham Hotspur.

EAST GERMANY (2)
Dynamo Berlin, Dynamo Dresden.

FINLAND (5)
FC Haka, HJK Helsinki, Kuusysi Lahti, MyPa 47, Oulu Palloseura.

FRANCE (8)
Auxerre, Bordeaux, Olimpique Marseille, Monaco, Paris St Germain, RC Strasbourg, St Etienne, Toulouse.

GERMANY (2)
Bayer Leverkusen, Borussia Dortmund (2001).

GREECE (3)
AEK Athens, Olympiakos, Panathinaikos.

HOLLAND (4)
Ajax Amsterdam, AZ '67 Alkmaar, PSV Eindhoven, Vitesse Arnhem.

HUNGARY (2)
Ferencvaros, Honved.

ICELAND (1)
Reykjavik.

LIVERPOOL'S EUROPEAN OPPONENTS

ISRAEL (1)
Maccabi Haifa.
ITALY (5)
AC Milan, AS Roma, Genoa, Inter Milan,
Juventus.
LITHUANIA (1)
FBK Kaunas.
LUXEMBOURG (1)
Jeunesse D'Esch.
NORTHERN IRELAND (1)
Crusaders.
NORWAY (2)
Brann Bergen, Stromsgodset.
POLAND (3)
Lech Poznan, Slask Wroclaw, Widzew Lodz.
PORTUGAL (4)
Benfica, Boavista, FC Porto, Vitoria Setubal.
REPUBLIC OF IRELAND (1)
Dundalk.
ROMANIA (4)
Dinamo Bucharest, Petrolul Ploesti,
Rapid Bucharest, Steaua Bucharest.
RUSSIA (4)
Dynamo Tblisi, Spartak Moscow,
Spartak Vladikavkaz, CSKA Moscow.
SCOTLAND (3)
Aberdeen, Celtic, Hibernian.
SLOVAKIA (1)
FC Kosice.
SLOVENIA (1)
Olimpija Ljubljana.
SPAIN (9)
Alaves, Atletico Bilbao, Barcelona, Celta Vigo,
Deportivo La Coruna, Real Betis, Real Madrid,
Real Sociedad, Valencia.
SWEDEN (1)
Malmo.
SWITZERLAND (4)
FC Basel, FC Sion, FC Zurich, Servette Geneva.
TURKEY (3)
Besiktas, Galatasaray, Trabzonspor.
WALES (1)
Total Network Solutions.
WEST GERMANY (7)
Bayern Munich, Borussia Moenchengladbach,
Borussia Dortmund (1966), FC Cologne,
Eintracht Frankfurt, Hamburg, 1860 Munich.
UKRAINE (1)
Dynamo Kiev.
YUGOSLAVIA (1)
Red Star Belgrade.

**Liverpool in action for the first time in
European competition against Toulouse,
Besiktas and Arsenal in 2007/08**

LIVERPOOL IN EUROPE: CLUB-BY-CLUB RECORD

OPPOSITION	PLAYED	WON	DRAWN	LOST	FOR	AGAINST
Aberdeen	2	2	0	0	5	0
AC Milan	2	1	0	1	4	5
AEK Athens	2	2	0	0	6	1
Ajax Amsterdam	2	0	1	1	3	7
Alaves	1	1	0	0	5	4
Anderlecht	6	5	0	1	11	4
Apollon Limassol	2	2	0	0	8	2
Arsenal	2	1	1	0	5	3
AS Monaco	2	1	0	1	2	1
AS Roma	5	3	1	1	5	2
Athletic Bilbao	4	2	1	1	4	3
Austria Vienna	2	1	1	0	5	2
Auxerre	4	3	0	1	6	2
AZ '67 Alkmaar	2	1	1	0	5	4
Basel FC	2	0	2	0	4	4
Bayer Leverkusen	4	3	0	1	9	6
Bayern Munich	7	2	4	1	9	7
Benfica	8	5	0	3	14	8
Besiktas	2	1	0	1	9	2
Boavista	2	0	2	0	2	2
Bordeaux	2	2	0	0	4	0
Borussia Dortmund	3	1	1	1	3	2
Bor. Moenchengladbach	5	3	0	2	10	5
Brann Bergen	2	1	1	0	4	1
Brondby	2	0	1	1	0	1
Celta Vigo	2	0	0	2	1	4
Celtic	6	1	3	2	5	6
Chelsea	8	2	4	2	5	5
Club Brugge KV	3	2	1	0	5	3
Crusaders	2	2	0	0	7	0
CSKA Moscow	1	1	0	0	3	1
CSKA Sofia	6	4	0	2	10	5
Deportivo La Coruna	2	1	1	0	1	0
Dinamo Bucharest	4	3	1	0	7	2
Dundalk	4	4	0	0	19	1
Dynamo Berlin	2	1	1	0	3	1
Dynamo Dresden	6	4	1	1	11	4
Dynamo Kiev	2	2	0	0	3	1
Dynamo Tblisi	2	1	0	1	2	4
Eintracht Frankfurt	2	1	1	0	2	0
FC Barcelona	8	3	3	2	6	6
FC Cologne	3	0	3	0	2	2
FC Porto	4	2	2	0	7	2
Ferencvaros	6	1	3	2	3	4
Galatasaray	4	1	2	1	6	6
Genoa	2	0	0	2	1	4
Graz AK	2	1	0	1	2	1
Haka FC	2	2	0	0	9	1
Hamburg	2	1	1	0	7	1
Hibernian	4	3	0	1	6	2
HJK Helsinki	2	1	0	1	5	1
Honved	2	1	1	0	2	0

LIVERPOOL IN EUROPE: CLUB-BY-CLUB RECORD

OPPOSITION	PLAYED	WON	DRAWN	LOST	FOR	AGAINST
Inter Milan	4	3	0	1	6	4
Jeunesse D'Esch	2	1	1	0	3	1
Juventus	6	2	1	3	4	5
Kaunas FBK	2	2	0	0	5	1
Kosice FC	2	2	0	0	8	0
Kuusysi Lahti	2	1	0	1	6	2
Lech Poznan	2	2	0	0	5	0
Leeds United	2	0	1	1	0	1
Levski Sofia	2	2	0	0	6	2
Maccabi Haifa	2	1	1	0	3	2
Malmo	2	2	0	0	4	1
Munich 1860	2	1	0	1	9	2
MyPa 47	2	2	0	0	4	1
Nottingham Forest	2	0	1	1	0	2
Odense	2	2	0	0	6	0
Olimpija Ljubljana	2	1	1	0	4	1
Olympiakos	4	2	1	1	7	4
Olympique Marseille	4	1	1	2	6	4
Oulu Palloseura	4	3	1	0	19	2
Panathinaikos	2	2	0	0	5	0
Paris St Germain	2	1	0	1	2	3
Petrolul Ploesti	3	2	0	1	5	3
PSV Eindhoven	4	3	1	0	6	0
Rapid Bucharest	2	1	1	0	1	0
RC Strasbourg	2	1	0	1	2	3
Real Betis	2	1	1	0	2	1
Real Madrid	1	1	0	0	1	0
Real Sociedad	2	2	0	0	9	1
Red Star Belgrade	2	0	0	2	2	4
Reykjavik	2	2	0	0	11	1
St Etienne	2	1	0	1	3	2
Servette Geneva	2	1	0	1	3	2
Sion FC	2	2	0	0	8	4
Slask Wroclaw	2	2	0	0	5	1
Slovan Liberec	2	2	0	0	4	2
Spartak Moscow	4	2	0	2	10	7
Spartak Vladikavkaz	2	1	1	0	2	1
Standard Liege	2	2	0	0	5	2
Steaua Bucharest	2	1	1	0	2	1
Stromsgodset	2	2	0	0	12	0
Swarowski Tirol	2	2	0	0	6	0
Total Network Solutions	2	2	0	0	6	0
Tottenham Hotspur	2	1	0	1	2	2
Toulouse	2	2	0	0	5	0
Trabzonspor	2	1	0	1	3	1
Valencia	4	0	2	2	2	5
Vitesse Arnhem	2	2	0	0	2	0
Vitoria Setubal	2	1	0	1	3	3
Widzew Lodz	2	1	0	1	3	4
Zurich FC	2	2	0	0	6	1
OVERALL	**288**	**164**	**61**	**63**	**525**	**234**

Games decided on toss of coin (Petrolul) in a third game counted as a draw. One-game ties decided on penalties count as wins or losses.

THAT WAS THE SEASON THAT...

The highs and lows of the 2007/08 season were recorded for posterity as they happened. In the following pages we take a look at events, the injuries, the comings and goings, the quotes - and anything else of relevance.

August
Sebastian Leto is given international clearance to make his Liverpool bow in the 2-0 friendly victory over Shanghai Shenhua, during which Fernando Torres nets his first goal for the club. The Reds are drawn to face Toulouse in the Champions League third-qualifying round - the French club will be Liverpool's 100th opponents in European football. Jose Reina picks up the Barclays Golden Glove award for the second successive season ahead of the new campaign, after keeping 19 clean sheets during 2006/07.
The Reds get off to the perfect start in the Premiership, claiming a 2-1 win at Aston Villa courtesy of a late Steven Gerrard free-kick, while Champions League qualification is all but assured following a 1-0 first-leg triumph in Toulouse. Andriy Voronin is the scorer, his first for the club in sweltering conditions in the south of France.
Fernando Torres impresses in a goalscoring home debut against Chelsea, where only a controversial penalty award denies the Reds victory.
Liverpool fail in their bid to sign Gabriel Heinze from Manchester United, the Argentine only being contractually obliged to move to an overseas club – he leaves for Real Madrid.
Momo Sissoko's first goal for the club in his 76th appearance sets Liverpool on the way to a 2-0 win at Sunderland.
The 4-0 defeat of Toulouse puts Liverpool in the Champions League group phase. The players wore black armbands and observed a minute's silence ahead of the game in memory of 11-year-old Rhys Jones.
The draw sees Porto, Marseille (including old boys Bolo Zenden and Djibril Cisse) and Besiktas as future Group A opponents, while Steven Gerrard is named in the England squad for Euro 2008 qualifiers against Israel and Russia despite a toe injury.

Incoming:
Charles Itandje (Lens), Peter Gulacsi (MTK Hungaria, loan), Mikel San Jose (Athletic Bilbao), Emiliano Insua (Boca Juniors), Damien Plessis (Lyon).

Outgoing:
Lee Peltier (Yeovil Town, loan), Paul Anderson (Swansea City, loan), Florent Sinama-Pongolle (Recreativo Huelva), Scott Carson (Aston Villa, loan), Jimmy Ryan (Shrewsbury Town, loan), Miki Roque (Xerez CD, loan), Nikolay Mihaylov (FC Twente, loan), Gabriel Paletta (Boca Juniors), Besian Idrizaj (Crystal Palace, loan), Anthony Le Tallec (Le Mans, loan).

Injuries:
Harry Kewell (thigh), Steven Gerrard (toe), Jamie Carragher (rib), Sami Hyypia (nose).

Landmarks:
The opening-day triumph at Aston Villa takes Liverpool's all-time Premiership points total to over 1,000. It was also the Reds' first opening-day win for five years.
Peter Crouch makes his 100th Liverpool appearance against Chelsea.
Daniel Agger made his 50th Liverpool appearance against Sunderland.
Momo Sissoko's first goal for the club, at Sunderland, is the club's 7,000th in the league.

Quote of the month:
"This is the first time in my Anfield career that I see genuine competition for every place in the team."

Steven Gerrard, positive for the season ahead

AUGUST

THE GAMES

11	Aston Villa	A	2-1	(Laursen o.g, Gerrard)
15	**Toulouse**	**A**	**1-0**	(Voronin)
19	Chelsea	H	1-1	(Torres)
25	Sunderland	A	2-0	(Sissoko, Voronin)
28	**Toulouse**	**H**	**4-0**	(Crouch, Hyypia, Kuyt 2)

WHERE THEY STOOD

1	Chelsea
2	Manchester City
3	Wigan Athletic
4	**Liverpool**
5	Everton
6	Arsenal
7	Newcastle United

RAFA SAYS . . .

'We will fight to cope with our difficult kick-off times and all the other decisions... going against us.'

THAT WAS THE SEASON THAT...

September

Liverpool storm to the top of the Premiership (the first time under Rafael Benitez) following the 6-0 hammering of Derby County, Xabi Alonso and Fernando Torres scoring twice. A trip to Reading awaits the Reds in the third round of the Carling Cup.

Steven Gerrard plays in England's vital Euro 2008 qualifiers against Israel and Russia despite struggling with a hairline fracture in his toe. The Liverpool skipper helps inspire his country to back-to-back 3-0 wins. Fernando Torres and John Arne Riise are also on target for their countries in qualifying action.

Former boss Gerard Houllier is appointed technical director for the French Football Federation for a second time. Rafael Benitez, along with Sir Alex Ferguson, voices displeasure over early kick-offs ahead of the trip to Portsmouth.

Liverpool secure a hard-earned 1-1 draw at Porto in their first Champions League group game, holding on with 10 men after Jermaine Pennant is sent off for two yellow cards.

It is confirmed that LFC TV will be launched on September 20th, with John Barnes confirmed as one of the presenters. Rafael Benitez suggests that defender Sami Hyypia could be offered a contract extension.

Fernando Torres' first hat-trick for the club earns a 4-2 at Reading in the Carling Cup, with Yossi Benayoun netting the other, his first in a red shirt. The draw for the fourth round sees a return to Anfield for Robbie Fowler and his Cardiff City team-mates.

Outgoing:

Jimmy Ryan (Shrewsbury Town, loan extended).

Injuries:

Steve Finnan (knee), John Arne Riise (groin), Xabi Alonso (foot), Daniel Agger (foot).

Landmarks:

The clean sheet at Wigan – the fifth of the league season – equalled the club's best defensive start to a season (set in 1977). Reina has also equalled Ray Clemence's 1978/79 record for goals conceded in the opening seven league games.

Quotes of the month:

"I feel as if I have been at Liverpool for a long time. I intend to stay here for many years to come and I am really pleased with everything – my new team-mates, the fans, the city, the stadium and, of course with my first goal at Anfield versus Chelsea."

Fernando Torres, settling in at Liverpool

"He was an icon at Atletico Madrid and had to make a personal decision, one that I respect. There is a different air about him now, and it looks like he is enjoying the experience. This is a new challenge, though I am sure that he will triumph."

Raul, on Fernando Torres

"I knew he was good before I arrived because my Valencia team had played against Liverpool. I knew all the players but it was clear watching him with his team-mates how important he was."

Rafael Benitez, impressed with Jamie Carragher

"Fernando Torres...he kills defenders."

Rafael Benitez reveals the key to the Spanish hitman's success!

SEPTEMBER

THE GAMES

1	Derby County	H	6-0	(Alonso 2, Babel, Torres 2, Voronin)
15	Portsmouth	A	0-0	
18	**FC Porto**	**A**	**1-1**	(Kuyt)
22	Birmingham C.	H	0-0	
25	Reading	A	4-2	(Benayoun, Torres 3)
29	Wigan Athletic	A	1-0	(Benayoun)

WHERE THEY STOOD

1   Arsenal
2   Manchester United
3   Manchester City
4   **Liverpool**
5   Everton
6   Portsmouth
7   Blackburn Rovers

RAFA SAYS . . .

'The team is better than before Athens...I'm pleased now because of the players we can use.'

THAT WAS THE SEASON THAT...

October

The reserves lose their unbeaten record against Sunderland, while the first team suffer a shock 1-0 home defeat to Marseille in the Champions League, a performance Rafael Benitez describes as the worst since his time in charge. Steven Gerrard, Peter Crouch and on-loan Scott Carson are named in the England squad for upcoming Euro 2008 qualifiers against Estonia and Russia. A last-minute Fernando Torres equaliser preserves the Reds' unbeaten league start against Tottenham.

Harry Kewell is set to return to training after recovering from a groin injury picked up during the Asian Cup with Australia over the summer.

Steven Gerrard, winning his 60th cap, captains England in the absence of John Terry in their 3-0 defeat of Estonia, although the Liverpool skipper suffers disappointment in Russia, the hosts coming from behind to win 2-1, and it now looks unlikely that the national side will participate in Euro 2008. Ryan Babel is dropped from the Holland starting line-up for their 1-0 loss in Romania.

Former midfield favourite and Reds coach Sammy Lee is dismissed as boss of Bolton, the first Premiership casualty of the season. Lee was in charge for less than six months.

Steve Finnan rescues a point for the Republic of Ireland against Cyprus, his second international goal, but the 1-1 draw means Steve Staunton's team can now not qualify for the Euro 2008 finals. Rafael Benitez insists striker Peter Crouch will not leave the club in the January transfer window. The Reds win the 206th Merseyside derby at Goodison, sweet revenge for last season. Dirk Kuyt's two penalties, the second in injury time, earn a 2-1 win as the Blues end the game with nine men.

Former star Steve Staunton agrees to step down as the Republic of Ireland manager, while the 2-1 defeat at Besiktas leaves the Reds' Champions League ambitions for this season hanging in the balance.

Harry Kewell makes a scoring return in the reserves' 2-1 victory over Newcastle United, the Australian midfielder playing the first half.

Steven Gerrard smashes home the opener against Arsenal, but the Reds are unable to hold on as Arsene Wenger's men earn a 1-1 draw in an entertaining tussle at Anfield.

FA Youth Cup winner Jimmy Ryan looks likely to make his move to Shrewsbury Town permanent during the January transfer window.

Injuries:

Dirk Kuyt (hamstring), Fernando Torres (thigh), Jermaine Pennant (tibia), Xabi Alonso (metatarsal), Javier Mascherano (foot), Fernando Torres (adductor).

Landmarks:

Fernando Torres' late equaliser against Spurs was the 300th goal of Benitez's tenure.

Steven Gerrard marks his 400th Liverpool appearance with an early goal in the 1-1 draw with in-form Arsenal. He is the 26th Liverpool player to reach this milestone.

Steve Finnan made his 400th club career start in the game.

Quotes of the month:

"Liverpool were always my number one choice to stay, but you cannot always have what you want in football. I still have my house here and have no plans to sell, and I get back to the area whenever I can. I feel bonded to this club."

Djibril Cisse, glad to be back at Anfield with Marseille

"A Championship medal is what's missing for me. It would be a great achievement for the club, for the team and for me to win the Premier League."

Sami Hyypia aiming to complete his personal collection

"We showed them we are a better team because we played better this time. You could see our reaction after the game – you could see what it meant for us. But it was not only on the pitch, it was the same atmosphere in the dressing room afterwards."

Dirk Kuyt reveals post-derby delight

OCTOBER

THE GAMES

3	Marseille	H	0-1	
7	Tottenham H.	H	2-2	(Voronin, Torres)
20	Everton	A	2-1	(Kuyt 2 pens)
24	**Besiktas**	**A**	**1-2**	(Gerrard)
28	Arsenal	H	1-1	(Gerrard)
31	Cardiff City	H	2-1	(El Zhar, Gerrard)

WHERE THEY STOOD

3	Manchester City
4	Chelsea
5	Blackburn Rovers
6	**Liverpool**
7	Portsmouth
8	Newcastle United
9	Everton

RAFA SAYS . . .

'When teams spend, people expect. We want to win every trophy. Managers need time to build a team to win the title. '

THAT WAS THE SEASON THAT...

November

The Reds must travel to Chelsea in the Carling Cup quarter-final, while Blackburn's run of seven successive wins is ended at Ewood Park as the points are shared in a 0-0 draw.

The Reds earn a stunning Champions League record 8-0 victory over Besiktas to keep alive their hope of qualifying for the last 16.

Rafael Benitez indicates that he would be keen to sign on-loan midfielder Javier Mascherano on a permanent deal, and celebrates his 200th game in charge with a 2-0 win over Fulham at Anfield.

Peter Crouch scores the winner in England's 1-0 win in Austria, with on-loan Scott Carson making his international debut. Harry Kewell also plays the full 90 minutes in Australia's 1-0 defeat of Nigeria. Fernando Torres is confident of a sustained title challenge this season.

Liverpool and England captain (in the absence of the injured John Terry) Steven Gerrard warns his England team-mates not to freeze against Croatia – although, unfortunately, his warning goes unheeded as they lose 3-2, failing to qualify for a major tournament for the first time since 1994. Crouch equalises after Steve McClaren's side go in 2-0 down at the break – the first goal unfortunate for Carson – before a goal 13 minutes from time ends the country's hopes – and loses the manager his job. There are international disappointments elsewhere for Sami Hyypia and John Arne Riise, who also fail to qualify with their respective countries.

Ian Callaghan and Gerry Byrne are to be awarded World Cup winners medals after being in the England squad in 1966 – a rule only brought in for the 1978 World Cup (to award medals to each squad member).

Former Reds reserve Paul Jewell is appointed Derby County boss, while the Reds keep their Champions League hopes alive courtesy of a 4-1 defeat of Porto. Steven Gerrard is on target, equalling Michael Owen's European goals record in the process.

Outgoing:

Craig Lindfield (Notts County, loan), Ryan Flynn (Hereford United, loan).

Injuries:

Yossi Benayoun (groin).

Landmarks:

The 8-0 romp over Besiktas is a Champions League record.

Yossi Benayoun notched his first hat-trick for the Reds in the demolition of Besiktas.

Steven Gerrard equals Michael Owen's Reds European scoring record.

Quotes of the month:

"He kept on at me all night, which is really good. I might have a little bit of earache but it's all good. It's quality to be playing against Robbie Fowler. He said: 'Aright Jacko' at the start of the game. I think I did alright against him...we won 2-1 and got through to the next round, so happy days."

Jack Hobbs, after making his first Liverpool start alongside Jamie Carragher

"I was tired after a lot of running but the audience gave me a lot of extra energy. When they were singing 'we want 10' when we were leading 5-0, it gave us a lot of energy and we went for 10."

John Arne Riise, post Besiktas

"I want to play for Liverpool, I want to sign a permanent deal. I want roots, and I want them here. I don't want to move again next summer but if I do not sign for Liverpool then I will not play for another club in England."

Javier Mascherano, keen on permanent Anfield switch

NOVEMBER

THE GAMES

3	Blackburn R.	A	0-0	
6	**Besiktas**	**H**	**8-0**	(Crouch 2, Benayoun 3, Gerrard, Babel 2)
10	Fulham	H	2-0	(Torres, Gerrard)
24	Newcastle U.	A	3-0	(Gerrard, Kuyt, Babel)
28	**FC Porto**	**H**	**4-1**	(Torres 2, Gerrard pen, Crouch)

WHERE THEY STOOD

2	Manchester United
3	Manchester City
4	Chelsea
5	**Liverpool**
6	Aston Villa
7	Portsmouth
8	Everton

RAFA SAYS . . .

'I am really happy with my club, my squad, my supporters...'

THAT WAS THE SEASON THAT...

December
The 4-0 defeat of Bolton Wanderers at Anfield means the Reds have now scored 21 goals in their last five games. The game also sees reserve-team captain Jack Hobbs make his league debut as a second-half substitute.

The Reds must travel to Luton Town in the third round of the FA Cup. The Reds' reserves come out on top in the mini-derby, two goals from Krisztian Nemeth helping to secure a 3-0 win.

Reading inflict Liverpool's first league defeat of the season, the Royals winning 3-1

The Reds cruise to a 4-0 win in France, with Steven Gerrard, Fernando Torres, Dirk Kuyt and Ryan Babel on target. The skipper's goal means he is now the club's top scorer in European competition. The club release a statement confirming that a meeting between Rafael Benitez and club owners George Gillett and Tom Hicks is concluded amicably. It is thought team strengthening in January was one of the key topics. Liverpool go down 1-0 to Manchester United, in the first of a Sunday 'Grand Slam' double-header, Arsenal winning the other match by the same score against Chelsea. Jamie Carragher insists he will not make a U-turn on his decision to quit international football, while a weakened Reds side bow out of the Carling Cup quarter-finals at Chelsea, going down 2-0. Italian champions Inter Milan will be the club's opponents in the last 16 of the Champions League. Fernando Torres scores twice as Liverpool defeat Champions League candidates Portsmouth 4-1 at Anfield. A last-minute Steven Gerrard goal earns victory at Derby, while 16-year-old winger Alex Cooper agrees to join the club from Ross County. Leaving is defender James Smith, who has agreed a six-month deal with Stockport County.

Injuries:
Jamie Carragher (rib), Steve Finnan (calf), Steven Gerrard (illness), Sami Hyypia (hamstring, ankle), Alvaro Arbeloa (illness).

Quotes:
"I played many times against him in Spain and I think I am one of his favourite goalkeepers because I have conceded many goals against him, but thankfully he is becoming my friend now!"
Pepe Reina, finds a new friend at Anfield in Fernando Torres

"The most important word in the team talk was 'cup final'. When the manager said it was a cup final situation, you know you've got to give everything you've got."
Steven Gerrard revels in the crucial victory in Marseille

"He's definitely one of the best players in the world. For me he'll go down alongside Kenny Dalglish as one of the greatest players ever to have played for Liverpool and at the moment he's probably in the top four or five players in the world."
Jamie Carragher, impressed with the skipper

"I have been in England for five years and I have never seen a Liverpool side looking so strong in the league at this point of the season."
Carlos Queiroz, impressed with the Reds

"I am not sure how to stop Steven. We shall have to find a way but I do know if you give him space and time and the chance to run forward with or without the ball, he is incredible."
Sven Goran Eriksson, another figure impressed with Steven Gerrard

DECEMBER

THE GAMES

2	Bolton W.	H	4-0	(Hyypia, Torres, Gerrard pen, Babel)
8	Reading	A	1-3	(Gerrard)
11	**Marseille**	**A**	**4-0**	(Gerrard, Torres, Kuyt, Babel)
16	Man Utd	H	0-1	
19	Chelsea	A	0-2	
22	Portsmouth	H	4-1	(Benayoun, Distin o.g., Torres 2)
26	Derby C.	A	2-1	(Torres, Gerrard)
30	Man City	A	0-0	

WHERE THEY STOOD

1 Arsenal
2 Manchester United
3 Chelsea
4 **Liverpool**
5 Manchester City
6 Everton
7 Aston Villa

RAFA SAYS . . .

'For me the sporting achievement is more important than the money in the Champions League. You want to win more trophies.'

THAT WAS THE SEASON THAT...

January

Javier Mascherano reveals his concern that the club have yet to make his loan move permanent. Jermaine Pennant returns to the Reds side in the 1-1 draw with Wigan after a three-month injury absence, while a late John Arne Riise own goal earns cash-strapped Luton Town a replay at Anfield in the FA Cup third round.

Peter Crouch reiterates his desire to stay at the club, while former Liverpool favourite Kevin Keegan makes a surprise return to Newcastle United, becoming their manager for a second time. Lee Peltier goes on trial at Championship side Norwich City (eventually joining Yeovil Town). One-time favourite of the Kop Jari Litmanen goes on trial at Fulham, signing a permanent deal until the end of the campaign. Steve Finnan announces his international retirement.

The Reds survive a scare against Blue Square South side Havant & Waterlooville in the FA Cup fourth round, twice being behind – and level at half-time – before winning through 5-2 thanks to a Yossi Benayoun treble. They will meet Championship strugglers Barnsley at Anfield in round five. Momo Sissoko completes his £8.2m move to Italian giants Juventus. Liverpool go down to a 1-0 defeat at West Ham, Mark Noble scoring the winner in the last minute from the penalty spot. Steven Gerrard and Peter Crouch are included in Fabio Capello's first England squad, while Gary McAllister is appointed Leeds boss.

Incoming:

Alex Cooper (Ross County), Martin Skrtel (Zenit St Petersburg).

Outgoing:

James Smith (Stockport County), Craig Lindfield (Chester City, loan), Robbie Threlfall (Hereford United, loan), Jack Hobbs (Scunthorpe United, loan), Momo Sissoko (Juventus), Lee Peltier (Yeovil), Besian Idrizaj (Wacker Tirol).

Injuries:

Fabio Aurelio (hamstring), Alvaro Arbeloa (calf, adominal strain), Steven Gerrard (calf), Daniel Agger (foot), Andriy Voronin (ankle).

Landmarks:

Xabi Alonso makes his 100th league appearance for the club in the 1-1 draw at Middlesbrough. Jamie Carragher becomes the 12th player to reach 500 appearances for the club in the 5-0 FA Cup third-round replay defeat of Luton Town at Anfield. Steven Gerrard's hat-trick in the match is the first by a Liverpool player in the competition for 12 years.

Quote of the month:

"I don't think I have played against a plumber before! In Spain that would not happen because the teams that are in the cup are all professional. You can only play teams up to two divisions below you. But that is all part of the glamour and the prestige that the FA Cup has. This is why it is so interesting."

Xabi Alonso, ahead of the Havant FA Cup tie

"As the Kop was singing 'You'll Never Walk Alone', I couldn't help myself and joined in. I was singing it at the top of my voice and he (Steven Gerrard) looked at me like I was a weirdo, like I was an alien. But then I don't suppose he gets that too much in the Premier League!"

Jamie Collins, the Havant skipper, relives his big day at Anfield

"The Liverpool fans were amazing, they clapped us on and off the pitch, they're probably the best fans in the country."

Alfie Potter, Havant's second goalscorer

JANUARY

THE GAMES

2	Wigan Athletic	H	1-1	(Torres)
6	Luton Town	A	1-1	(Crouch)
12	Middlesbrough	A	1-1	(Torres)
15	Luton Town	H	5-0	(Babel, Gerrard 3, Hyypia)
21	Aston Villa	H	2-2	(Benayoun, Crouch)
26	Havant & Wat.	H	5-2	(Lucas, Benayoun 3, Crouch)
30	West Ham Utd	A	0-1	

WHERE THEY STOOD

4	Everton
5	Aston Villa
6	Manchester City
7	**Liverpool**
8	Blackburn Rovers
9	Portsmouth
10	West Ham United

RAFA SAYS . . .

'I have two more years and if I can stay for more than two I'll be happy. I want to stay. Finish.'

THAT WAS THE SEASON THAT...

February

Alvaro Arbeloa is named in the Spanish squad for the first time, for their friendly against France – unfortunately injury forces the defender out of the reckoning for an international bow.

Steven Gerrard captains England in their 2-1 friendly defeat of Switzerland, Fabio Capello's first game in charge of the national side. Fernando Torres suffers an injury though in Spain's 1-0 win over France. Premier League clubs approve a plan to explore the possibility of staging an extra round of league fixtures across the world.

The Reds earn a creditable 0-0 draw at Chelsea, the first time they have not lost at a top three ground under Rafael Benitez in the league.

Gary Ablett's reserve side go top of the table after seeing off Sunderland 1-0. Holders Liverpool bow out of the FA Youth Cup, 5-3 after extra time at Sunderland.

On-loan Danny Guthrie reveals that he could make his move to Bolton permanent in the summer. FIFA chief Sepp Blatter insists plans by the Premier League clubs to play games abroad would not go ahead while he was in charge of the world game.

The Reds are dumped out of the FA Cup, a last-gasp Brian Howard strike earning a 2-1 win for Barnsley at Anfield, Liverpool having led at half-time. However, the next game sees 10-man Inter Milan beaten 2-0 at Anfield in the first leg of the Champions League last 16 clash – the Italians' first defeat in five months.

Fernando Torres' second hat-trick for the Reds ensures a 3-2 victory over Middlesbrough, moving the club up to fourth above Everton. Sami Hyypia, out of contract in the summer, is hopeful of earning a new deal. Javier Mascherano completes his permanent deal with the club.

Incoming:

Javier Mascherano (West Ham United).

Injuries:

Fernando Torres (hamstring), Martin Skrtel (calf).

Landmarks:

Pepe Reina's clean sheet against Sunderland means it took the Spanish stopper 92 games to keep 50 clean sheets in the league, beating the former record set by Ray Clemence by three games.

Steven Gerrard's goal against Inter Milan saw him become the first Liverpool player to score in five successive European Champions League/Cup games.

Quotes of the month:

"Normally (an injury) it is a week when a player goes off like this. It is difficult to be calm about it. You can always blame someone, but any solution would be better than this. Every time we have an international break we are talking of a solution and a way to improve things, but nothing happens."

Rafael Benitez, not a fan of international friendlies

"We are not good enough. It is not one particular 'this' or 'that'. It is just that other teams have been playing better than us. We have obviously got to improve both as individuals and as a team."

Jamie Carragher, blunt in his views

"The dressing room has always been happy. We are together and we have always been strong."

Pepe Reina, remaining positive

FEBRUARY

THE GAMES

2	Sunderland	H	3-0	(Crouch, Torres, Gerrard pen)
10	Chelsea	A	0-0	
16	Barnsley	H	1-2	(Kuyt)
19	Inter Milan	H	2-0	(Kuyt, Gerrard)
23	Middlesbrough	H	3-2	(Torres 3)

WHERE THEY STOOD

2	Manchester United
3	Chelsea
4	Everton
5	Liverpool
6	Aston Villa
7	Portsmouth
8	Manchester City

RAFA SAYS . . .

'This is a very, very special club and we are really lucky because we have the support of the best fans in the world.'

THAT WAS THE SEASON THAT...

March

Rafael Benitez reveals his hope of earning a new contract. Liverpool's recent Reebok Stadium hoodoo is ended as the Reds win 3-1 at Bolton. Rafael Benitez tips reserve striker Krisztian Nemeth to shine after seeing the young Hungarian net six goals in six games.

Liverpool win their game in hand 4-0 over West Ham to regain fourth in the Premier League – Fernando Torres scoring a second successive Anfield hat-trick. Ian Rush backs the Reds to finish above Everton, while Torres is named PFA Player of the Month for February.

Fernando Torres makes it 25 for the season in the 3-0 defeat of Newcastle.

Liverpool secure their quarter-final passage into the Champions League following a 1-0 victory over Inter Milan at the San Siro – 3-0 on aggregate – with Fernando Torres again on target.

The quarter-final draw pairs them with Arsenal, meaning the two teams will play three times in the space of six days, with a Premier League encounter sandwiched in between.

Liverpool record their seventh successive win, 2-1 over Reading with Javier Mascherano netting his first goal for the club – while Fernando Torres' winner is his 20th league goal of the season, the first Liverpool player to reach that mark since Robbie Fowler in 1995/96. His achievements are rewarded with February's Premiership Player of the Month award.

Harry Kewell, who had been named Australia captain for their upcoming World Cup qualifier in China, reveals his hope of earning a new deal, while Steven Gerrard and Peter Crouch feature in England's 1-0 defeat in France.

Javier Mascherano is sent off as the Reds are downed 3-0 at Manchester United.

Alvaro Arbeloa makes his Spain debut in the 1-0 friendly win over Italy.

Liverpool complete the derby double over Everton, securing a deserved 1-0 win.

Injuries:

Javier Mascherano (dead leg), Daniel Agger (metatarsal), Harry Kewell (groin), Fernando Torres (ankle, ribs).

Landmarks:

Jamie Carragher makes his 100th appearance in Europe in the 1-0 defeat of Inter Milan in the San Siro – the first player in the club's history to reach this milestone.

Quotes of the month:

"As captain of the team, a rallying cry is sometimes needed. We are disappointed about where we are in the league. It's important we do rally, that we do stick together and keep fighting."

Steven Gerrard, delighted with Bolton win

"He's on his way to the top, if he's not there already. He can only be proud of what he's done. He could score 30 this season. If we can keep playing like this, we know we can give the chances to Fernando. He's scoring nearly every game and if he keeps doing that, we are going to make fourth."

Dirk Kuyt, hails the Reds' star striker

"We're more suited to it than the Premier League, which is more about power and pace. We have good thinkers – players who know the game. Because it's a bit slower in Europe, it suits us. There's a bit of mystique about us – the home crowd's a big thing."

Jamie Carragher, eyeing continued European success

"To score one for Liverpool – and in front of the Kop as well – was really special. I can't really describe the feeling but I know I celebrated like I had gone crazy. Some of the lads in the dressing room said I was like Inzaghi in the Champions League final."

Javier Mascherano, on his goal celebration

MARCH

THE GAMES

2	Bolton W.	A	3-1	(Jaaskelainen o.g., Babel, Aurelio)
5	West Ham	H	4-0	(Torres 3, Gerrard)
8	Newcastle U.	A	3-0	(Pennant, Torres, Gerrard)
11	**Inter Milan**	**A**	**1-0**	(Torres)
15	Reading	H	2-1	(Mascherano, Torres)
23	Man Utd	A	0-3	
30	Everton	H	1-0	(Torres)

WHERE THEY STOOD

1 Manchester United
2 Chelsea
3 Arsenal
4 **Liverpool**
5 Everton
6 Portsmouth
7 Blackburn Rovers

RAFA SAYS . . .

'Steven (Gerrard) can realise his ambitions here. We are progressing, going in the right direction.'

THAT WAS THE SEASON THAT...

April

A 1-1 draw at Arsenal in the Champions League quarter-final, first leg sets the Reds up for the return at Anfield in six days' time – Dirk Kuyt the man on the mark.

Javier Mascherano's initial three-match ban for his dismissal at Manchester United is extended by a further two games. Sami Hyypia agrees a new one-year deal with the club while the Reds record another 1-1 draw against Arsenal – this time in the league at the Emirates, Peter Crouch netting for the visitors. The game sees the Reds make eight changes, including a debut for reserve midfielder Damien Plessis.

A dramatic 4-2 win – 5-3 on aggregate – secures the Reds a third semi-final in four years in the Champions League, with Chelsea again set to be their opponents. The Gunners were ahead on the away goals rule when they hit back to level at 2-2 on the night with six minutes left – only for Steven Gerrard's penalty and Ryan Babel to earn victory.

Robbie Fowler could end the season playing in the FA Cup final after his Cardiff side beat Barnsley to book a return ticket to Wembley.

The 3-1 defeat of Blackburn Rovers sees Fernando Torres reach 30 goals for the season – and cements the Reds' position in the top four.

An injury-time own goal from John Arne Riise denies the Reds victory in the Champions League semi-final, first leg at Anfield. The 2-2 draw at Birmingham, coupled with Everton being held by Aston Villa, ensures 4th spot is confirmed. Steven Gerrard and Fernando Torres are named in the PFA Team of the Year. Despite scoring at Stamford Bridge for the first time in over four years and eight games, the Reds miss out on reaching the first-ever all-English Champions League final, going down 3-2 after extra time – 4-3 on aggregate.

Injuries:

Jermaine Pennant (hamstring), Peter Crouch (toe), Steven Gerrard (neck), Fabio Aurelio (abductor), Fernando Torres (hamstring).

Landmarks:

Fernando Torres reaches 30 goals for the season, while his goal against Blackburn is the seventh consecutive home game in which he has scored – a club record in the top flight.

Torres' 22 league goals is one short of Ruud van Nistelrooy's record for a player in their debut Premier League season.

Steven Gerrard makes his 300th league appearance against Blackburn.

Liverpool reach a century of goals for the season against Blackburn.

Sami Hyypia plays his 300th league game against Fulham.

Jamie Carragher reaches 500 starts in the home Champions League semi-final against Chelsea.

Quotes of the month:

"It is fantastic. For me, Stevie Gerrard is the best player, he is the hero of the fans. So when I hear them sing the song they have for me it makes me feel very pleased."
Fernando Torres enjoys a song

"It's been a while and I thought I'd be a bit rusty. It was nice to score and to remind people that I'm still alive. It's frustrating when you're not involved in the big games."
Peter Crouch, following his league goal at Arsenal

"The atmosphere there is the best in the world. You see the pure football at Anfield. The crowd and the team are as one together. The crowd lifts the team in any situation and that is fantastic."
Manuel Almunia, impressed by Reds' fans

APRIL

THE GAMES

2	Arsenal	A	1-1	(Kuyt)
5	Arsenal	A	1-1	(Crouch)
8	Arsenal	H	4-2	(Hyypia, Torres, Gerrard pen, Babel)
13	Blackburn R.	H	3-1	(Gerrard, Torres, Voronin)
19	Fulham	A	2-0	(Pennant, Crouch)
22	Chelsea	H	1-1	(Kuyt)
26	Birmingham C	A	2-2	(Crouch, Benayoun)
30	Chelsea	A	2-3 aet	(Torres, Babel)

WHERE THEY STOOD

1   Manchester United
2   Chelsea
3   Arsenal
4   **Liverpool**
5   Everton
6   Aston Villa
7   Portsmouth

RAFA SAYS . . .

'Success for us is to win trophies, that is clear, but when you cannot, you must try to do the right things.'

THAT WAS THE SEASON THAT...

May

Javier Mascherano looks likely to miss games at the start of next season after being named in Argentina's Olympics squad. Pepe Reina is confirmed as the golden gloves winner for the third successive season, eventually keeping 18 clean sheets in the league. There could be more Olympics woe for the Reds with Lucas Leiva hopeful of a Brazil call-up.

Liverpool reserves are crowned national champions after defeating Aston Villa 3-0. Dirk Kuyt is recalled to the Holland squad, being named in the initial 30-man squad for Euro 2008.

First-team coach Alex Miller will leave the club to manage J League side JEF United Chiba.

The Reds finish the season on a high, winning 2-0 at Tottenham with Fernando Torres on target to break Ruud van Nistelrooy's record for goals scored in the Premier League in a debut season by an overseas player. Steven Gerrard and Peter Crouch are in the England squad for end-of-season friendlies against the USA and Trinidad & Tobago.

Sammy Lee returns to the club as No 2 to Rafael Benitez, while reserve keeper David Martin signs a new contract, keeping him at Anfield until 2010. Jose Reina, Alvaro Arbeloa, Xabi Alonso and Fernando Torres are named in Spain's Euro 2008 squad.

Robbie Fowler fails to recover from injury as Cardiff lose the FA Cup final 1-0 to Portsmouth.

The Reds confirm a friendly with La Liga runners-up Villarreal for late July. Dirk Kuyt and Ryan Babel are on target in Holland's 3-0 friendly defeat of Ukraine – both are in the squad for Euro 2008. Steven Gerrard nets in England's 2-0 defeat of the USA – his 13th international goal, while John Arne Riise is also on target for Norway in their 2-2 draw with Uruguay. Javier Mascherano is included in Argentina's squad for friendlies against the USA and Mexico. New signing Philipp Degen is in Switzerland's Euro 2008 squad.

Former Reds favourite Patrik Berger returns to his homeland, joining Sparta Prague.

Dirk Kuyt and Ryan Babel feature in Holland's 1-1 draw with Denmark – but the latter is ruled out of Euro 2008 after tearing ankle ligaments in training. Philipp Degen, who will officially join the club on July 1, features in Switzerland's 3-0 defeat of Liechtenstein.

Incoming:

Philipp Degen (Borussia Dortmund).

Injuries:

Ryan Babel (ankle ligaments).

Landmarks:

Fernando Torres equals Roger Hunt's record for scoring in eight consecutive league games at Anfield following the 1-0 defeat of Manchester City.

Liverpool end the season having scored 119 goals - more than any other team in England.

Fernando Torres beats Ruud Van Nistelrooy's record for goals by an overseas player in their first season in English football after hitting his 24th league goal of the season at Tottenham.

2007/08 was the club's third-best Premiership campaign:

82 points - 2005/06; 80 points - 2001/02; 76 points - 2007/08.

Quotes of the month:

"We want to win trophies every season. Maybe next season – we will have to keep improving. We are a strong team and we can win every game."

Fernando Torres, eyeing silverware

"Everyone knows what this club means to me and it's a great pleasure to be back. When a club the size of Liverpool comes in for you and when a manager of the magnitude of Rafael Benitez wants you then you can't say no. When I found out they were interested in me I was really thrilled."

Sammy Lee, delighted to be back at the club

MAY

THE GAMES

4	Man City	H	1-0	(Torres)
11	Tottenham H.	A	2-0	(Voronin, Torres)

WHERE THEY FINISHED

1	Manchester United
2	Chelsea
3	Arsenal
4	**Liverpool**
5	Everton
6	Aston Villa
7	Blackburn Rovers

RAFA SAYS . . .

'Torres is young and hungry. He is a good striker...I don't like to say he is the best but he is the best for us.'

■ Game played
■ Substituted player
■ Unused sub

1 Goal scored
■ Used Sub
■ Substituted sub

2007/08

BARCLAYS PREMIER LEAGUE

Player columns: Steve Finnan, Sami Hyypia, Daniel Agger, John Arne Riise, Harry Kewell, Steven Gerrard, Fernando Torres, Andriy Voronin, Yossi Benayoun, Fabio Aurelio, Xabi Alonso, Peter Crouch, Jermaine Pennant, Alvaro Arbeloa, Dirk Kuyt, Ryan Babel, Javier Mascherano, Lucas, Jamie Carragher, Pepe Reina

Column numbers: 3 4 5 6 7 8 9 10 11 12 13 14 15 16 17 18 19 20 21 22 23 24 25

DATE	OPPONENTS		RES	ATT
Sat 11 Aug	Aston Villa	A	2-1*	42,640
Wed 15 Aug	Toulouse (CL Q3 1st)	A	1-0	30,380
Sun 19 Aug	Chelsea	H	1-1	43,294
Sat 25 Aug	Sunderland	A	2-0	45,645
Tue 28 Aug	Toulouse (CL Q3 2nd)	H	4-0	43,118
Sat 1 Sept	Derby	H	6-0	44,076
Sat 15 Sept	Portsmouth	A	0-0	20,388
Tue 18 Sept	Porto (CL Group game 1)	A	1-1	41,208
Sat 22 Sept	Birmingham	H	0-0	44,215
Tue 25 Sept	Reading (C Cup 3rd)	A	4-2	23,563
Sat 29 Sept	Wigan	A	1-0	24,311
Wed 3 Oct	Marseille (CL Group game 2)	H	0-1	41,355
Sun 7 Oct	Tottenham	H	2-2	43,986
Sat 20 Oct	Everton	A	2-1	40,049
Wed 24 Oct	Besiktas (CL Group game 3)	A	1-2	32,500
Sun 28 Oct	Arsenal	H	1-1	44,122
Wed 31 Oct	Cardiff (C Cup 4th)	H	2-1	41,780
Sat 3 Nov	Blackburn	A	0-0	30,033
Tue 6 Nov	Besiktas (CL Group game 4)	H	8-0	41,143
Sat 10 Nov	Fulham	H	2-0	43,073
Sat 24 Nov	Newcastle	A	3-0	52,307
Wed 28 Nov	Porto (CL Group game 5)	H	4-1	41,095
Sun 2 Dec	Bolton	H	4-0	43,270
Sat 8 Dec	Reading	A	1-3	24,022
Tue 11 Dec	Marseille (CL Group game 6)	A	4-0	53,000
Sun 16 Dec	Man United	H	0-1	44,459
Wed 19 Dec	Chelsea (C Cup 5th)	A	0-2	41,366
Sat 22 Dec	Portsmouth	H	4-1*	43,071
Wed 26 Dec	Derby	A	2-1	33,029
Sun 30 Dec	Man City	A	0-0	47,321
Wed 2 Jan	Wigan	H	1-1	42,308
Sun 6 Jan	Luton (FA Cup 3rd)	A	1-1	10,226
Sat 12 Jan	Middlesbrough	A	1-1	33,035
Tue 15 Jan	Luton (FA Cup 3rd replay)	H	5-0	41,446
Mon 21 Jan	Aston Villa	H	2-2	42,590
Sat 26 Jan	Havant & W'loovile (FAC4)	H	5-2	42,566
Wed 30 Jan	West Ham	A	0-1	34,977
Sat 2 Feb	Sunderland	H	3-0	43,244
Sun 10 Feb	Chelsea	A	0-0	41,788
Sat 16 Feb	Barnsley (FA Cup 5th)	H	1-2	42,449
Tue 19 Feb	Inter Milan (CL last 16 1st)	H	2-0	41,999
Sat 23 Feb	Middlesbrough	H	3-2	43,612
Sun 2 Mar	Bolton	A	3-1*	24,004
Wed 5 Mar	West Ham	H	4-0	42,954
Sat 8 Mar	Newcastle	H	3-0	44,031
Tue 11 Mar	Inter Milan (CL last 16 2nd)	A	1-0	80,000
Sat 15 Mar	Reading	H	2-1	43,524
Sun 23 Mar	Man United	A	0-3	76,000
Sun 30 Mar	Everton	H	1-0	44,295
Wed 2 Apr	Arsenal (CL QF 1st)	A	1-1	60,041
Sat 5 Apr	Arsenal	A	1-1	60,111
Tue 8 Apr	Arsenal (CL QF 2nd)	H	4-2	41,985
Sun 13 Apr	Blackburn	H	3-1	43,283
Sat 19 Apr	Fulham	A	2-0	25,311
Tue 22 Apr	Chelsea (CL SF 1st)	H	1-1	42,180
Sat 26 Apr	Birmingham	A	2-2	29,252
Wed 30 Apr	Chelsea (CL SF 2nd)	A	2-3^	38,900
Sun 4 May	Man City	H	1-0	43,074
Sun 11 May	Tottenham	A	2-0	36,063

^ After extra time*Own goal v Aston Villa (Laursen)*Own goal v Portsmouth (Distin)
*Own goal v Bolton (Jaaskelainen)

	Charles Itandje	Sebastian Leto	Jay Spearing	Ray Putterill	Ryan Flynn	Martin Skrtel	Craig Lindfield	Stephen Darby	David Martin	Nabil El Zhar	Mikel San Jose	Jack Hobbs	Damien Plessis	Emiliano Insua	Mohamed Sissoko
	30	33	34	35	36	37	38	39	40	42	45	46	47	48	

FINAL TABLE

BARCLAYS PREMIER LEAGUE   **2007/08**

	Team	Pd	W	D	L	F	A	W	D	L	F	A	Pts	GD
			HOME					**AWAY**						
1	Man Utd	38	17	1	1	47	7	10	5	4	33	15	87	+58
2	Chelsea	38	12	7	0	36	13	13	3	3	29	13	85	+39
3	Arsenal	38	14	5	0	37	11	10	6	3	37	20	83	+43
4	**Liverpool**	**38**	**12**	**6**	**1**	**43**	**13**	**9**	**7**	**3**	**24**	**15**	**76**	**+39**
5	Everton	38	11	4	4	34	17	8	4	7	21	16	65	+22
6	Aston Villa	38	10	3	6	34	22	6	9	4	37	29	60	+20
7	Blackburn	38	8	7	4	26	19	7	6	6	24	29	58	+2
8	Portsmouth	38	7	8	4	24	14	9	1	9	24	26	57	+8
9	Man City	38	11	4	4	28	20	4	6	9	17	33	55	-8
10	West Ham	38	7	7	5	24	24	6	3	10	18	26	49	-8
11	Tottenham	38	8	5	6	46	34	3	8	8	20	27	46	+5
12	Newcastle	38	8	5	6	25	26	3	5	11	20	39	43	-20
13	Middlesbro	38	7	5	7	27	23	3	7	9	16	30	42	-10
14	Wigan	38	8	5	6	21	17	2	5	12	13	34	40	-17
15	Sunderland	38	9	3	7	23	21	2	3	14	13	38	39	-23
16	Bolton	38	7	5	7	23	18	2	5	12	13	36	37	-18
17	Fulham	38	5	5	9	22	31	3	7	9	16	29	36	-22
18	Reading	38	8	2	9	19	25	2	4	13	22	41	36	-25
19	Birmingham	38	6	8	5	30	23	2	3	14	16	39	35	-16
20	Derby	38	1	5	13	12	43	0	3	16	8	46	11	-69

New-boy Robbie Keane is welcomed to the club by Rafa Benitez

PLAYER STATISTICS 2007/2008

PLAYER	PLAYED	SUBSTITUTED	SUB NOT USED	GOALS
FINNAN	31 + 4	0	6	0
HYYPIA	40 + 4	5	10	4
AGGER	5 + 1	1	3	0
RIISE	31 + 13	4	8	0
KEWELL	9 + 6	9	2	0
GERRARD	47 + 5	10	1	21
TORRES	41 + 5	19	4	33
VORONIN	18 + 10	11	4	6
BENAYOUN	26 + 21	12	5	11
AURELIO	23 + 6	6	0	1
ALONSO	24 + 3	6	6	2
CROUCH	21 + 15	7	11	11
PENNANT	18 + 7	11	3	2
ARBELOA	38 + 3	3	6	0
KUYT	36 + 12	11	4	11
BABEL	29 + 20	23	4	10
MASCHERANO	39 + 2	7	6	1
LUCAS	20 + 12	6	8	1
SISSOKO	10 + 4	2	3	1
CARRAGHER	53 + 2	3	1	0
REINA	52	0	0	0
ITANDJE	7	0	47	0
LETO	4	3	0	0
PUTTERILL	0	0	1	0
SKRTEL	19 + 1	1	3	0
MARTIN	0	0	12	0
EL ZHAR	1 + 2	1	0	1
SAN JOSE	0	0	1	0
HOBBS	3 + 2	0	3	0
PLESSIS	2	0	0	0
INSUA	2 + 1	0	0	0

Tribute to Carra - Who surpassed 500 Liverpool appearances during 2007/08

MINUTES ON PITCH 2007/2008

PLAYER	LEAGUE	FA CUP	LEAGUE CUP	CHAMP. LEAGUE	TOTAL
FINNAN	1956	270	90	549	2865
HYYPIA	2026	354	0	1170	3550
AGGER	434	0	0	81	515
RIISE	1987	360	21	590	2958
KEWELL	605	21	19	112	757
GERRARD	2843	93	103	1157	4196
TORRES	2537	73	90	886	3586
VORONIN	1123	19	90	342	1574
BENAYOUN	1575	247	135	676	2633
AURELIO	1123	17	249	581	1970
ALONSO	1467	254	59	377	2157
CROUCH	925	335	227	474	1961
PENNANT	1135	180	0	180	1495
ARBELOA	2273	90	270	751	3384
KUYT	2164	223	0	936	3323
BABEL	1422	320	163	704	2609
MASCHERANO	2157	102	3	1184	3446
LUCAS	1108	271	267	226	1872
SISSOKO	553	0	180	183	916
CARRAGHER	3043	276	270	1200	4789
REINA	3420	0	0	1290	4710
ITANDJE	0	360	270	0	630
LETO	0	0	152	127	279
SKRTEL	1190	90	0	382	1662
EL ZHAR	0	5	102	0	107
HOBBS	130	0	181	0	311
PLESSIS	180	0	0	0	180
INSUA	205	0	0	0	205

PLAYER GOALS 2007/2008 SEASON

PLAYER	1ST HALF	2ND HALF	EXTRA TIME	TOTAL
TORRES	10	23	0	33
GERRARD	4	17	0	21
BENAYOUN	5	6	0	11
CROUCH	3	8	0	11
KUYT	4	7	0	11
BABEL	2	7	1	10
VORONIN	2	4	0	6
HYYPIA	2	2	0	4
OWN GOALS	3	0	0	3
ALONSO	1	1	0	2
PENNANT	2	0	0	2
AURELIO	0	1	0	1
EL ZHAR	0	1	0	1
LUCAS	1	0	0	1
MASCHERANO	1	0	0	1
SISSOKO	1	0	0	1
TOTAL	41	77	1	119

APPEARANCES & GOALS FOR LIVERPOOL

AT END OF 2007/08 SEASON – CURRENT SQUAD ONLY

L'POOL	LGE GMS	LGE GLS	FA GMS	FA GLS	L. CUP GMS	L. CUP GLS	EURO GMS (inc Spr Cup)	EURO GLS (inc C. Shield & C. World)	OTHER GMS	OTHER GLS	L'POOL GMS	GLS
FINNAN	145	1	13	0	6	0	51	0	2	0	217	1
HYYPIA	302	21	28	2	17	2	94	8	4	0	445	33
AGGER	36	2	1	0	2	1	13	1	1	0	53	4
RIISE	234	21	17	3	13	2	79	4	5	1	348	31
KEWELL	93	12	10	0	5	1	30	3	1	0	139	16
GERRARD	302	55	23	8	19	7	91	25	4	1	439	96
TORRES	33	24	1	0	1	3	11	6	0	0	46	33
VORONIN	19	5	1	0	1	0	7	1	0	0	28	6
BENAYOUN	30	4	3	3	3	1	11	3	0	0	47	11
AURELIO	33	1	2	0	4	0	14	0	1	0	54	1
ALONSO	110	11	9	2	3	0	38	1	3	0	163	14
CROUCH	85	22	11	5	5	1	30	11	3	3	134	42
PENNANT	52	3	3	0	2	0	19	0	1	0	77	3
ARBELOA	37	1	1	0	3	0	14	0	0	0	55	1
KUYT	66	15	5	2	2	0	23	8	0	0	96	25
BABEL	30	4	4	1	2	0	13	5	0	0	49	10
MASCHERANO	32	1	2	0	1	0	17	0	0	0	52	1
LUCAS	18	0	4	1	3	0	7	0	0	0	32	1
CARRAGHER	360	3	29	0	26	0	104	1	4	0	523	4
REINA	106	0	5	0	1	0	41	0	3	0	156	0
ITANDJE	0	0	4	0	3	0	0	0	0	0	7	0
LETO	0	0	0	0	2	0	2	0	0	0	4	0
SKRTEL	14	0	1	0	0	0	5	0	0	0	20	0
EL ZHAR	3	0	1	0	2	1	0	0	0	0	6	1
HOBBS	2	0	0	0	3	0	0	0	0	0	5	0
PLESSIS	2	0	0	0	0	0	0	0	0	0	2	0
INSUA	5	0	0	0	0	0	0	0	0	0	5	0
ROQUE	0	0	0	0	0	0	1	0	0	0	1	0
GUTHRIE	3	0	0	0	3	0	1	0	0	0	7	0
CARSON	4	0	1	0	1	0	3	0	0	0	9	0
LE TALLEC	17	0	4	0	2	0	9	1	0	0	32	1

MAN OF THE SEASON

There was one clear winner for the club's player of the year as voted by LFC Magazine. Possessor of numerous goalscoring records following a blistering first season in English football, record signing Fernando Torres was worth every penny of his fee, and his 33 goals in all competitions ensured the Spain star took the honours. His records/landmarks included:
• His 24 Premier League goals was a record for a foreign player in a debut season;
• The first player to score in eight consecutive top-flight league games at Anfield;
• First player to score 30 goals in a season since 1996/97;
• First Liverpool player to score back-to-back hat-tricks since 1946;
• His 24 goals at Anfield came in only 25 games;
• Became the first non-British player to score 15 goals in the Premier League for Liverpool.

MOST GOALS IN 2007/08

(ALL COMPETITIONS - FOOTBALL LEAGUE CLUBS ONLY)		
CLUB	**GOALS**	**GAMES PLAYED**	**AVERAGE PER GAME**
LIVERPOOL	**119**	**59**	**2.02**
ARSENAL	113	58	1.95
MANCHESTER UNITED	110	57	1.93
WEST BROMWICH ALBION	109	55	1.98
CHELSEA	106	62	1.71
SWANSEA CITY	104	59	1.76
PETERBOROUGH UNITED	102	54	1.89
TOTTENHAM HOTSPUR	102	57	1.79
MILTON KEYNES DONS	97	55	1.76

Man of the season - Fernando Torres

MOST POINTS WON BY TEAMS IN PREMIER LEAGUE HISTORY

07/08 POS.	POS.	CLUB	POINTS	HIGHEST POS	SEASONS IN PREMIERSHIP
1	1	MANCHESTER UNITED	1319	1st (10 times)	16
2	2	ARSENAL	1164	1st (3 times)	16
3	3	CHELSEA	1098	1st (2 times)	16
4	4	LIVERPOOL	1075	2nd (2001/2002)	16
6	5	ASTON VILLA	877	2nd (1992/1993)	16
5	6	NEWCASTLE UNITED	872	2nd (2 times)	15
7	7	TOTTENHAM HOTSPUR	834	5th (2 times)	16
8	8	BLACKBURN ROVERS	805	1st (1994/1995)	14
9	9	EVERTON	800	4th (2004/2005)	16
10	10	LEEDS UNITED	692	3rd (1999/2000)	12
11	11	WEST HAM UNITED	645	5th (1998/1999)	13
13	12	MIDDLESBROUGH	601	7th (2004/2005)	13
12	13	SOUTHAMPTON	587	8th (2002/2003)	13
14	14	MANCHESTER CITY	507	8th (2004/2005)	11
18	15	BOLTON WANDERERS	413	6th (2004/2005)	9
15	16	COVENTRY CITY	409	11th (2 times)	9
16	17	SHEFFIELD WEDNESDAY	392	7th (3 times)	8
17	18	WIMBLEDON (MK DONS)	391	6th (1993/1994)	8
19	19	CHARLTON ATHLETIC	361	7th (2003/2004)	8
20	20	LEICESTER CITY	342	8th (1999/2000)	8
21	21	FULHAM	311	9th (2003/2004)	7
22	22	DERBY COUNTY	274	8th (1998/1999)	7
24	23	SUNDERLAND	268	7th (2 times)	7
23	24	NOTTINGHAM FOREST	239	3rd (1994/1995)	5
29	25	PORTSMOUTH	233	8th (2007/2008)	5
25	26	IPSWICH TOWN	224	5th (2000/2001)	5
26	27	QUEENS PARK RANGERS	216	5th (1992/1993)	4
28	28	BIRMINGHAM CITY	212	10th (2003/2004)	5
27	29	NORWICH CITY	201	3rd (1992/1993)	4
30	30	CRYSTAL PALACE	160	18th (2004/2005)	4
31	31	SHEFFIELD UNITED	132	14th (1992/1993)	3
33	32	WIGAN ATHLETIC	129	10th (2005/2006)	3
36	33	READING	91	8th (2006/2007)	2
32	34	WEST BROMWICH ALBION	90	17th (2004/2005)	3
33	35	OLDHAM ATHLETIC	89	19th (1992/1993)	2
35	36	BRADFORD CITY	62	17th (1999/2000)	2
37	37	WATFORD	52	20th (1999/2000)	2
38	38	BARNSLEY	35	19th (1997/1998)	1
39	39	WOLVERHAMPTON W.	33	20th (2003/2004)	1
40	40	SWINDON TOWN	30	22nd (1994/1995)	1

THE LEAGUE FINISHES

DIVISION ONE/PREMIER LEAGUE - 93 SEASONS

POSITION	NUMBER OF TIMES	MOST RECENT FINAL POSITION
1st	18	1989/90
2nd	11	2001/02
3rd	7	2006/07
4th	8	2007/08
5th	9	2004/05
6th	2	1992/93
7th	4	1998/99
8th	4	1993/94
9th	4	1950/51
10th	2	1931/32
11th	5	1951/52
12th	4	1948/49
13th	2	1914/15
14th	1	1932/33
15th	1	1906/07
16th	4	1927/28
17th	3	1952/53
18th	2	1936/37
19th	1	1935/36
20th	0	-
21st	0	-
22nd	1	1953/54

DIVISION TWO - 11 SEASONS

POSITION	NUMBER OF TIMES	MOST RECENT FINAL POSITION
1st	4	1961/62
3rd	4	1960/61
4th	2	1958/59
11th	1	1954/55

Title celebrations from 1989/90

FULL LEAGUE RECORD - CLUB-BY-CLUB

	PLAYED	WON	DREW	LOST	FOR	AGAINST
ARSENAL	168	68	42	58	238	212
ASTON VILLA	166	78	37	51	293	244
BARNSLEY	12	7	2	3	23	15
BIRMINGHAM CITY	96	46	22	28	159	134
BLACKBURN ROVERS	120	49	37	34	211	164
BLACKPOOL	40	18	9	13	72	62
BOLTON WANDERERS	110	46	29	35	174	135
BRADFORD CITY	26	18	2	6	45	22
BRADFORD PARK AVENUE	6	3	1	2	10	8
BRENTFORD	10	4	3	3	16	16
BRIGHTON & HOVE ALBION	16	8	6	2	36	20
BRISTOL CITY	30	16	3	11	52	39
BRISTOL ROVERS	16	10	1	5	32	21
BURNLEY	74	29	19	26	117	95
BURTON SWIFTS	4	3	1	0	17	3
BURTON UNITED	2	1	0	1	3	2
BURTON WANDERERS	2	1	0	1	5	3
BURY	48	26	14	8	92	53
CARDIFF CITY	26	8	2	16	35	51
CARLISLE UNITED	2	2	0	0	3	0
CHARLTON ATHLETIC	56	29	8	19	93	70
CHELSEA	130	58	28	44	203	183
CHESTERFIELD	2	1	1	0	7	2
COVENTRY CITY	68	39	16	13	113	45
CREWE ALEXANDRA	4	4	0	0	20	1
CRYSTAL PALACE	26	15	6	5	57	17
DARWEN	2	1	1	0	4	0
DERBY COUNTY	126	66	28	32	248	156
DONCASTER ROVERS	10	5	2	3	19	13
EVERTON	178	67	55	56	241	213
FULHAM	42	24	11	7	82	41
GAINSBOROUGH TRINITY	2	2	0	0	8	2
GLOSSOP	4	3	1	0	11	5
GRIMSBY TOWN	36	18	10	8	87	47
HUDDERSFIELD TOWN	68	25	17	26	113	113
HULL CITY	6	5	1	0	15	7
IPSWICH TOWN	60	28	19	13	110	59
LEEDS UNITED	100	51	25	24	164	101
LEICESTER CITY	88	36	19	33	143	121
LEYTON ORIENT	14	9	2	3	37	15
LINCOLN CITY	20	11	4	5	42	28
LOUGHBOROUGH TOWN	2	2	0	0	5	2
LUTON TOWN	28	13	9	6	52	33
MANCHESTER CITY	144	73	34	37	259	188
MANCHESTER UNITED	150	49	43	58	192	209
MIDDLESBROUGH	132	56	39	37	227	169
MIDDLESBROUGH IRONOPOLIS	2	2	0	0	8	0
MILLWALL	4	3	1	0	6	3
NEWCASTLE UNITED	146	69	37	40	251	183
NORTHAMPTON TOWN	2	1	1	0	5	0
NORTHWICH VICTORIA	2	2	0	0	7	2

FULL LEAGUE RECORD - CLUB-BY-CLUB

	PLAYED	WON	DREW	LOST	FOR	AGAINST
NORWICH CITY	46	24	11	11	84	47
NOTTINGHAM FOREST	100	50	24	26	167	99
NOTTS COUNTY	60	34	12	14	110	63
OLDHAM ATHLETIC	24	14	4	6	39	30
OXFORD UNITED	6	5	1	0	20	3
PLYMOUTH ARGYLE	10	5	3	2	22	15
PORTSMOUTH	56	22	15	19	98	85
PORT VALE	12	7	3	2	38	20
PRESTON NORTH END	64	26	17	21	114	99
QUEENS PARK RANGERS	40	28	6	6	68	34
READING	4	3	0	1	7	5
ROTHERHAM UNITED	20	14	3	3	57	21
SCUNTHORPE UNITED	8	6	2	0	17	8
SHEFFIELD UNITED	118	55	27	36	192	153
SHEFFIELD WEDNESDAY	116	54	26	36	197	165
SOUTHAMPTON	74	35	18	21	112	86
STOKE CITY	106	53	27	26	176	113
SUNDERLAND	142	62	31	49	239	210
SWANSEA CITY	20	10	4	6	51	27
SWINDON TOWN	2	1	1	0	7	2
TOTTENHAM HOTSPUR	130	61	34	35	207	145
WALSALL	4	2	2	0	11	3
WATFORD	16	12	1	3	37	16
WEST BROMWICH ALBION	114	53	33	28	176	127
WEST HAM UNITED	102	53	28	21	166	93
WIGAN ATHLETIC	6	5	1	0	12	1
WIMBLEDON	28	11	10	7	41	31
WOLVERHAMPTON WANDERERS	88	43	16	29	136	106

Liverpool against Nottingham Forest - Ton-up in league meetings

PREMIER LEAGUE NUMBERS GAME

SQUAD NUMBERS

NUMBER PLAYERS (PREMIER LEAGUE APPEARANCES IN BRACKETS)

1	Grobbelaar (29),	James (171),	Westerveld (75),	Dudek (92)	
2	R.Jones (125),	Henchoz (135),	Kromkamp (14),	Arbeloa (9)	
3	Burrows (4),	Dicks (24),	Scales (3),	Kvarme (45),	Ziege (16),
	Xavier (14),	Finnan (145)			
4	Nicol (35),	McAteer (100),	Song (34),	Hyypia (229)	
5	M.Wright (104),	Staunton (44),	Baros (68),	Agger (36)	
6	Hutchison (11),	Babb (128),	Babbel (42),	Riise (131)	
7	Clough (39),	McManaman (101),	Smicer (91),	Kewell (93)	
8	Stewart (8),	Collymore (61),	Leonhardsen (37),		Heskey (150),
	Gerrard (132)				
9	Rush (98),	Fowler (144),	Anelka (20),	Diouf (55),	Cisse (49),
	Torres (33)				
10	Barnes (135),	Owen (178),	Garcia (77),	Voronin (19)	
11	Walters (35),	Redknapp (103),	Smicer (30),	Fowler (14),	Gonzalez (25),
	Benayoun (30)				
12	Whelan (23),	Scales (62),	Harkness (38),	Hyypia (73),	Dudek (35),
	P.Jones (2),	Pellegrino (12),	Aurelio (33)		
13	James (14),	Riedle (60),	Murphy (130),	Le Tallec (4)	
14	Molby (25),	Ruddock (19),	Heggem (54),	Alonso (110)	
15	Redknapp (99),	Berger (148),	Diao (11),	Crouch (85)	
16	Thomas (99),	Dundee (3),	Hamann (191),	Pennant (52)	
17	McManaman (108),	Ince (65),	Gerrard (129),	Josemi (21)	
	Bellamy (27),				
	Arbeloa (28)				
18	Rosenthal (3),	Owen (38),	Ferri (2),	Meijer (24),	Riise (103),
	Nunez (18),	Kuyt (66)			
19	Piechnik (1),	Kennedy (16),	Friedel (14),	Arphexad (2),	Morientes (41),
	Babel (30)				
20	Bjornebye (128),	Barmby (32),	Le Tallec (13),	Carson (4),	Mascherano (32)
21	Marsh (2),	Matteo (127),	McAllister (55),	Diao (26),	Traore (48),
	Lucas (18)				
22	Harkness (43),	Camara (33),	Kirkland (25),	Sissoko (51)	
23	Fowler (108),	Carragher (360)			
24	L.Jones (3),	Murphy (40),	Diomede (2),	S-Pongolle (38),	
25	Ruddock (96),	Thompson (48),	Biscan (72),	Reina (106)	
27	Vignal (11)				
28	Gerrard (41),	Cheyrou (31),	Warnock (40)		
29	Friedel (11),	S.Wright (14),	Luzi (1),	Paletta (3)	
30	Traore (40),	Zenden (7),	Padelli (1)		
31	Raven (1)				
32	Newby (1),	Welsh (4),	Zenden (16)		
33	Mellor (12)				
34	Potter (2)				
35	Guthrie (3)				
36	Otsemobor (4)				
37	Litmanen (26),	Skrtel (14)			
42	El Zhar (3)				
46	Hobbs (2)				
47	Plessis (2)				
48	Insua (5)				

MOST APPEARANCES IN PREMIER LEAGUE

1	Jamie Carragher	360
2	Steven Gerrard	302
=	Sami Hyypia	302
4	Robbie Fowler	266
5	Steve McManaman	240
6	John Arne Riise	234
7	Jamie Redknapp	231
8	Michael Owen	216
9	David James	214
10	Dietmar Hamann	191
11	Danny Murphy	170
12	John Barnes	162
13	Rob Jones	155
14	Emile Heskey	150
15	Patrik Berger	148
16	Steve Finnan	145
17	Stig Inge Bjornebye	139
18	Mark Wright	137
19	Stephane Henchoz	135
20	Ian Rush	130
21	Phil Babb	128
22	Jerzy Dudek	127
=	Dominic Matteo	127
24	Vladimir Smicer	121
25	Neil Ruddock	115

Steve Finnan - At number 16

MOST GOALS IN PREMIER LEAGUE

1	Robbie Fowler	128
2	Michael Owen	118
3	Steven Gerrard	55
4	Ian Rush	45
5	Steve McManaman	41
6	Emile Heskey	39
7	Jamie Redknapp	29
8	Patrik Berger	28
=	Own Goals	28
10	Stan Collymore	26
11	Danny Murphy	25
12	Fernando Torres	24
13	John Barnes	22
=	Peter Crouch	22
15	Sami Hyypia	21
=	John Arne Riise	21
17	Milan Baros	19
18	Luis Garcia	18
19	Dirk Kuyt	15
20	Paul Ince	14
21	Djibril Cisse	13
22	Harry Kewell	12

Left to right: Fowler, Redknapp, Collymore - all in the top 10

PREMIER LEAGUE FACTS & FIGURES

LEAGUE RECORD								
Season	P	W	D	L	F	A	Pts	Pos
1992/1993	42	16	11	15	62	55	59	6
1993/1994	42	17	9	16	59	55	60	8
1994/1995	42	21	11	10	65	37	74	4
1995/1996	38	20	11	7	70	34	71	3
1996/1997	38	19	11	8	62	37	68	4
1997/1998	38	18	11	9	68	42	65	3
1998/1999	38	15	9	14	68	49	54	7
1999/2000	38	19	10	9	51	30	67	4
2000/2001	38	20	9	9	71	39	69	3
2001/2002	38	24	8	6	67	30	80	2
2002/2003	38	18	10	10	61	41	64	5
2003/2004	38	16	12	10	55	37	60	4
2004/2005	38	17	7	14	52	41	58	5
2005/2006	38	25	7	6	57	25	82	3
2006/2007	38	20	8	10	57	27	68	3
2007/2008	38	21	13	4	67	28	76	4

Joint second - Liverpool's 6-0 victory over Derby County

PREMIER LEAGUE FACTS & FIGURES

BIGGEST WINS (ALL HOME UNLESS STATED)

DATE	OPPONENTS	SCORE	LIVERPOOL SCORERS	ATT.
16th Jan 1999	Southampton	7-1	Fowler 3, Matteo, Carragher, Owen, Thompson	44,011
1st Sept 2007	Derby County	6-0	Alonso 2, Babel, Torres 2, Voronin	44,076
26th Apr 2003	West Brom	6-0	Owen 4, Baros 2	27,128*
9th Feb 2002	Ipswich Town	6-0	Abel Xavier, Heskey 2, Hyypia, Owen 2	25,608**
28th Oct 1995	Manchester City	6-0	Rush 2, Redknapp, Fowler 2, Ruddock	39,267

(*At The Hawthorns)
(**At Portman Road)

BIGGEST DEFEATS (ALL AWAY UNLESS STATED)

DATE	OPPONENTS	SCORE	LIVERPOOL SCORER	ATT.
19th Dec 1992	Coventry City	1-5	Redknapp	19,779
5th Apr 2003	Manchester Utd	0-4		67,639
2nd Oct 2005	Chelsea	1-4	Gerrard	44,235*
16th Dec 2001	Chelsea	0-4		41,174
25th Apr 1998	Chelsea	1-4	Riedle	34,639
3rd Apr 1992	Blackburn Rovers	1-4	Rush	15,032

(*At Anfield)

AVERAGE HOME ATTENDANCES

Season	High	Low	Average	High/Low
1992/1993	44,619	29,574	37,009	
1993/1994	44,601	24,561	38,503	LOWEST ATTENDANCE, v QPR
1994/1995	40,014	27,183	34,175	LOWEST SEASON AVERAGE
1995/1996	40,820	34,063	39,552	
1996/1997	40,892	36,126	39,776	
1997/1998	44,532	34,705	40,628	
1998/1999	44,852	36,019	43,321	
1999/2000	44,929	40,483	44,074	
2000/2001	44,806	38,474	43,698	
2001/2002	44,371	37,153	43,389	
2002/2003	44,250	41,462	43,243	
2003/2004	44,374	34,663	42,677	
2004/2005	44,224	35,064	42,587	
2005/2006	44,983	42,293	44,236	HIGHEST SEASON AVERAGE / HIGHEST ATTENDANCE, v SPURS
2006/2007	44,403	41,370	43,561	
2007/2008	44,459	42,308	43,532	

AWAY GOALSCORERS IN THE PREMIER LEAGUE

FIRST 400 GOALS

Jermaine Pennant's goal at Fulham in April 2008 saw Liverpool reach the significant landmark, and the following tables highlight who has been the most prolific away from Anfield, and who reached each milestone for the club.

GOALS	PLAYER	GOALS	PLAYER
55	Michael Owen	2	Julian Dicks
43	Robbie Fowler	2	Dietmar Hamann
23	Steve McManaman	2	Paul Ince
22	Emile Heskey	2	Oyvind Leonhardsen
21	Ian Rush	2	Fernando Morientes
19	Steven Gerrard	2	Ronny Rosenthal
12	Danny Murphy	2	Fernando Torres
12	John Arne Riise	2	Mark Walters
11	John Barnes	2	Ronnie Whelan
11	Jamie Redknapp	2	Mark Wright
10	Milan Baros	1	Nicolas Anelka
10	Sami Hyypia	1	Alvaro Arbeloa
10	Own Goals	1	Fabio Aurelio
8	Patrik Berger	1	Phil Babb
8	Djibril Cisse	1	Markus Babbel
8	Luis Garcia	1	Yossi Benayoun
7	Stan Collymore	1	Igor Biscan
7	Peter Crouch	1	Stig Inge Bjornebye
7	Karlheinz Riedle	1	Nigel Clough
6	Dirk Kuyt	1	Salif Diao
5	Titi Camara	1	Steve Harkness
5	Craig Bellamy	1	Vegard Heggem
5	Harry Kewell	1	Jason McAteer
5	Vladimir Smicer	1	Mike Marsh
4	Don Hutchison	1	Steve Nicol
4	Neil Ruddock	1	Jermaine Pennant
4	Michael Thomas	1	Florent Sinama-Pongolle
3	Xabi Alonso	1	Momo Sissoko
3	Jari Litmanen	1	David Thompson
3	Gary McAllister	1	Andriy Voronin
3	Jan Molby	1	Abel Xavier
2	Ryan Babel	1	Christian Ziege
2	Bruno Cheyrou		

LANDMARK GOALSCORERS

GOAL	PLAYER	DATE/SCORE/OPPOSITION
1	Mark Walters	25th August 1992 - 2-2 v Ipswich Town
50	Robbie Fowler	20th August 1994 - 6-1 v Crystal Palace
100	John Barnes	17th August 1996 - 3-3 v Middlesbrough
150	Michael Owen	16th August 1998 - 2-1 v Southampton
200	Emile Heskey	15th October 2000 - 4-0 v Derby County
250	Abel Xavier	9th February 2002 - 6-0 v Ipswich Town
300	Emile Heskey	2nd November 2003 - 2-1 v Fulham
350	Luis Garcia	2nd January 2006 - 2-2 v Bolton Wanderers
400	Jermaine Pennant	19th April 2008 - 2-0 v Fulham

LIVERPOOL'S PREMIER LEAGUE RED CARDS

DATE	PLAYER	OPPONENTS	VENUE	MINUTE OF DISMISSAL	SCORE AT TIME	FINAL SCORE (IN FAVOUR OF L'POOL)
19/12/92	Jamie Redknapp	Coventry City	Away	69	1-3	1-5
01/05/93	David James	Norwich City	Away	61	0-0	0-1
05/05/93	Don Hutchison	Oldham Ath.	Away	76	2-3	2-3
01/09/93	Rob Jones	Coventry City	Away	70	0-1	0-1
04/02/95	Phil Babb	Nottingham F.	Away	52	0-1	1-1
16/04/97	Robbie Fowler	Everton	Away	82	1-1	1-1
01/11/97	Robbie Fowler	Bolton Wan.	Away	76	1-0	1-1
10/04/98	Michael Owen	Man Utd	Away	41	1-1	1-1
31/10/98	Jason McAteer	Leicester City	Away	85	0-1	0-1
06/02/99	Dominic Matteo	Middlesbrough	Home	64	3-0	3-1
13/02/99	Jamie Carragher	Charlton Ath.	Away	68	0-0	0-1
18/09/99	David Thompson	Leicester City	Away	90	2-2	2-2
27/09/99	Sander Westerveld	Everton	Home	75	0-1	0-1
27/09/99	Steven Gerrard	Everton	Home	90	0-1	0 1
02/10/99	Steve Staunton	Aston Villa	Away	31*	0-0	0-0
21/08/00	Gary McAllister	Arsenal	Away	39	0-1	0-2
21/08/00	Dietmar Hamann	Arsenal	Away	78*	0-1	0-2
31/03/01	Danny Murphy	Man Utd	Home	69	2-0	2-0
13/04/01	Steven Gerrard	Leeds United	Home	71	1-2	1-2
16/04/01	Igor Biscan	Everton	Away	77	2-1	3-2
08/09/01	Steven Gerrard	Aston Villa	Home	74	1-2	1-3
27/10/01	Stephen Wright	Charlton Ath.	Away	88	2-0	2-0
25/11/01	Dietmar Hamann	Sunderland	Home	44	1-0	1-0
01/01/03	Salif Diao	Newcastle U.	Away	65	0-1	0-1
05/04/03	Sami Hyypia	Man Utd	Away	4	0-0	0-4
11/05/03	Steven Gerrard	Chelsea	Away	90	1-2	1-2
07/01/04	El-Hadji Diouf	Chelsea	Away	86	1-0	1-0
16/10/04	Josemi	Fulham	Away	77	2-2	4-2
20/03/05	Milan Baros	Everton	Home	77	2-0	2-1
30/11/05	Mohamed Sissoko	Sunderland	Away	65	2-0	2-0
05/02/06	Pepe Reina	Chelsea	Away	82	0-2	0-2
12/03/06	Xabi Alonso	Arsenal	Away	81	1-1	1-2
25/03/06	Steven Gerrard	Everton	Home	18	0-0	3-1
26/04/06	Luis Garcia	West Ham	Away	82	2-1	2-1
23/03/08	Javier Mascherano	Man Utd	Away	44	0-1	0-3

* Later rescinded

PLAYERS SENT OFF AGAINST LIVERPOOL IN PREMIER LEAGUE

DATE	PLAYER	OPPONENTS	VENUE	MINUTE OF DISMISSAL	SCORE AT TIME (IN FAVOUR OF L'POOL)	FINAL SCORE
31/01/93	Nigel Winterburn	Arsenal	Away	87	1-0	1-0
27/02/93	Nigel Worthington	Sheff. Wed.	Away	65	1-0	1-1
14/08/93	Carlton Palmer	Sheff. Wed.	Home	12	0-0	2-0
08/12/93	Simon Barker	QPR	Home	78	2-2	3-2
08/12/93	Les Ferdinand	QPR	Home	82	3-2	3-2
05/02/94	Bryan Gunn	Norwich City	Away	89	2-2	2-2
10/09/94	Tony Cottee	West Ham	Home	54	0-0	0-0
24/09/94	Philippe Albert	Newcastle U.	Away	80	1-1	1-1
09/11/94	Erland Johnsen	Chelsea	Home	72	3-1	3-1
26/12/94	Simon Grayson	Leicester City	Away	82	2-0	2-1
17/04/95	Mike Whitlow	Leicester City	Home	72	0-0	2-0
09/09/95	Vinnie Jones	Wimbledon	Away	23	0-0	0-1
16/09/95	Henning Berg	Blackburn R.	Home	50	3-0	3-0
22/10/95	Matt Le Tissier	Southampton	Away	68	2-1	3-1
20/01/96	Gary Kelly	Leeds United	Home	61	1-0	5-0
01/02/97	Daryl Powell	Derby County	Away	47	0-0	1-0
16/04/97	David Unsworth	Everton	Away	82	1-1	1-1
11/05/97	Matt Clarke	Sheff. Wed.	Away	83	0-1	1-1
05/10/97	Bernard Lambourde	Chelsea	Home	25	1-1	4-2
28/03/98	Darren Barnard	Barnsley	Away	53	1-1	3-2
28/03/98	Chris Morgan	Barnsley	Away	65	2-1	3-2
28/03/98	Darren Sheridan	Barnsley	Away	90	3-2	3-2
21/11/98	Stan Collymore	Aston Villa	Away	67	4-2	4-2
28/12/98	Dietmar Hamann	Newcastle U.	Home	30	0-1	4-2
01/05/99	Mauricio Taricco	Tottenham H.	Home	44	0-2	3-2
05/05/99	Denis Irwin	Man. Utd	Home	76	1-2	2-2
11/09/99	Andy Cole	Man. Utd	Home	72	2-3	2-3
18/09/99	Frank Sinclair	Leicester City	Away	51	2-1	2-2
27/09/99	Francis Jeffers	Everton	Home	75	0-1	0-1
16/10/99	Marcel Desailly	Chelsea	Home	73	1-0	1-0
16/10/99	Dennis Wise	Chelsea	Home	88	1-0	1-0
21/08/00	Patrick Vieira	Arsenal	Away	74	0-1	0-2
29/10/00	Thomas Gravesen	Everton	Home	77	2-1	3-1
17/12/00	Luke Chadwick	Man. Utd	Away	89	1-0	1-0
23/12/01	Gio van Bronckhorst	Arsenal	Home	36	0-0	1-2
13/04/02	Claudio Reyna	Sunderland	Away	89	1-0	1-0
21/09/02	Russell Hoult	WBA	Home	34	0-0	2-0
23/11/02	Alain Goma	Fulham	Away	70	1-3	2-3
19/04/03	David Weir	Everton	Away	82	2-1	2-1
19/04/03	Gary Naysmith	Everton	Away	90	2-1	2-1
13/09/03	Lucas Neill	Blackburn R.	Away	13	1-1	3-1
02/11/03	Luis Boa Morte	Fulham	Away	90	2-1	2-1
08/05/04	Kenny Cunningham	Birmingham	Away	64	2-0	3-0
21/08/04	Richard Dunne	Man. City	Home	85	2-1	2-1
19/12/04	Lee Bowyer	Newcastle U.	Home	77	3-1	3-1
26/12/04	Cosmin Contra	WBA	Away	39	1-0	5-0
15/01/05	Wes Brown	Man. Utd	Home	65	0-1	0-1

PLAYERS SENT OFF AGAINST LIVERPOOL IN PREMIER LEAGUE

DATE	PLAYER	OPPONENTS	VENUE	MINUTE OF DISMISSAL	SCORE AT TIME	FINAL SCORE (IN FAVOUR OF L'POOL)
13/08/05	Ugo Ehiogu	Middlesbrough	Away	74	0-0	0-0
20/08/05	Andrew Welsh	Sunderland	Home	74*	1-0	1-0
24/09/05	Neil Kilkenny	Birmingham	Away	82	1-2	2-2
15/10/05	Zurab Khizanishvili	Blackburn R.	Home	35	0-0	1-0
10/12/05	Chris Riggott	Middlesbrough	Home	84	2-0	2-0
26/12/05	Lee Bowyer	Newcastle U.	Home	66	2-0	2-0
28/12/05	Phil Neville	Everton	Away	68	3-1	3-1
28/12/05	Mikel Arteta	Everton	Away	90	3-1	3-1
14/01/06	Paul Stalteri	Tottenham H.	Home	87	1-0	1-0
01/02/06	Damien Johnson	Birmingham	Home	28	0-0	1-1
26/02/06	Joey Barton	Man. City	Home	52	1-0	1-0
19/03/06	Jean-Alain Boumsong	Newcastle U.	Away	51	2-1	3-1
25/03/06	Andy van der Meyde	Everton	Home	73	2-1	3-1
26/04/06	Hayden Mullins	West Ham	Away	82	2-1	2-1
17/09/06	Michael Ballack	Chelsea	Away	51	0-1	0-1
03/03/07	Paul Scholes	Man. Utd	Home	86	0-1	0-1
05/05/07	Papa Bouba Diop	Fulham	Away	90	0-1	0-1
20/10/07	Tony Hibbert	Everton	Away	53	0-1	2-1
20/10/07	Phil Neville	Everton	Away	90	1-1	2-1
23/02/08	Jeremie Aliadiere	Middlesbrough	Home	84	3-2	3-2

Jeremie Aliadiere - Given an 'early bath' in 2007/08 against the Reds

PREMIER LEAGUE PLAYERS' RECORD (A-G)

The following statistics are the full records of players who have played for Liverpool since the inception of the Premier League in 1992. However, the figures are their full record for the club, which includes the period prior to 1992 (all figures correct at end of 2007/08 season).

PLAYER	FIRST GAME-LAST GAME	LEAGUE		FA CUP		LEAGUE CUP		EUROPE		OTHER GAMES		LFC CAREER	
		A	G	A	G	A	G	A	G	A	G	A	G
Daniel Agger	2006-07	36	2	1	0	2	1	13	1	1	0	53	4
Xabi Alonso	2004-08	110	11	9	2	3	0	38	1	3	0	163	14
Nicolas Anelka	2001-02	20	4	2	1	0	0	0	0	0	0	22	5
Alvaro Arbeloa	2007-08	37	1	1	0	3	0	14	0	0	0	55	1
Pegguy Arphexad	2000-02	2	0	0	0	2	0	2	0	0	0	6	0
Fabio Aurelio	2006-08	33	1	2	0	4	0	14	0	1	0	54	1
Phil Babb	1994-99	128	1	12	0	16	0	14	0	0	0	170	1
Markus Babbel	2000-02	42	3	5	1	7	1	17	1	2	0	73	6
Ryan Babel	2007-08	30	4	4	1	2	0	13	5	0	0	49	10
Nick Barmby	2000-02	32	2	5	1	7	1	13	4	1	0	58	8
John Barnes	1987-97	314	84	51	16	26	3	12	3	4	2	407	108
Milan Baros	2002-05	68	19	3	0	8	4	28	4	1	0	108	27
Antonio Barragan	2005-05	0	0	0	0	0	0	1	0	0	0	1	0
Craig Bellamy	2006-07	27	7	0	0	2	0	12	2	1	0	42	9
Yossi Benayoun	2007-08	30	4	3	3	3	1	11	3	0	0	47	11
Patrik Berger	1996-03	148	28	8	0	11	3	28	4	1	0	196	35
Igor Biscan	2000-05	72	2	7	0	15	1	23	0	1	0	118	3
Stig I. Bjornebye	1992-99	139	2	13	0	16	0	16	2	0	0	184	4
David Burrows	1988-93	146	3	17	0	16	0	11	0	3	0	193	3
Titi Camara	1999-00	33	9	2	1	2	0	0	0	0	0	37	10
Jamie Carragher	1997-08	360	3	29	0	26	0	104	1	4	0	523	4
Scott Carson	2005-06	4	0	1	0	1	0	3	0	0	0	9	0
Phil Charnock	1992-92	0	0	0	0	1	0	1	0	0	0	2	0
Bruno Cheyrou	2002-04	31	2	6	2	2	0	8	1	1	0	48	5
Djibril Cisse	2004-06	49	13	6	2	0	0	23	9	1	0	79	24
Nigel Clough	1993-95	39	7	2	0	3	2	0	0	0	0	44	9
Stan Collymore	1995-97	61	26	9	7	4	0	7	2	0	0	81	35
Peter Crouch	2005-08	85	22	11	5	5	1	30	11	3	3	134	42
Salif Diao	2002-05	37	1	2	0	8	1	14	1	0	0	61	3
Julian Dicks	1993-94	24	3	1	0	3	0	0	0	0	0	28	3
Bernard Diomede	2000-01	2	0	0	0	0	0	3	0	0	0	5	0
El-Hadji Diouf	2002-04	55	3	4	0	7	3	13	0	1	0	80	6
Jerzy Dudek	2001-07	127	0	9	0	11	0	38	0	1	0	186	0
Sean Dundee	1998-99	3	0	0	0	1	0	1	0	0	0	5	0
Nabil El Zhar	2006-08	3	0	1	0	2	1	0	0	0	0	6	1
Jean Michel Ferri	1999-99	2	0	0	0	0	0	0	0	0	0	2	0
Steve Finnan	2003-08	145	1	13	0	6	0	51	0	2	0	217	1
Robbie Fowler	1993-07	266	128	24	12	35	29	44	14	0	0	369	183
Brad Friedel	1998-99	25	0	0	0	4	0	2	0	0	0	31	0
Luis Garcia	2004-07	77	18	4	1	5	0	32	11	3	0	121	30
Steven Gerrard	1998-08	302	55	23	8	19	7	91	25	4	1	439	96
Mark Gonzalez	2006-07	25	2	0	0	2	0	8	1	1	0	36	3
Bruce Grobbelaar	1981-94	440	0	62	0	70	0	38	0	18	0	628	0
Danny Guthrie	2006-07	3	0	0	0	3	0	1	0	0	0	7	0

PREMIER LEAGUE PLAYERS' RECORD (H-N)

PLAYER	FIRST GAME-LAST GAME	LEAGUE		FA CUP		LEAGUE CUP		EUROPE		OTHER GAMES		LFC CAREER	
		A	G	A	G	A	G	A	G	A	G	A	G
Dietmar Hamann	1999-06	191	8	16	1	12	0	61	2	3	0	283	11
Steve Harkness	1991-99	102	2	6	0	15	1	16	0	0	0	139	3
Vegard Heggem	1998-00	54	3	1	0	4	0	6	0	0	0	65	3
Stephane Henchoz	1999-04	135	0	15	0	16	0	37	0	2	0	205	0
Emile Heskey	2000-04	150	39	14	6	12	2	45	13	2	0	223	60
Jack Hobbs	2007-07	2	0	0	0	3	0	0	0	0	0	5	0
Mike Hooper	1986-93	51	0	5	0	10	0	4	0	3	0	73	0
Don Hutchison	1992-94	45	7	3	0	8	2	3	1	1	0	60	10
Sami Hyypia	1999-08	302	21	28	2	17	2	94	8	4	0	445	33
Paul Ince	1997-99	65	14	3	1	6	1	7	1	0	0	81	17
Emiliano Insua	2007-08	5	0	0	0	0	0	0	0	0	0	5	0
Charles Itandje	2007-08	0	0	4	0	3	0	0	0	0	0	7	0
David James	1992-99	214	0	19	0	22	0	22	0	0	0	277	0
Lee Jones	1994-96	3	0	0	0	1	0	0	0	0	0	4	0
Paul Jones	2004-04	2	0	0	0	0	0	0	0	0	0	2	0
Rob Jones	1991-98	183	0	27	0	22	0	11	0	0	0	243	0
Josemi	2004-05	21	0	0	0	1	0	12	0	1	0	35	0
Mark Kennedy	1995-98	16	0	1	0	2	0	2	0	0	0	21	0
Harry Kewell	2003-08	93	12	10	0	5	1	30	3	1	0	139	16
Frode Kippe	1999-01	0	0	0	0	2	0	0	0	0	0	2	0
Chris Kirkland	2001-04	25	0	3	0	6	0	11	0	0	0	45	0
Istvan Kozma	1992-92	6	0	2	0	1	0	0	0	1	0	10	0
Jan Kromkamp	2006-06	14	0	4	0	0	0	0	0	0	0	18	0
Dirk Kuyt	2006-08	66	15	5	2	2	0	23	8	0	0	96	25
Bjorn Tore Kvarme	1997-99	45	0	2	0	2	0	5	0	0	0	54	0
Lucas Leiva	2007-08	18	0	4	1	3	0	7	0	0	0	32	1
O. Leonhardsen	1997-99	37	7	1	0	6	0	5	0	0	0	49	7
Anthony Le Tallec	2003-05	17	0	4	0	2	0	9	1	0	0	32	1
Sebastian Leto	2007-07	0	0	0	0	2	0	2	0	0	0	4	0
Jari Litmanen	2001-02	26	5	3	1	3	0	11	3	0	0	43	9
Patrice Luzi	2004-04	1	0	0	0	0	0	0	0	0	0	1	0
Gary McAllister	2000-02	55	5	5	0	6	1	20	2	1	1	87	9
Jason McAteer	1995-99	100	3	12	3	13	0	14	0	0	0	139	6
Steve McManaman	1990-99	272	46	29	5	33	10	30	5	0	0	364	66
Mike Marsh	1989-93	69	2	8	0	11	3	12	1	1	0	101	6
Javier Mascherano	2007-08	32	1	2	0	1	0	17	0	0	0	52	1
Dominic Matteo	1993-00	127	1	8	1	9	0	11	0	0	0	155	2
Layton Maxwell	1999-99	0	0	0	0	1	1	0	0	0	0	1	1
Erik Meijer	1999-00	24	0	0	0	3	2	0	0	0	0	27	2
Neil Mellor	2002-05	12	2	2	0	6	3	2	1	0	0	22	6
Jan Molby	1984-95	218	44	28	4	28	9	7	1	11	3	292	61
F. Morientes	2005-06	41	8	5	1	3	0	11	3	1	0	61	12
Danny Murphy	1997-04	170	25	15	3	16	11	46	5	2	0	249	44
Jon Newby	1999-00	1	0	2	0	1	0	0	0	0	0	4	0
Steve Nicol	1982-94	343	36	50	3	42	4	20	2	13	1	468	46
Antonio Nunez	2004-05	18	0	1	0	3	1	5	0	0	0	27	1

PREMIER LEAGUE PLAYERS' RECORD (O-Z)

PLAYER	FIRST GAME-LAST GAME	LEAGUE		FA CUP		LEAGUE CUP		EUROPE		OTHER GAMES		LFC CAREER	
		A	G	A	G	A	G	A	G	A	G	A	G
Jon Otsemobor	2002-03	4	0	0	0	2	0	0	0	0	0	6	0
Michael Owen	1997-04	216	118	15	8	14	9	50	22	2	1	297	158
Daniele Padelli	2007-07	1	0	0	0	0	0	0	0	0	0	1	0
Gabriel Paletta	2006-07	3	0	0	0	3	1	2	0	0	0	8	1
Richie Partridge	2000-04	0	0	0	0	3	0	0	0	0	0	3	0
M. Pellegrino	2005-05	12	0	0	0	1	0	0	0	0	0	13	0
Lee Peltier	2006-07	0	0	0	0	3	0	1	0	0	0	4	0
Jermaine Pennant	2006-08	52	3	3	0	2	0	19	0	1	0	77	3
Torben Piechnik	1992-93	17	0	2	0	5	0	0	0	0	0	24	0
Damien Plessis	2008-08	2	0	0	0	0	0	0	0	0	0	2	0
Darren Potter	2004-05	2	0	1	0	5	0	9	0	0	0	17	0
David Raven	2004-05	1	0	1	0	2	0	0	0	0	0	4	0
Jamie Redknapp	1991-01	237	30	18	2	27	5	26	4	0	0	308	41
Jose Reina	2005-08	106	0	5	0	1	0	41	0	3	0	156	0
Karlheinz Riedle	1997-99	60	11	2	0	7	2	7	2	0	0	76	15
John Arne Riise	2001-08	234	21	17	3	13	2	79	4	5	1	348	31
Miki Roque	2006-06	0	0	0	0	0	0	1	0	0	0	1	0
Ronny Rosenthal	1990-93	74	21	8	0	9	1	4	0	2	0	97	22
Neil Ruddock	1993-97	115	11	11	0	20	1	6	0	0	0	152	12
Ian Rush	1980-96	469	229	61	39	78	48	38	20	14	10	660	346
Dean Saunders	1991-92	42	11	8	2	5	2	5	9	1	1	61	25
John Scales	1994-96	65	2	14	0	10	2	5	0	0	0	94	4
F. S-Pongolle	2003-06	38	4	5	2	8	1	12	2	3	0	66	9
Mohamed Sissoko	2005-07	51	1	6	0	4	0	23	0	3	0	87	1
Martin Skrtel	2008-08	14	0	1	0	0	0	5	0	0	0	20	0
Vladimir Smicer	1999-05	121	10	10	1	15	5	37	3	1	0	184	19
Jamie Smith	2006-06	0	0	0	0	1	0	0	0	0	0	1	0
Mark Smyth	2004-04	0	0	0	0	1	0	0	0	0	0	1	0
Rigobert Song	1999-00	34	0	1	0	2	0	1	0	0	0	38	0
Steve Staunton	1988-00	109	0	18	1	13	5	7	0	1	1	148	7
Paul Stewart	1992-93	32	1	1	0	6	0	2	2	1	0	42	3
Nick Tanner	1989-92	40	1	2	0	8	0	8	0	1	0	59	1
Michael Thomas	1991-98	124	9	17	2	10	1	12	0	0	0	163	12
David Thompson	1996-00	48	5	1	0	5	0	2	0	0	0	56	5
Fernando Torres	2007-08	33	24	1	0	1	3	11	6	0	0	46	33
Djimi Traore	1999-06	88	0	5	0	14	0	32	1	2	0	141	1
Gregory Vignal	2001-03	11	0	1	0	3	0	5	0	0	0	20	0
Andriy Voronin	2007-08	19	5	1	0	1	0	7	1	0	0	28	6
Mark Walters	1991-95	94	14	9	0	12	4	8	1	1	0	124	19
Stephen Warnock	2004-07	40	1	3	0	8	0	15	0	1	0	67	1
John Welsh	2002-05	4	0	1	0	3	0	2	0	0	0	10	0
Sander Westerveld	1999-01	75	0	8	0	5	0	14	0	1	0	103	0
Ronnie Whelan	1981-94	362	46	41	7	50	14	24	6	16	0	493	73
Zak Whitbread	2004-05	0	0	1	0	4	0	2	0	0	0	7	0
Mark Wright	1991-97	158	5	18	0	16	2	17	2	1	0	210	9
Stephen Wright	2000-02	14	0	2	0	2	0	3	1	0	0	21	1
Abel Xavier	2002-02	14	1	0	0	1	0	5	1	1	0	21	2
Boudewijn Zenden	2005-07	23	2	0	0	2	0	21	0	1	0	47	2
Christian Ziege	2000-01	16	1	3	0	4	1	9	0	0	0	32	2

PREMIER LEAGUE CAPTAINS

LIVERPOOL CAPTAINS IN PREMIER LEAGUE GAMES (MOST SUCCESSFUL FIRST)

CAPTAIN	PLD	W	D	L	PTS	WIN %	AVE PTS. PER GAME
Steve Nicol	9	6	2	1	20	66.67	2.22
Steve McManaman	8	5	1	2	16	62.50	2.00
Jamie Carragher	14	8	4	2	28	57.14	2.00
Steven Gerrard	155	81	40	34	283	52.26	1.83
Robbie Fowler	22	12	4	6	40	54.55	1.82
Sami Hyypia	131	69	32	30	239	52.67	1.82
John Barnes	87	43	25	19	154	49.43	1.77
Ian Rush	87	40	20	27	140	45.98	1.61
Jamie Redknapp	22	10	5	7	35	45.45	1.59
Paul Ince	65	28	18	19	102	43.08	1.57
Neil Ruddock	2	0	2	0	2	0.00	1.00
Mark Wright	17	4	4	9	16	23.53	0.94
Phil Babb	1	0	0	1	0	0.00	0.00
TOTAL	**620**	**306**	**157**	**157**	**1075**	**49.35**	**1.73**

BEST PREMIER LEAGUE GOAL DIFFERENCE

LIVERPOOL RECORD SINCE 1992

SEASON	GOAL DIFFERENCE	GOALS FOR	GOALS AGAINST	FINAL POSITION
2007/08	39	67	28	4th
2001/02	37	67	30	2nd
1995/96	36	70	34	3rd
2000/01	32	71	39	3rd
2005/06	32	57	25	3rd
2006/07	30	57	27	3rd
1994/95	28	65	37	4th
1997/98	26	68	42	3rd
1996/97	25	62	37	4th
1999/00	21	51	30	4th
2002/03	20	61	41	5th
1998/99	19	68	49	7th
2003/04	18	55	37	4th
2004/05	11	52	41	5th
1992/93	7	62	55	6th
1993/94	4	59	55	8th

EVER-PRESENTS

PLAYERS WHO HAVE PLAYED EVERY LEAGUE GAME FOR LIVERPOOL DURING ONE SEASON

SEASON	GAMES	PLAYER
1894/95	30	Tom Bradshaw
1896/97	30	John McCartney
1897/98	30	Thomas Cleghorn, Harry Storer
1899/00	34	Billy Dunlop, Tom Robertson
1900/01	34	Bill Goldie, Bill Perkins, Tom Robertson
1901/02	34	Bill Goldie
1902/03	34	Bill Goldie
1904/05	34	Ned Doig
1905/06	38	Arthur Goddard
1909/10	38	Tom Chorlton
1910/11	38	Robbie Robinson
1912/13	38	Robert Ferguson
1913/14	38	Thomas Fairfoul
1914/15	38	Jimmy Nicholl
1920/21	42	Walter Wadsworth
1921/22	42	Dick Forshaw, Fred Hopkin
1922/23	42	Dick Forshaw, Donald McKinlay, Elisha Scott
1923/24	42	Elisha Scott
1924/25	42	Danny Shone
1925/26	42	Harry Chambers
1926/27	42	Harry Chambers
1927/28	42	Tom Bromilow, Dick Edmed
1928/29	42	James Jackson, Tom Morrison
1930/31	42	Tommy Lucas, Archie McPherson
1931/32	42	Tom Bradshaw, Gordon Gunson
1932/33	42	Willie Steel
1936/37	42	Alf Hanson
1938/39	42	Jack Balmer, Matt Busby
1948/49	42	Jack Balmer
1950/51	42	Eddie Spicer
1955/56	42	Geoff Twentyman
1956/57	42	Ronnie Moran
1958/59	42	Dick White
1959/60	42	Alan A'Court, Ronnie Moran
1960/61	42	Bert Slater, Dick White
1961/62	42	Alan A'Court, Gerry Byrne, Jimmy Melia, Gordon Milne
1962/63	42	Roger Hunt
1963/64	42	Ian Callaghan, Gordon Milne, Peter Thompson
1965/66	42	Gerry Byrne, Ian Callaghan, Tommy Lawrence, Tommy Smith, Ron Yeats
1966/67	42	Chris Lawler, Tommy Smith, Peter Thompson
1967/68	42	Chris Lawler, Tommy Lawrence
1968/69	42	Ian Callaghan, Chris Lawler, Tommy Lawrence, Tommy Smith, Peter Thompson
1969/70	42	Bobby Graham, Chris Lawler
1971/72	42	Ray Clemence, Emlyn Hughes, Chris Lawler
1972/73	42	Ian Callaghan, Chris Lawler, Larry Lloyd
1973/74	42	Ian Callaghan, Ray Clemence, Peter Cormack, Emlyn Hughes, Kevin Keegan
1974/75	42	Ray Clemence, Emlyn Hughes

EVER-PRESENTS

SEASON	GAMES	PLAYER
PLAYERS WHO HAVE PLAYED EVERY LEAGUE GAME FOR LIVERPOOL DURING ONE SEASON		
1975/76	42	Ray Clemence, Phil Neal
1976/77	42	Ray Clemence, Emlyn Hughes, Phil Neal
1977/78	42	Kenny Dalglish, Phil Neal
1978/79	42	Ray Clemence, Kenny Dalglish, Ray Kennedy, Phil Neal
1979/80	42	Kenny Dalglish, Phil Neal, Phil Thompson
1980/81	42	Phil Neal
1981/82	42	Kenny Dalglish, Bruce Grobbelaar, Phil Neal
1982/83	42	Kenny Dalglish, Bruce Grobbelaar, Alan Kennedy, Phil Neal
1983/84	42	Bruce Grobbelaar, Alan Hansen, Alan Kennedy, Mark Lawrenson, Sammy Lee
1984/85	42	Bruce Grobbelaar, Phil Neal
1985/86	42	Bruce Grobbelaar
1986/87	42	Ian Rush
1987/88	40	Steve McMahon, Steve Nicol
1988/89	38	Ray Houghton, Steve Nicol
1989/90	38	Bruce Grobbelaar, Steve McMahon
1993/94	42	Ian Rush
1994/95	42	Robbie Fowler, David James
1995/96	38	Steve McManaman, Robbie Fowler, David James
1996/97	38	Stig Inge Bjornebye, David James
1999/00	38	Sami Hyypia
2000/01	38	Markus Babbel, Sander Westerveld
2001/02	38	John Arne Riise
2003/04	38	Sami Hyypia
2004/05	38	Jamie Carragher
2007/08	38	Jose Reina

Ray Kennedy - Ever present in 1978/79

THE FA CUP RESULTS

(*1970-2008 - Full record available in The Official Guides 2006-2008*)

Date	Round	Venue	Opponents	Opponent Division	Score	Scorers	Att
1969/70	**(WINNERS - CHELSEA)**						
7th Jan	3	(a)	Coventry City	1	1-1	Graham	33,688
12th Jan	3 Rep	(h)	Coventry City	1	3-0	Ross, Thompson, Graham	51,261
24th Jan	4	(h)	Wrexham	4	3-1	Graham 2, St John	54,096
7th Feb	5	(h)	Leicester City	2	0-0		53,785
11th Feb	5 Rep	(a)	Leicester City	2	2-0	Evans 2	42,100
21st Feb	6	(a)	Watford	2	0-1		34,047
1970/71	**(WINNERS - ARSENAL)**						
2nd Jan	3	(h)	Aldershot	4	1-0	McLaughlin	45,500
23rd Jan	4	(h)	Swansea Town	3	3-0	Toshack, St John, Lawler	47,229
13th Feb	5	(h)	Southampton	1	1-0	Lawler	50,226
6th Mar	6	(h)	Tottenham Hotspur	1	0-0		54,731
16th Mar	6 Rep	(a)	Tottenham Hotspur	1	1-0	Heighway	56,283
27th Mar	S.F.	Old Trafford	Everton	1	2-1	Evans, Hall	62,144
8th May	Final	Wembley	Arsenal	1	1-2 aet	Heighway	100,000
1971/72	**(WINNERS - LEEDS UNITED)**						
15th Jan	3	(a)	Oxford United	2	3-0	Keegan 2, Lindsay	18,000
5th Feb	4	(h)	Leeds United	1	0-0		56,300
9th Feb	4 Rep	(a)	Leeds United	1	0-2		45,821
1972/73	**(WINNERS - SUNDERLAND)**						
13th Jan	3	(a)	Burnley	2	0-0		35,730
16th Jan	3 Rep	(h)	Burnley	2	3-0	Toshack 2, Cormack	56,124
3rd Feb	4	(h)	Manchester City	1	0-0		56,296
7th Feb	4 Rep	(a)	Manchester City	1	0-2		49,572
1973/74	**(WINNERS - LIVERPOOL)**						
5th Jan	3	(h)	Doncaster Rovers	4	2-2	Keegan 2	31,483
8th Jan	3 Rep	(a)	Doncaster Rovers	4	2-0	Heighway, Cormack	22,499
26th Jan	4	(h)	Carlisle United	2	0-0		47,211
29th Jan	4 Rep	(a)	Carlisle United	2	2-0	Boersma, Toshack	21,262
16th Feb	5	(h)	Ipswich Town	1	2-0	Hall, Keegan	45,340
9th Mar	6	(a)	Bristol City	2	1-0	Toshack	37,671
30th Mar	S.F.	Old Trafford	Leicester City	1	0-0		60,000
3rd Apr	S.F. Rep	Villa Park	Leicester City	1	3-1	Hall, Keegan, Toshack	55,619
4th May	Final	Wembley	Newcastle United	1	3-0	Keegan 2, Heighway	100,000
1974/75	**(WINNERS - WEST HAM UNITED)**						
4th Jan	3	(h)	Stoke City	1	2-0	Heighway, Keegan	48,723
25th Jan	4	(a)	Ipswich Town	1	0-1		34,708
1975/76	**(WINNERS - SOUTHAMPTON)**						
3rd Jan	3	(a)	West Ham United	1	2-0	Keegan, Toshack	32,363
24th Jan	4	(a)	Derby County	1	0-1		38,200

THE FA CUP RESULTS

Date	Round	Venue	Opponents	Opponent Division	Score	Scorers	Att
1976/77	**(WINNERS - MANCHESTER UNITED)**						
8th Jan	3	(h)	Crystal Palace	3	0-0		44,730
11th Jan	3 Rep	(a)	Crystal Palace	3	3-2	Keegan, Heighway 2	42,644
29th Jan	4	(h)	Carlisle United	2	3-0	Keegan, Toshack, Heighway	45,358
26th Feb	5	(h)	Oldham Athletic	2	3-1	Keegan, Case, Neal (pen)	52,455
19th Mar	6	(h)	Middlesbrough	1	2-0	Fairclough, Keegan	55,881
23rd Apr	S.F.	Maine Rd	Everton	1	2-2	McDermott, Case	52,637
27th Apr	S.F. Rep	Maine Rd	Everton	1	3-0	Neal (pen), Case, Kennedy	52,579
21st May	Final	Wembley	Manchester United	1	1-2	Case	100,000
1977/78	**(WINNERS - IPSWICH TOWN)**						
7th Jan	3	(a)	Chelsea	1	2-4	Johnson, Dalglish	45,449
1978/79	**(WINNERS - ARSENAL)**						
10th Jan	3	(a)	Southend United	3	0-0		31,033
17th Jan	3 Rep	(h)	Southend United	3	3-0	Case, Dalglish, R.Kennedy	37,797
30th Jan	4	(h)	Blackburn Rovers	2	1-0	Dalglish	43,432
28th Feb	5	(h)	Burnley	2	3-0	Johnson 2, Souness	47,161
10th Mar	6	(a)	Ipswich Town	1	1-0	Dalglish	31,322
31st Mar	S.F.	Maine Rd	Manchester United	1	2-2	Dalglish, Hansen	52,584
4th Apr	S.F. Rep	Goodison	Manchester United	1	0-1		53,069
1979/80	**(WINNERS - WEST HAM UNITED)**						
5th Jan	3	(h)	Grimsby Town	3	5-0	Souness, Johnson 3, Case	49,706
26th Jan	4	(a)	Nottingham Forest	1	2-0	Dalglish, McDermott (pen)	33,277
16th Feb	5	(h)	Bury	3	2-0	Fairclough 2	43,769
8th Mar	6	(a)	Tottenham Hotspur	1	1-0	Mc Dermott	48,033
12th Apr	S.F.	Hillsborough	Arsenal	1	0-0		50,174
16th Apr	S.F. Rep	Villa Park	Arsenal	1	1-1 aet	Fairclough	40,679
28th Apr	S.F.Rep (2)	Villa Park	Arsenal	1	1-1 aet	Dalglish	42,975
1st May	S.F.Rep (3)	Highfield Rd	Arsenal	1	0-1		35,335
1980/81	**(WINNERS - TOTTENHAM HOTSPUR)**						
3rd Jan	3	(h)	Altrincham	Non Lge	4-1	McDermott, Dalglish 2, R.Kennedy	37,170
24th Jan	4	(a)	Everton	1	1-2	Case	53,804
1981/82	**(WINNERS - TOTTENHAM HOTSPUR)**						
2nd Jan	3	(a)	Swansea City	1	4-0	Hansen, Rush 2, Lawrenson	24,179
23rd Jan	4	(a)	Sunderland	1	3-0	Dalglish 2, Rush	28,582
13th Feb	5	(a)	Chelsea	2	0-2		41,422
1982/83	**(WINNERS - MANCHESTER UNITED)**						
8th Jan	3	(a)	Blackburn Rovers	2	2-1	Hodgson, Rush	21,967
29th Jan	4	(h)	Stoke City	1	2-0	Dalglish, Rush	36,666
20th Feb	5	(h)	Brighton	1	1-2	Johnston	44,868
1983/84	**(WINNERS - EVERTON)**						
6th Jan	3	(h)	Newcastle United	2	4-0	Robinson, Rush 2, Johnston	33,566
29th Jan	4	(a)	Brighton	2	0-2		19,057

THE FA CUP RESULTS

Date	Round	Venue	Opponents	Opponent Division	Score	Scorers	Att
1984/85	**(WINNERS - MANCHESTER UNITED)**						
5th Jan	3	(h)	Aston Villa	1	3-0	Rush 2, Wark	36,877
27th Jan	4	(h)	Tottenham Hotspur	1	1-0	Rush	27,905
16th Feb	5	(a)	York City	3	1-1	Rush	13,485
20th Feb	5 Rep	(h)	York City	3	7-0	Whelan 2, Wark 3, Neal, Walsh	43,010
10th Mar	6	(a)	Barnsley	2	4-0	Rush 3, Whelan	19,838
13th Apr	S.F.	Goodison	Manchester United	1	2-2 aet	Whelan, Walsh	51,690
17th Apr	S.F. Rep	Maine Rd	Manchester United	1	1-2	McGrath o.g.	45,775
1985/86	**(WINNERS - LIVERPOOL)**						
4th Jan	3	(h)	Norwich City	2	5-0	MacDonald, Walsh, McMahon Whelan, Wark	29,082
26th Jan	4	(a)	Chelsea	1	2-1	Rush, Lawrenson	33,625
15th Feb	5	(a)	York City	3	1-1	Molby (pen)	12,443
18th Feb	5 Rep	(h)	York City	3	3-1 aet	Wark, Molby, Dalglish	29,362
11th Mar	6	(h)	Watford	1	0-0		36,775
17th Mar	6 Rep	(a)	Watford	1	2-1 aet	Molby (pen), Rush	28,097
5th Apr	S.F.	Tottenham	Southampton	1	2-0 aet	Rush 2	44,605
10th May	Final	Wembley	Everton	1	3-1	Rush 2, Johnston	98,000
1986/87	**(WINNERS - COVENTRY CITY)**						
11th Jan	3	(a)	Luton Town	1	0-0		11,085
26th Jan	3 Rep	(h)	Luton Town	1	0-0 aet		34,822
28th Jan	3 Rep (2)	(a)	Luton Town	1	0-3		14,687
1987/88	**(WINNERS - WIMBLEDON)**						
9th Jan	3	(a)	Stoke City	2	0-0		31,979
12th Jan	3 Rep	(h)	Stoke City	2	1-0	Beardsley	39,147
31st Jan	4	(a)	Aston Villa	2	2-0	Barnes, Beardsley	46,324
21st Feb	5	(a)	Everton	1	1-0	Houghton	48,270
13th Mar	6	(a)	Manchester City	2	4-0	Houghton, Beardsley (pen) Johnston, Barnes	44,077
9th Apr	S.F.	Hillsborough	Nottingham Forest	1	2-1	Aldridge 2 (1 pen)	51,627
14th May	Final	Wembley	Wimbledon	1	0-1		98,203
1988/89	**(WINNERS - LIVERPOOL)**						
7th Jan	3	(a)	Carlisle United	4	3-0	Barnes, McMahon 2	18,556
29th Jan	4	(a)	Millwall	1	2-0	Aldridge, Rush	23,615
18th Feb	5	(a)	Hull City	2	3-2	Barnes, Aldridge 2	20,058
18th Mar	6	(h)	Brentford	3	4-0	McMahon, Barnes, Beardsley 2	42,376
7th May	S.F.	Old Trafford	Nottingham Forest	1	3-1	Aldridge, Laws o.g.	38,000
20th May	Final	Wembley	Everton	1	3-2aet	Aldridge, Rush 2	82,800
1989/90	**(WINNERS - MANCHESTER UNITED)**						
6th Jan	3	(a)	Swansea City	3	0-0		16,098
9th Jan	3 Rep	(h)	Swansea City	3	8-0	Barnes 2, Whelan, Rush 3, Beardsley, Nicol	29,194
28th Jan	4	(a)	Norwich City	1	0-0		23,152
31st Jan	4 Rep	(h)	Norwich City	1	3-1	Nicol, Barnes, Beardsley (pen)	29,339
17th Feb	5	(h)	Southampton	1	3-0	Rush, Beardsley, Nicol	35,961
11th Mar	6	(a)	QPR	1	2-2	Barnes, Rush	21,057
14th Mar	6 Rep	(h)	QPR	1	1-0	Beardsley	38,090
8th Apr	S.F.	Villa Park	Crystal Palace	1	3-4 aet	Rush, McMahon, Barnes (pen)	38,389

THE FA CUP RESULTS

Date	Round	Venue	Opponents	Opponent Division	Score	Scorers	Att
1990/91	**(WINNERS - TOTTENHAM HOTSPUR)**						
5th Jan	3	(a)	Blackburn Rovers	2	1-1	Atkins o.g.	18,524
8th Jan	3 Rep	(h)	Blackburn Rovers	2	3-0	Houghton, Rush, Staunton	34,175
26th Jan	4	(h)	Brighton	2	2-2	Rush 2	32,670
30th Jan	4 Rep	(a)	Brighton	2	3-2 aet	McMahon 2, Rush	14,392
17th Feb	5	(h)	Everton	1	0-0		38,323
20th Feb	5 Rep	(a)	Everton	1	4-4 aet	Beardsley 2, Rush, Barnes	37,766
27th Feb	5 Rep (2)	(a)	Everton	1	0-1		40,201
1991/92	**(WINNERS - LIVERPOOL)**						
6th Jan	3	(a)	Crewe Alexandra	4	4-0	McManaman, Barnes 3 (1 pen)	7,400
5th Feb	4	(a)	Bristol Rovers	2	1-1	Saunders	9,464
11th Feb	4 Rep	(h)	Bristol Rovers	2	2-1	McManaman, Saunders	30,142
16th Feb	5	(a)	Ipswich Town	2	0-0		26,140
26th Feb	5 Rep	(h)	Ipswich Town	2	3-2 aet	Houghton, Molby, McManaman	27,335
8th Mar	6	(h)	Aston Villa	1	1-0	Thomas	29,109
5th Apr	S.F.	Highbury	Portsmouth	2	1-1 aet	Whelan	41,869
13th Apr	S.F. Rep	Villa Park	Portsmouth	2	0-0 aet		40,077
			(Liverpool won 3-1 on penalties)				
9th May	Final	Wembley	Sunderland	2	2-0	Thomas, Rush	79,544
1992/93	**(WINNERS - ARSENAL)**						
3rd Jan	3	(a)	Bolton Wanderers	2	2-2	Winstanley o.g., Rush	21,502
13th Jan	3 Rep	(h)	Bolton Wanderers	2	0-2		34,790
1993/94	**(WINNERS - MANCHESTER UNITED)**						
19th Jan	3	(a)	Bristol City	1	1-1	Rush	21,718
25th Jan	3 Rep	(h)	Bristol City	1	0-1		36,720
1994/95	**(WINNERS - EVERTON)**						
7th Jan	3	(a)	Birmingham City	2	0-0		25,326
18th Jan	3 Rep	(h)	Birmingham City	2	1-1 aet	Redknapp	36,275
			(Liverpool won 2-0 on penalties)				
28th Jan	4	(a)	Burnley	1	0-0		20,551
7th Feb	4 Rep	(h)	Burnley	1	1-0	Barnes	32,109
19th Feb	5	(h)	Wimbledon	Prem	1-1	Fowler	25,124
28th Feb	5 Rep	(a)	Wimbledon	Prem	2-0	Barnes, Rush	12,553
11th Mar	6	(h)	Tottenham Hotspur	Prem	1-2	Fowler	39,592
1995/96	**(WINNERS - MANCHESTER UNITED)**						
6th Jan	3	(h)	Rochdale	3	7-0	Fowler, Collymore 3, Valentine o.g., Rush, McAteer	28,126
18th Feb	4	(a)	Shrewsbury Town	2	4-0	Collymore, Walton o.g., Fowler McAteer	7,752
28th Feb	5	(h)	Charlton Athletic	1	2-1	Fowler, Collymore	36,818
10th Mar	6	(a)	Leeds United	Prem	0-0		34,632
20th Mar	6 Rep	(h)	Leeds United	Prem	3-0	McManaman 2, Fowler	30,812
31st Mar	S.F	Old Trafford	Aston Villa	Prem	3-0	Fowler 2, McAteer	39,072
11th May	Final	Wembley	Manchester United	Prem	0-1		79,007
1996/97	**(WINNERS - CHELSEA)**						
4th Jan	3	(h)	Burnley	2	1-0	Collymore	33,252
26th Jan	4	(a)	Chelsea	Prem	2-4	Fowler, Collymore	27,950

THE FA CUP RESULTS

Date	Round	Venue	Opponents	Opponent Division	Score	Scorers	Att
1997/98	**(WINNERS - ARSENAL)**						
3rd Jan	3	(h)	Coventry City	Prem	1-3	Redknapp	33,888
1998/99	**(WINNERS - MANCHESTER UNITED)**						
3rd Jan	3	(a)	Port Vale	1	3-0	Owen (pen), Ince, Fowler	16,557
24th Jan	4	(a)	Manchester United	Prem	1-2	Owen	54,591
1999/2000	**(WINNERS - CHELSEA)**						
12th Dec	3	(a)	Huddersfield Town.	1	2-0	Camara, Matteo	23,678
10th Jan	4	(h)	Blackburn Rovers	1	0-1		32,839
2000/01	**(WINNERS - LIVERPOOL)**						
6th Jan	3	(h)	Rotherham United	2	3-0	Heskey 2, Hamann	30,689
27th Jan	4	(a)	Leeds United	Prem	2-0	Barmby, Heskey	37,108
18th Feb	5	(h)	Manchester City	Prem	4-2	Litmanen (pen), Heskey, Smicer (pen), Babbel	36,231
11th Mar	6	(a)	Tranmere Rovers	1	4-2	Murphy, Owen, Gerrard Fowler (pen)	16,334
8th Apr	S.F.	Villa Park	Wycombe W.	2	2-1	Heskey, Fowler	40,037
12th May	Final	Cardiff	Arsenal	Prem	2-1	Owen 2	74,200
2001/02	**(WINNERS - ARSENAL)**						
5th Jan	3	(h)	Birmingham City	1	3-0	Owen 2, Anelka	40,875
27th Jan	4	(a)	Arsenal	Prem	0-1		38,092
2002/03	**(WINNERS - ARSENAL)**						
5th Jan	3	(a)	Manchester City	Prem	1-0	Murphy (pen)	28,586
26th Jan	4	(a)	Crystal Palace	1	0-0		26,054
5th Feb	4 Rep	(h)	Crystal Palace	1	0-2		35,109
2003/04	**(WINNERS - MANCHESTER UNITED)**						
4th Jan	3	(a)	Yeovil Town	3	2-0	Heskey, Murphy (pen)	9,348
24th Jan	4	(h)	Newcastle United	Prem	2-1	Cheyrou 2	41,365
15th Feb	5	(h)	Portsmouth	Prem	1-1	Owen	34,669
22nd Feb	5 Rep	(a)	Portsmouth	Prem	0-1		19,529
2004/05	**(WINNERS - ARSENAL)**						
18th Jan	3	(a)	Burnley	Champ	0-1		19,033
2005/06	**(WINNERS - LIVERPOOL)**						
7th Jan	3	(a)	Luton Town	Champ	5-3	Gerrard, Sinama-Pongolle 2, Alonso 2	10,170
29th Jan	4	(a)	Portsmouth	Prem	2-1	Gerrard (pen), Riise	17,247
18th Feb	5	(h)	Manchester United	Prem	1-0	Crouch	44,039
21st Mar	6	(a)	Birmingham City	Prem	7-0	Hyypia, Crouch 2, Morientes, Riise, Tebily o.g., Cisse	27,378
22nd Apr	S.F.	Old Trafford	Chelsea	Prem	2-1	Riise, Garcia	64,575
13th May	Final	Cardiff	West Ham United (Liverpool won 3-1 on penalties)	Prem	3-3 aet	Cisse, Gerrard 2	74,000
2006/07	**(WINNERS - CHELSEA)**						
6th Jan	3	(h)	Arsenal	Prem	1-3	Kuyt	43,619
2007/08	**(WINNERS - PORTSMOUTH)**						
6th Jan	3	(a)	Luton Town	1	1-1	Crouch	10,226
15th Jan	3 Rep	(h)	Luton Town	1	5-0	Babel, Gerrard 3, Hyypia	41,446
26th Jan	4	(h)	Havant & Water.	Non Lge	5-2	Lucas, Benayoun 3, Crouch	42,566
16th Feb	5	(h)	Barnsley	Champ	1-2	Kuyt	42,449

FA CUP - DID YOU KNOW?

- John Barnes and David James have each played in a record three FA Cup finals with different clubs. Barnes played for Watford, Liverpool and Newcastle, with James wearing the colours of Liverpool, Aston Villa and Portsmouth.

- Liverpool's first-ever final appearance came in 1914. Their 1-0 defeat to Burnley was the last time the final was played at the Crystal Palace ground.

- John Miller recorded Liverpool's first-ever hat-trick in the Cup, doing so in the club's first-ever game in the competition against Nantwich in 1892.

- When Liverpool beat Everton in the 1986 final not one of the players in the Reds' starting line-up was registered as English. Mark Lawrenson was born in Preston, but was a Republic of Ireland International.

- Only one player scored in two FA Cup finals in the 1970s. Steve Heighway found the net in 1971 against Arsenal, and three years later in the win over Newcastle United.

- Ian Rush was the first Liverpool substitute to score twice in the final. In that 3-2 defeat of Everton in 1989, Blues' substitute Stuart McCall also netted two.

- Steven Gerrard found the back of the net three times in their 2006 final defeat of West Ham United in 2006. He scored twice in the 120 minutes, and then in the penalty shoot-out. The Hammers were the first team to score three goals in a final and lose since 1953 when Blackpool beat Bolton Wanderers 4-3.

- Ian Rush scored a 20th-century record 44 goals in the competition. Thirty-nine came in a Liverpool shirt, while his last was scored for Newcastle United against Everton!

- Rushy's tally of five goals in finals is also a record.

- Bruce Grobbelaar, Steve Nicol and Ian Rush have won three FA Cup winners' medals. Only Mark Hughes (four) has won more at Wembley.

- Kenny Dalglish, in 1986, was the first player-manager to win the Cup.

- Ian Callaghan played in a record 88 games in the FA Cup, 79 with Liverpool. That total is one more than John Barnes, who appeared 51 times for the Reds out of his 87.

- When Liverpool played Yeovil Town in the third round in 2004 they fielded a team of 11 different nationalities. The line-up consisted of one each from Poland, Switzerland, Finland, Norway, Croatia, Czech Republic, England, Germany, Australia, Senegal and France.

- Gary Ablett and Ray Clemence are the only two players to win the FA Cup with Liverpool and another club. Ablett won with Liverpool in 1989 and Everton in 1995, while Clemence achieved the feat with the Reds in 1974 and Tottenham Hotspur eight years later.

- Liverpool's most regular opponents in the competition have been Everton 15, Arsenal 12, Manchester United 11 and Burnley 10.

- Since Liverpool became a Football League club in 1893, the only players to play all their games for the club in the FA Cup are Fred Nickson (3), Fred Finney (2) and Dave Rylands, who made his only appearance in 1974 against Doncaster Rovers.

THE LEAGUE CUP

(*1969-2008 - Full record available in The Official Guides 2006-2008*)

Date	Round	Venue	Opponents	Opponent Division	Score	Scorers	Att
1969/70	**(WINNERS - MANCHESTER CITY)**						
3rd Sept	2	(a)	Watford	2	2-1	Slater o.g., St John	21,149
24th Sept	3	(a)	Manchester City	1	2-3	A.Evans, Graham	28,019
1970/71	**(WINNERS - TOTTENHAM HOTSPUR)**						
8th Sept	2	(a)	Mansfield Town	3	0-0		12,532
22nd Sept	2 Rep	(h)	Mansfield Town	3	3-2 aet	Hughes, Smith (pen), A.Evans	31,087
6th Oct	3	(a)	Swindon Town	2	0-2		23,992
1971/72	**(WINNERS - STOKE CITY)**						
7th Sept	2	(h)	Hull City	2	3-0	Lawler, Heighway, Hall (pen)	31,612
5th Oct	3	(h)	Southampton	1	1-0	Heighway	28,964
27th Oct	4	(a)	West Ham United	1	1-2	Graham	40,878
1972/73	**(WINNERS - TOTTENHAM HOTSPUR)**						
5th Sept	2	(a)	Carlisle United	2	1-1	Keegan	16,257
19th Sept	2 Rep	(h)	Carlisle United	2	5-1	Keegan, Boersma 2, Lawler, Heighway	22,128
3rd Oct	3	(a)	West Bromwich Alb.	1	1-1	Heighway	17,756
10th Oct	3 Rep	(h)	West Bromwich Alb.	1	2-1 aet	Hughes, Keegan	26,461
31st Oct	4	(h)	Leeds United	1	2-2	Keegan, Toshack	44,609
22nd Nov	4 Rep	(a)	Leeds United	1	1-0	Keegan	34,856
4th Dec	5	(h)	Tottenham Hotspur	1	1-1	Hughes	48,677
6th Dec	5 Rep	(a)	Tottenham Hotspur	1	1-3	Callaghan	34,565
1973/74	**(WINNERS - WOLVERHAMPTON WANDERERS)**						
8th Oct	2	(a)	West Ham United	1	2-2	Cormack, Heighway	25,823
29th Oct	2 Rep	(h)	West Ham United	1	1-0	Toshack	26,002
21st Nov	3	(a)	Sunderland	2	2-0	Keegan, Toshack	36,208
27th Nov	4	(a)	Hull City	2	0-0		19,748
4th Dec	4 Rep	(h)	Hull City	2	3-1	Callaghan 3	17,120
19th Dec	5	(a)	Wolverhampton W.	1	0-1		15,242
1974/75	**(WINNERS - ASTON VILLA)**						
10th Sept	2	(h)	Brentford	4	2-1	Kennedy, Boersma	21,413
8th Oct	3	(a)	Bristol City	2	0-0		25,573
16th Oct	3 Rep	(h)	Bristol City	2	4-0	Heighway 2, Kennedy 2	23,694
12th Nov	4	(h)	Middlesbrough	1	0-1		24,906
1975/76	**(WINNERS - MANCHESTER CITY)**						
10th Sept	2	(a)	York City	2	1-0	Lindsay (pen)	9,421
7th Oct	3	(h)	Burnley	1	1-1	Case	24,607
14th Oct	3 Rep	(a)	Burnley	1	0-1		20,022
1976/77	**(WINNERS - ASTON VILLA)**						
31st Aug	2	(h)	West Bromwich Alb.	1	1-1	Callaghan	23,378
6th Sept	2 Rep	(a)	West Bromwich Alb.	1	0-1		22,662
1977/78	**(WINNERS - NOTTINGHAM FOREST)**						
30th Aug	2	(h)	Chelsea	1	2-0	Dalglish, Case	33,170
26th Oct	3	(h)	Derby County	1	2-0	Fairclough 2	30,400
29th Nov	4	(h)	Coventry City	1	2-2	Fairclough, Neal (pen)	33,817
20th Dec	4 Rep	(a)	Coventry City	1	2-0	Case, Dalglish	36,105

THE LEAGUE CUP

Date	Round	Venue	Opponents	Opponent Division	Score	Scorers	Att
1977/78	**(WINNERS - NOTTINGHAM FOREST)**						
17th Jan	5	(a)	Wrexham	3	3-1	Dalglish 3	25,641
7th Feb	S.F.Leg 1	(h)	Arsenal	1	2-1	Dalglish, Kennedy	44,764
14th Feb	S.F.Leg 2	(a)	Arsenal	1	0-0		49,561
18th Mar	Final	Wembley	Nottingham Forest	1	0-0 aet		100,000
22nd Mar	Final Rep.	Old Trafford	Nottingham Forest	1	0-1		54,375
1978/79	**(WINNERS - NOTTINGHAM FOREST)**						
28th Aug	2	(a)	Sheffield United	2	0-1		35,753
1979/80	**(WINNERS - WOLVERHAMPTON WANDERERS)**						
29th Aug	2 Leg 1	(a)	Tranmere Rovers	4	0-0		16,759
4th Sept	2 Leg 2	(h)	Tranmere Rovers	4	4-0	Thompson, Dalglish 2, Fairclough	24,785
25th Sept	3	(h)	Chesterfield	3	3-1	Fairclough, Dalglish, McDermott	20,960
30th Oct	4	(h)	Exeter City	3	2-0	Fairclough 2	21,019
5th Dec	5	(a)	Norwich City	1	3-1	Johnson 2, Dalglish	23,000
22nd Jan	S.F.Leg 1	(a)	Nottingham Forest	1	0-1		32,234
12th Feb	S.F.Leg 2	(h)	Nottingham Forest	1	1-1	Fairclough	50,880
1980/81	**(WINNERS - LIVERPOOL)**						
27th Aug	2 Leg 1	(a)	Bradford City	4	0-1		16,232
2nd Sept	2 Leg 2	(h)	Bradford City	4	4-0	Dalglish 2, R.Kennedy, Johnson	21,017
23rd Sept	3	(h)	Swindon Town	3	5-0	Lee 2, Dalglish, Cockerill o.g., Fairclough	16,566
28th Oct	4	(h)	Portsmouth	3	4-1	Dalglish, Johnson 2, Souness	32,021
5th Dec	5	(h)	Birmingham City	1	3-1	Dalglish, McDermott, Johnson	30,236
14th Jan	S.F.Leg 1	(a)	Manchester City	1	1-0	R.Kennedy	48,045
10th Feb	S.F.Leg 2	(h)	Manchester City	1	1-1	Dalglish	46,711
14th Mar	Final	Wembley	West Ham United	2	1-1 aet	A.Kennedy	100,000
1st Apr	Final Rep	Villa Park	West Ham United	2	2-1	Dalglish, Hansen	36,693
1981/82	**(WINNERS - LIVERPOOL)**						
7th Oct	2 Leg 1	(h)	Exeter City	3	5-0	Rush 2, McDermott, Dalglish, Whelan	11,478
28th Oct	2 Leg 2	(a)	Exeter City	3	6-0	Rush 2, Dalglish, Neal, Sheedy, Marker o.g.	11,740
10th Nov	3	(h)	Middlesbrough	1	4-1	Sheedy, Rush, Johnson 2	16,145
1st Dec	4	(a)	Arsenal	1	0-0		37,917
8th Dec	4 Rep	(h)	Arsenal	1	3-0 aet	Johnston, McDermott (pen), Dalglish	21,375
12th Jan	5	(h)	Barnsley	2	0-0		33,707
19th Jan	5 Rep	(a)	Barnsley	2	3-1	Souness, Johnson, Dalglish	29,639
2nd Feb	S.F.Leg 1	(a)	Ipswich Town	1	2-0	McDermott, Rush	26,690
9th Feb	S.F.Leg 2	(h)	Ipswich Town	1	2-2	Rush, Dalglish	34,933
13th Mar	Final	Wembley	Tottenham Hotspur	1	3-1 aet	Whelan 2, Rush	100,000
1982/83	**(WINNERS - LIVERPOOL)**						
5th Oct	2 Leg 1	(a)	Ipswich Town	1	2-1	Rush 2	19,328
26th Oct	2 Leg 2	(h)	Ipswich Town	1	2-0	Whelan, Lawrenson	17,698
11th Nov	3	(h)	Rotherham United	2	1-0	Johnston	20,412
30th Nov	4	(h)	Norwich City	1	2-0	Lawrenson, Fairclough	13,235
18th Jan	5	(h)	West Ham United	1	2-1	Hodgson, Souness	23,953
8th Feb	S.F.Leg 1	(h)	Burnley	2	3-0	Souness, Neal (pen), Hodgson	33,520
15th Feb	S.F.Leg 2	(a)	Burnley	2	0-1		20,000
26th Mar	Final	Wembley	Manchester United	1	2-1 aet	Kennedy, Whelan	100,000

THE LEAGUE CUP

Date	Round	Venue	Opponents	Opponent Division	Score	Scorers	Att
1983/84	**(WINNERS - LIVERPOOL)**						
5th Oct	2 Leg 1	(a)	Brentford	3	4-1	Rush 2, Robinson, Souness	17,859
25th Oct	2 Leg 2	(h)	Brentford	3	4-0	Souness (pen), Hodgson, Dalglish, Robinson	9,902
8th Nov	3	(a)	Fulham	2	1-1	Rush	20,142
22nd Nov	3 Rep	(h)	Fulham	2	1-1 aet	Dalglish	15,783
29th Nov	3 Rep (2)	(a)	Fulham	2	1-0 aet	Souness	20,905
20th Dec	4	(a)	Birmingham City	1	1-1	Souness	17,405
22nd Dec	4 Rep	(h)	Birmingham City	1	3-0	Nicol, Rush 2 (1 pen)	11,638
17th Jan	5	(a)	Sheffield Wed.	2	2-2	Nicol, Neal (pen)	49,357
25th Jan	5 Rep	(h)	Sheffield Wed.	2	3-0	Rush 2, Robinson	40,485
7th Feb	S.F.Leg 1	(h)	Walsall	3	2-2	Whelan 2	31,073
14th Feb	S.F.Leg 2	(a)	Walsall	3	2-0	Rush, Whelan	19,591
25th Mar	Final	Wembley	Everton	1	0-0 aet		100,000
28th Mar	Final Rep	Maine Rd	Everton	1	1-0	Souness	52,089
1984/85	**(WINNERS - NORWICH CITY)**						
24th Sept	2 Leg 1	(a)	Stockport County	4	0-0		11,169
9th Oct	2 Leg 2	(h)	Stockport County	4	2-0 aet	Robinson, Whelan	13,422
31st Oct	3	(a)	Tottenham Hotspur	1	0-1		38,690
1985/86	**(WINNERS - OXFORD UNITED)**						
24th Sept	2 Leg 1	(h)	Oldham Athletic	2	3-0	McMahon 2, Rush	16,150
9th Oct	2 Leg 2	(a)	Oldham Athletic	2	5-2	Whelan 2, Wark, Rush, MacDonald	7,719
29th Oct	3	(h)	Brighton	2	4-0	Walsh 3, Dalglish	15,291
26th Nov	4	(h)	Manchester United	1	2-1	Molby 2 (1 pen)	41,291
21st Jan	5	(h)	Ipswich Town	1	3-0	Walsh, Whelan, Rush	19,762
12th Feb	S.F.Leg 1	(a)	QPR	1	0-1		15,051
5th Mar	S.F.Leg 2	(h)	QPR	1	2-2	McMahon, Johnston	23,863
1986/87	**(WINNERS - ARSENAL)**						
23rd Sept	2 Leg 1	(h)	Fulham	3	10-0	Rush 2, Wark 2, Whelan, McMahon 4, Nicol	13,498
7th Oct	2 Leg 2	(a)	Fulham	3	3-2	McMahon, Parker o.g., Molby (pen)	7,864
29th Oct	3	(h)	Leicester City	1	4-1	McMahon 3, Dalglish	20,248
19th Nov	4	(a)	Coventry City	1	0-0		26,385
26th Nov	4 Rep	(h)	Coventry City	1	3-1	Molby 3 (3 pens)	19,179
21st Jan	5	(a)	Everton	1	1-0	Rush	53,325
11th Feb	S.F.Leg 1	(a)	Southampton	1	0-0		22,818
25th Feb	S.F.Leg 2	(h)	Southampton	1	3-0	Whelan, Dalglish, Molby	38,481
5th Apr	Final	Wembley	Arsenal	1	1-2	Rush	96,000
1987/88	**(WINNERS - LUTON TOWN)**						
23rd Sept	2 Leg 1	(a)	Blackburn Rovers	2	1-1	Nicol	13,924
6th Oct	2 Leg 2	(h)	Blackburn Rovers	2	1-0	Aldridge	28,994
28th Oct	3	(h)	Everton	1	0-1		44,071
1988/89	**(WINNERS - NOTTINGHAM FOREST)**						
28th Sept	2 Leg 1	(h)	Walsall	2	1-0	Gillespie	18,084
12th Oct	2 Leg 2	(a)	Walsall	2	3-1	Barnes, Rush, Molby (pen)	12,015
2nd Nov	3	(h)	Arsenal	1	1-1	Barnes	31,951
9th Nov	3 Rep	(a)	Arsenal	1	0-0		54,029
23rd Nov	3 Rep (2)	Villa Park	Arsenal	1	2-1	McMahon, Aldridge	21,708
30th Nov	4	(a)	West Ham United	1	1-4	Aldridge (pen)	26,971

THE LEAGUE CUP

Date	Round	Venue	Opponents	Opponent Division	Score	Scorers	Att
1989/90	**(WINNERS - NOTTINGHAM FOREST)**						
19th Sept	2 Leg 1	(h)	Wigan Athletic	3	5-2	Hysen, Rush 2, Beardsley, Barnes	19,231
4th Oct	2 Leg 2	(a)	Wigan Athletic (match played at Anfield)	3	3-0	Staunton 3	17,954
25th Oct	3	(a)	Arsenal	1	0-1		40,814
1990/91	**(WINNERS - SHEFFIELD WEDNESDAY)**						
25th Sept	2 Leg 1	(h)	Crewe Alexandra	3	5-1	McMahon, Gillespie, Houghton, Rush 2	17,228
9th Oct	2 Leg 2	(a)	Crewe Alexandra	3	4-1	Rush 3, Staunton	7,200
31st Oct	3	(a)	Manchester United	1	1-3	Houghton	42,033
1991/92	**(WINNERS - MANCHESTER UNITED)**						
25th Sept	2 Leg 1	(h)	Stoke City	3	2-2	Rush 2	18,389
9th Oct	2 Leg 2	(a)	Stoke City	3	3-2	McManaman, Saunders, Walters	22,335
29th Oct	3	(h)	Port Vale	2	2-2	McManaman, Rush	21,553
20th Nov	3 Rep	(a)	Port Vale	2	4-1	McManaman, Walters, Houghton, Saunders	18,725
3rd Dec	4	(a)	Peterborough Utd	3	0-1		14,114
1992/93	**(WINNERS - ARSENAL)**						
22nd Sept	2 Leg 1	(h)	Chesterfield	3	4-4	Rosenthal, Hutchison, Walters Wright	12,533
6th Oct	2 Leg 2	(a)	Chesterfield	3	4-1	Hutchison, Redknapp, Walters Rush	10,632
28th Oct	3	(a)	Sheffield United	Prem	0-0		17,856
11th Nov	3 Rep	(h)	Sheffield United	Prem	3-0	McManaman 2, Marsh (pen)	17,654
1st Dec	4	(h)	Crystal Palace	Prem	1-1	Marsh (pen)	18,525
16th Dec	4 Rep	(a)	Crystal Palace	Prem	1-2 aet	Marsh (pen)	19,622
1993/94	**(WINNERS - ASTON VILLA)**						
22nd Sept	2 Leg 1	(a)	Fulham	2	3-1	Rush, Clough, Fowler	13,599
5th Oct	2 Leg 2	(h)	Fulham	2	5-0	Fowler 5	12,541
27th Oct	3	(h)	Ipswich Town	Prem	3-2	Rush 3	19,058
1st Dec	4	(h)	Wimbledon	Prem	1-1	Molby (pen)	19,290
14th Dec	4 Rep	(a)	Wimbledon (Liverpool lost 3-4 on penalties)	Prem	2-2 aet	Ruddock, Segers o.g.	11,343
1994/95	**(WINNERS - LIVERPOOL)**						
21st Sept	2 Leg 1	(h)	Burnley	1	2-0	Scales, Fowler	23,359
5th Oct	2 Leg 2	(a)	Burnley	1	4-1	Redknapp 2, Fowler, Clough	19,032
25th Oct	3	(h)	Stoke City	1	2-1	Rush 2	32,060
30th Nov	4	(a)	Blackburn Rovers	Prem	3-1	Rush 3	30,115
11th Jan	5	(h)	Arsenal	Prem	1-0	Rush	36,004
15th Feb	S.F.Leg 1	(h)	Crystal Palace	Prem	1-0	Fowler	25,480
8th Mar	S.F.Leg 2	(a)	Crystal Palace	Prem	1-0	Fowler	18,224
2nd Apr	Final	Wembley	Bolton Wanderers	1	2-1	McManaman 2	75,595

THE LEAGUE CUP

Date	Round	Venue	Opponents	Opponent Division	Score	Scorers	Att
1995/96	**(WINNERS - ASTON VILLA)**						
20th Sept	2 Leg 1	(h)	Sunderland	1	2-0	McManaman, Thomas	25,579
4th Oct	2 Leg 2	(a)	Sunderland	1	1-0	Fowler	20,560
25th Oct	3	(h)	Manchester City	Prem	4-0	Scales, Fowler, Rush, Harkness	29,394
29th Nov	4	(h)	Newcastle United	Prem	0-1		40,077
1996/97	**(WINNERS - LEICESTER CITY)**						
23rd Oct	3	(a)	Charlton Athletic	1	1-1	Fowler	15,000
13th Nov	3 Rep	(h)	Charlton Athletic	1	4-1	Wright, Redknapp, Fowler 2	20,714
27th Nov	4	(h)	Arsenal	Prem	4-2	McManaman, Fowler 2 (1 pen) Berger	32,814
8th Jan	5	(a)	Middlesbrough	Prem	1-2	McManaman	28,670
1997/98	**(WINNERS - CHELSEA)**						
15th Oct	3	(a)	West Bromwich Alb.	1	2-0	Berger, Fowler	21,986
18th Nov	4	(h)	Grimsby Town	2	3-0	Owen 3	28,515
7th Jan	5	(a)	Newcastle United	Prem	2-0 aet	Owen, Fowler	33,207
27th Jan	S.F.Leg 1	(h)	Middlesbrough	1	2-1	Redknapp, Fowler	33,438
18th Feb	S.F.Leg 2	(a)	Middlesbrough	1	0-2		29,828
1998/99	**(WINNERS - TOTTENHAM HOTSPUR)**						
27th Oct	3	(h)	Fulham	2	3-1	Morgan o.g., Fowler (pen), Ince	22,296
10th Nov	4	(h)	Tottenham Hotspur	Prem	1-3	Owen	20,772
1999/2000	**(WINNERS - LEICESTER CITY)**						
14th Sept	2 Leg 1	(a)	Hull City	3	5-1	Murphy 2, Meijer 2, Staunton	10,034
21st Sept	2 Leg 2	(h)	Hull City	3	4-2	Murphy, Maxwell, Riedle 2	24,318
13th Oct	3	(a)	Southampton	Prem	1-2	Owen	13,822
2000/01	**(WINNERS - LIVERPOOL)**						
1st Nov	3	(h)	Chelsea	Prem	2-1 aet	Murphy, Fowler	29,370
29th Nov	4	(a)	Stoke City	2	8-0	Ziege, Smicer, Babbel, Fowler 3 (1 pen), Hyypia, Murphy	27,109
13th Dec	5	(h)	Fulham	1	3-0 aet	Owen, Smicer, Barmby	20,144
10th Jan	S.F.Leg 1	(a)	Crystal Palace	1	1-2	Smicer	25,933
24th Jan	S.F.Leg 2	(h)	Crystal Palace	1	5-0	Smicer, Murphy 2, Biscan Fowler	41,854
25th Feb	Final	Cardiff	Birmingham City	1	1-1 aet	Fowler	73,500
			(Liverpool won 5-4 on penalties)				
2001/02	**(WINNERS - BLACKBURN ROVERS)**						
9th Oct	3	(h)	Grimsby Town	1	1-2 aet	McAllister (pen)	32,672
2002/03	**(WINNERS - LIVERPOOL)**						
6th Nov	3	(h)	Southampton	Prem	3-1	Berger, Diouf, Baros	35,870
4th Dec	4	(h)	Ipswich Town	1	1-1	Diouf (pen)	26,305
			(Liverpool won 5-4 on penalties)				
18th Dec	5	(a)	Aston Villa	Prem	4-3	Murphy 2, Baros, Gerrard	38,530
8th Jan	S.F.Leg 1	(a)	Sheffield United	1	1-2	Mellor	30,095
21st Jan	S.F.Leg 2	(h)	Sheffield United	1	2-0 aet	Diouf, Owen	43,837
2nd Mar	Final	Cardiff	Manchester United	Prem	2-0	Gerrard, Owen	74,500
2003/04	**(WINNERS - MIDDLESBROUGH)**						
29th Oct	3	(a)	Blackburn Rovers	Prem	4-3	Murphy (pen), Heskey 2, Kewell	16,918
3rd Dec	4	(h)	Bolton Wanderers	Prem	2-3	Murphy, Smicer	33,185

THE LEAGUE CUP

Date	Round	Venue	Opponents	Opponent Division	Score	Scorers	Att
2004/05	**(WINNERS - CHELSEA)**						
26th Oct	3	(a)	Millwall	Champ	3-0	Diao, Baros 2	17,655
10th Nov	4	(h)	Middlesbrough	Prem	2-0	Mellor 2	28,176
1st Dec	5	(a)	Tottenham Hotspur	Prem	1-1 aet	Sinama-Pongolle (pen)	36,100
			(Liverpool won 4-3 on penalties)				
11th Jan	S.F.Leg 1	(h)	Watford	Champ	1-0	Gerrard	35,739
25th Jan	S.F.Leg 2	(a)	Watford	Champ	1-0	Gerrard	19,797
27th Feb	Final	Cardiff	Chelsea	Prem	2-3 aet	Riise, Nunez	71,622
2005/06	**(WINNERS - MANCHESTER UNITED)**						
25th Oct	3	(a)	Crystal Palace	Champ	1-2	Gerrard	19,673
2006/07	**(WINNERS - CHELSEA)**						
25th Oct	3	(h)	Reading	Prem	4-3	Fowler, Riise, Paletta, Crouch	42,445
8th Nov	4	(a)	Birmingham City	Champ	1-0	Agger	23,061
9th Jan	5	(h)	Arsenal	Prem	3-6	Fowler, Gerrard, Hyypia	42,614
2007/08	**(WINNERS - TOTTENHAM HOTSPUR)**						
25th Sept	3	(a)	Reading	Prem	4-2	Benayoun, Torres 3	23,563
31st Oct	4	(h)	Cardiff City	Champ	2-1	El Zhar, Gerrard	41,780
19th Dec	5	(a)	Chelsea	Prem	0-2		41,366

LEAGUE CUP - DID YOU KNOW?

- Steve Staunton is the only player in the club's history to score a hat-trick after coming on as a substitute. Replacing Ian Rush at half-time of a second round, second-leg tie against Wigan Athletic at Anfield in October 1989, he netted all the goals in a 3-0 victory.

- Robbie Fowler's first goal for Liverpool came in the competition. He scored on his debut against Fulham at Craven Cottage in September 1993, whilst in the return at Anfield two weeks later he hit all five in a 5-0 win.

- Alan Hansen only scored one League Cup goal for Liverpool - but it was one that will live long in the memory. His goal proved to be the winner in the 1981 final replay at Villa Park as the Reds came from behind to beat West Ham United 2-1. His goal gave the club a first final success in the competition.

- Ian Callaghan scored only one hat-trick in his career, and it came in the League Cup against Hull City in December 1973. It was the first time a Liverpool player had scored three in a game in the competition. The match was played at Anfield on a weekday afternoon owing to electrical power cuts at the time.

- In December 1986 Jan Molby became the only player to score a hat-trick of penalties for the club. He did so in a fourth-round replay against Coventry City. In the Sky Blues' goal that night at Anfield was former Reds 'keeper Steve Ogrizovic.

- Steve Nicol played for Liverpool between 1981-1995 but in that time never made a final appearance, despite playing in 42 games in the competition.

- Two players have scored a record 49 League Cup goals. Geoff Hurst, with West Ham and Stoke, and Ian Rush, who scored 48 times for the Reds and once for Newcastle.

CLUB WORLD CHAMPIONSHIP

Date	Round	Venue	Opponents	Opponent Country	Score	Scorers	Att
1981							
13th Dec	Final	Tokyo	Flamengo	Bra	0-3		62,000
1984							
9th Dec	Final	Tokyo	Independiente	Arg	0-1		62,000
2005							
15th Dec	S.F.	Yokohama	Saprissa	CRi	3-0	Crouch 2, Gerrard	43,902
18th Dec	Final	Yokohama	Sao Paulo	Bra	0-1		66,821

FA CHARITY SHIELD/FA COMMUNITY SHIELD

Date	Round	Venue	Opponents	Opponent Division	Score	Scorers	Att
1922							
10th May		Old Trafford	Huddersfield Town	1	0-1		20,000
1964							
15th Aug		Anfield	West Ham United	1	2-2	Wallace, Byrne	38,858
1965							
14th Aug		Old Trafford	Manchester United	1	2-2	Stevenson, Yeats	48,502
1966							
13th Aug		Goodison P	Everton	1	1-0	Hunt	63,329
1971							
7th Aug		Filbert St	Leicester City	1	0-1		25,014
1974							
10th Aug		Wembley	Leeds United (Liverpool won 6-5 on penalties)	1	1-1	Boersma	67,000
1976							
14th Aug		Wembley	Southampton	2	1-0	Toshack	76,500
1977							
13th Aug		Wembley	Manchester United	1	0-0		82,000
1979							
11th Aug		Wembley	Arsenal	1	3-1	McDermott 2, Dalglish	92,000
1980							
9th Aug		Wembley	West Ham United	2	1-0	McDermott	90,000
1982							
21st Aug		Wembley	Tottenham Hotspur	1	1-0	Rush	82,500
1983							
20th Aug		Wembley	Manchester United	1	0-2		92,000
1984							
18th Aug		Wembley	Everton	1	0-1		100,000
1986							
16th Aug		Wembley	Everton	1	1-1	Rush	88,231
1988							
20th Aug		Wembley	Wimbledon	1	2-1	Aldridge 2	54,887
1989							
12th Aug		Wembley	Arsenal	1	1-0	Beardsley	63,149
1990							
18th Aug		Wembley	Manchester United	1	1-1	Barnes	66,558
1992							
8th Aug		Wembley	Leeds United	Prem	3-4	Rush, Saunders, Strachan o.g.	61,291
2001							
12th Aug		Cardiff	Manchester United	Prem	2-1	McAllister (pen), Owen	70,227
2002							
11th Aug		Cardiff	Arsenal	Prem	0-1		67,337
2006							
13th Aug		Cardiff	Chelsea	Prem	2-1	Riise, Crouch	56,275

The 1980 Liverpool team pose following the FA Charity Shield defeat of West Ham United

SCREEN SPORT SUPER CUP

Date	Round	Venue	Opponents	Opponent Division	Score	Scorers	Att
1985/86							
			Group stage				
17th Sept	Group	(h)	Southampton	1	2-1	Molby, Dalglish	16,189
22nd Oct	Group	(a)	Southampton	1	1-1	Walsh	10,503
3rd Dec	Group	(h)	Tottenham Hotspur	1	2-0	MacDonald, Walsh	14,855
14th Jan	Group	(a)	Tottenham Hotspur	1	3-0	Rush 2, Lawrenson	10,078
5th Feb	SF Leg 1	(a)	Norwich City	1	1-1	Dalglish	15,330
6th May	SF Leg 2	(h)	Norwich City	1	3-1	MacDonald, Molby (pen), Johnston	26,696
1986/87							
16th Sept	F Leg 1	(h)	Everton	1	3-1	Rush 2, McMahon	20,660
30th Sept	F Leg 2	(a)	Everton	1	4-1	Rush 3, Nicol	26,068

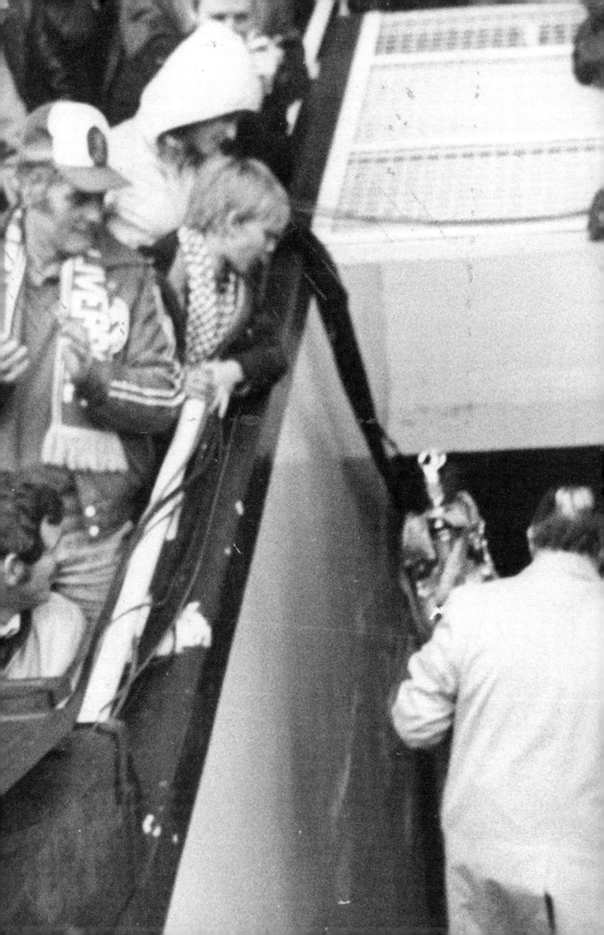

RECORD APPEARANCES & GOALS

TOTAL APPEARANCES		
	PLAYER	**APPS**
1	Ian Callaghan	857
2	Ray Clemence	665
=	Emlyn Hughes	665
4	Ian Rush	660
5	Phil Neal	650
6	Tommy Smith	638
7	Bruce Grobbelaar	628
8	Alan Hansen	620
9	Chris Lawler	549
10	Billy Liddell	534
11	Jamie Carragher	523
12	Kenny Dalglish	515
13	Ronnie Whelan	493
14	Roger Hunt	492
15	Phil Thompson	477

TOTAL GOALS			
	PLAYER	**APPS**	**GLS**
1	Ian Rush	660	346
2	Roger Hunt	492	286
3	Gordon Hodgson	377	241
4	Billy Liddell	534	228
5	Robbie Fowler	369	183
6	Kenny Dalglish	515	172
7	Michael Owen	297	158
8	Harry Chambers	339	151
9	Jack Parkinson	222	130
10	Sam Raybould	226	128
11	Dick Forshaw	288	124
12	Ian St John	425	118
13	Jack Balmer	310	110
14	John Barnes	407	108
15	Kevin Keegan	323	100

LEAGUE APPEARANCES		
	PLAYER	**APPS**
1	Ian Callaghan	640
2	Billy Liddell	492
3	Emlyn Hughes	474
4	Ray Clemence	470
5	Ian Rush	469
6	Tommy Smith	467
7	Phil Neal	455
8	Bruce Grobbelaar	440
9	Alan Hansen	434
10	Elisha Scott	430
11	Chris Lawler	406
12	Roger Hunt	404
13	Donald Mackinlay	393
14	Arthur Goddard	387
15	Ronnie Whelan	362

LEAGUE GOALS			
	PLAYER	**APPS**	**GLS**
1	Roger Hunt	404	245
2	Gordon Hodgson	358	233
3	Ian Rush	469	229
4	Billy Liddell	492	215
5	Harry Chambers	310	135
6	Robbie Fowler	266	128
7	Jack Parkinson	203	125
8	Sam Raybould	211	119
9	Michael Owen	216	118
=	Kenny Dalglish	355	118
11	Dick Forshaw	266	117
12	Jack Balmer	291	98
13	Ian St John	336	95
14	John Barnes	314	84

Kenny Dalglish - A feature in the LFC records

RECORD FA CUP APPEARANCES & GOALS

	FA CUP APPEARANCES				FA CUP GOALS		
	PLAYER	**APPS**			**PLAYER**	**APPS**	**GLS**
1	Ian Callaghan	79		1	Ian Rush	61	39
2	Bruce Grobbelaar	62		2	Roger Hunt	44	18
=	Emlyn Hughes	62		3	Harry Chambers	28	16
4	Ian Rush	61		=	John Barnes	51	16
5	Alan Hansen	58		5	Kevin Keegan	28	14
6	Ray Clemence	54		6	Kenny Dalglish	37	13
7	Tommy Smith	52		=	Billy Liddell	42	13
8	John Barnes	51		8	Jack Balmer	21	12
9	Steve Nicol	50		=	Robbie Fowler	24	12
=	Ron Yeats	50		=	Ian St John	49	12
11	Ian St John	49		11	Peter Beardsley	25	11
12	Chris Lawler	47		=	Billy Lacey	28	11
13	Phil Neal	45		13	Willie Fagan	24	10
14	Roger Hunt	44		14	Sam Raybould	14	9
15	Tommy Lawrence	42		15	John Aldridge	12	8
=	Billy Liddell	42					

	LEAGUE CUP APPEARANCES				LEAGUE CUP GOALS		
	PLAYER	**APPS**			**PLAYER**	**APPS**	**GLS**
1	Ian Rush	78		1	Ian Rush	78	48
2	Bruce Grobbelaar	70		2	Robbie Fowler	35	29
3	Alan Hansen	68		3	Kenny Dalglish	59	27
4	Phil Neal	66		4	Ronnie Whelan	50	14
5	Kenny Dalglish	59		5	Steve McMahon	27	13
6	Ray Clemence	55		6	Danny Murphy	16	11
7	Mark Lawrenson	50		7	David Fairclough	20	10
=	Ronnie Whelan	50		=	Steve McManaman	33	10
9	Emlyn Hughes	46		9	Michael Owen	14	9
10	Alan Kennedy	45		=	David Johnson	19	9
=	Graeme Souness	45		=	Jan Molby	28	9
12	Phil Thompson	43		=	Graeme Souness	45	9
13	Ian Callaghan	42		13	Steven Gerrard	19	7
=	Steve Nicol	42		=	Steve Heighway	38	7
15	Sammy Lee	39		=	Ian Callaghan	42	7

Ian Rush - Prominent in the Liverpool record books

OLDEST/YOUNGEST LIVERPOOL PLAYERS

OLDEST PLAYER

PLAYER	FINAL GAME	AGE
Ted Doig	April 11 1908	41 years & 165 days

OLDEST PLAYER (POST-WAR)

PLAYER	FINAL GAME	AGE
Kenny Dalglish	May 1 1990	39 years & 58 days
Billy Liddell	August 31 1960	38 years & 234 days
Gary McAllister	May 11 2002	37 years & 137 days
Paul Jones	January 17 2004	36 years & 274 days
Bruce Grobbelaar	February 19 1994	36 years & 136 days
Phil Taylor	December 25 1953	36 years & 98 days
Jack Balmer	February 16 1952	36 years & 10 days
Ian Callaghan	February 4 1978	35 years 300 days
Berry Nieuwenhuys	February 1 1947	35 years 88 days
Bob Paisley	March 13 1954	35 years 49 days

YOUNGEST PLAYER (POST-WAR)

PLAYER	DEBUT	AGE
Max Thompson	May 8 1974	17 years & 128 days
Michael Owen	May 6 1997	17 years & 143 days
Johnny Morrissey	September 23 1957	17 years & 158 days
Reginald Blore	October 17 1959	17 years & 213 days
Phil Charnock	September 16 1992	17 years & 215 days

YOUNGEST-EVER GOALSCORERS FOR LIVERPOOL

PLAYER	DEBUT	AGE	OPPONENTS
Michael Owen	6th May 1997	17 years & 143 days	Wimbledon
Jimmy Melia	17th December 1955	18 years & 46 days	Nottingham Forest
Jamie Redknapp	7th December 1991	18 years & 165 days	Southampton
Alan A'Court	14th March 1953	18 years & 165 days	Sunderland
Robbie Fowler	22nd September 1993	18 years & 166 days	Fulham
John McLaughlin	22nd August 1970	18 years & 178 days	Huddersfield Town
Phil Taylor	28th March 1936	18 years & 192 days	Derby County
Brian Jackson	10th November 1951	18 years & 223 days	Bolton Wanderers
Gordon Wallace	8th May 1963	18 years & 329 days	Birmingham City
Jamie Carragher	18th January 1997	18 years & 356 days	Aston Villa

MOST GOALS IN A LEAGUE SEASON

NAME	SEASON	DIVISION	GAMES	GOALS	GOAL AVERAGE
Roger Hunt	1961/62	2	41	41	1
Gordon Hodgson	1930/31	1	40	36	1.11
Ian Rush	1983/84	1	41	32	1.28
Sam Raybould	1902/03	1	33	31	1.06
Roger Hunt	1963/64	1	41	31	1.32
Jack Parkinson	1909/10	1	31	30	1.03
Gordon Hodgson	1928/29	1	38	30	1.27
Billy Liddell	1954/55	2	40	30	1.33
Ian Rush	1986/87	1	42	30	1.4
Roger Hunt	1965/66	1	37	29	1.28
John Evans	1954/55	2	38	29	1.31
Robbie Fowler	1995/96	Prem	38	28	1.36
Dick Forshaw	1925/26	1	32	27	1.19
Gordon Hodgson	1934/35	1	34	27	1.26
Billy Liddell	1955/56	2	39	27	1.44
John Aldridge	1987/88	1	36	26	1.38
Gordon Hodgson	1931/32	1	39	26	1.5
George Allan	1895/96	2	20	25	0.8
Roger Hunt	1964/65	1	40	25	1.6
Roger Hunt	1967/68	1	40	25	1.6
Robbie Fowler	1994/95	Prem	42	25	1.68

MOST GOALS IN A SEASON - ALL COMPETITIONS

NAME	SEASON	GAMES	GOALS	GOAL AVERAGE
Ian Rush	1983/84	65	47	1.38
Roger Hunt	1961/62	46	42	1.1
Ian Rush	1986/87	57	40	1.43
Roger Hunt	1964/65	58	37	1.57
Gordon Hodgson	1930/31	41	36	1.14
Robbie Fowler	1995/96	53	36	1.47
John Evans	1954/55	42	33	1.27
Billy Liddell	1955/56	44	33	1.33
Roger Hunt	1963/64	46	33	1.39
Roger Hunt	1965/66	46	33	1.39
Fernando Torres	2007/08	46	33	1.39
Ian Rush	1985/86	56	33	1.7
Sam Raybould	1902/03	34	32	1.06
Gordon Hodgson	1928/29	41	32	1.28
Billy Liddell	1954/55	44	31	1.42
Robbie Fowler	1996/97	44	31	1.42
John Aldridge	1988/89	47	31	1.52
Ian Rush	1982/83	51	31	1.65
Robbie Fowler	1994/95	57	31	1.84
Kenny Dalglish	1977/78	62	31	2
Jack Parkinson	1909/10	32	30	1.07
Ian Rush	1981/82	49	30	1.63
Roger Hunt	1967/68	57	30	1.9

DEBUT GOALSCORERS

(SINCE RETURNING TO TOP-FLIGHT IN 1962)

PLAYER	DATE	OPPONENTS	COMPETITION	GOALS SCORED	RESULT
Bobby Graham	14/09/64	Reykjavik (h)	European Cup	1	6-1
John Sealey	26/04/65	Wolves (a)	League	1	3-1
Alun Evans	21/09/68	Leicester City (h)	League	1	4-0
Alec Lindsay	16/09/69	Dundalk (h)	Fairs Cup	1	10-0
Kevin Keegan	14/08/71	Nottingham Forest (h)	League	1	3-1
Ray Kennedy	31/08/74	Chelsea (a)	League	1	3-0
Sammy Lee	08/04/78	Leicester City (h)	League	1	3-2
Ronnie Whelan	03/04/81	Stoke City (h)	League	1	3-0
John Wark	31/03/84	Watford (a)	League	1	2-0
David Speedie	03/02/91	Manchester United (a)	League	1	1-1
Nigel Clough	14/08/93	Sheffield Wed. (h)	League	2	2-0
Robbie Fowler	22/09/93	Fulham (a)	League Cup	1	3-1
Stan Collymore	19/08/95	Sheffield Wed. (h)	League	1	1-0
Michael Owen	06/05/97	Wimbledon (a)	League	1	1-2
Titi Camara	07/08/99	Sheffield Wed. (a)	League	1	2-1
Leyton Maxwell	21/09/99	Hull City (h)	League Cup	1	4-2
Abel Xavier	09/02/02	Ipswich Town (a)	League	1	6-0
Craig Bellamy	09/08/06	Maccabi Haifa (h)	European Cup	1	2-1
Mark Gonzalez	09/08/06	Maccabi Haifa (h)	European Cup	1	2-1
Gabriel Paletta	25/10/06	Reading (h)	League Cup	1	4-3

* Kenny Dalglish scored at Middlesbrough on 20/08/77 but had played in the FA Charity Shield a week earlier.

SUPER SUBS

LIVERPOOL'S MOST PROLIFIC GOALSCORING SUBSTITUTES

	LEAGUE	FA CUP	LGE CUP	EUROPE	OTHERS	TOTAL
David Fairclough	7	2	7	2	0	18
Ryan Babel	2	0	0	5	0	7
Djibril Cisse	2	1	0	4	0	7
Michael Owen	4	0	1	1	0	6
Ian Rush	2	3	0	1	0	6
Vladimir Smicer	4	0	1	1	0	6
Robbie Fowler	3	1	0	1	0	5
Emile Heskey	2	3	0	0	0	5
David Johnson	3	0	1	1	0	5
Milan Baros	1	0	2	1	0	4
Phil Boersma	0	0	2	2	0	4
Jimmy Case	2	1	0	1	0	4
Peter Crouch	3	0	0	1	0	4
Luis Garcia	4	0	0	0	0	4
Craig Johnston	2	1	1	0	0	4
Jari Litmanen	3	0	0	1	0	4
Danny Murphy	4	0	0	0	0	4
Ronny Rosenthal	4	0	0	0	0	4
Florent Sinama-Pongolle	1	2	0	1	0	4

DOUBLE FIGURES

SEASON	NO. OF PLAYERS	SCORERS
2007/08	6	Torres 33, Gerrard 21, Benayoun 11, Crouch 11, Kuyt 11, Babel 10
1985/86	6	Rush 33, Molby 21, Walsh 18, Whelan 14, McMahon 11, Johnston 10
1972/73	6	Keegan 22, Toshack 17, Boersma 13, Hughes 12, Cormack 10, Heighway 10

DOUBLE-FIGURE GOALSCORERS IN A SEASON

LIVERPOOL HAT-TRICK MEN

FULL RECORD OF LIVERPOOL HAT-TRICKS

17 Gordon Hodgson

16 Ian Rush

12 Roger Hunt

10 Robbie Fowler, Michael Owen

8 Dick Forshaw, Jack Parkinson

6 Sam Raybould

5 Harry Chambers, Billy Liddell

4 George Allan, Joe Hewitt

3 John Aldridge, Jack Balmer, Kenny Dalglish, Tony Hateley, Fred Howe, Albert Stubbins, John Toshack, **Fernando Torres,** John Wark

2 John Barnes, Harold Barton, Frank Becton, **Yossi Benayoun**, Jimmy Case, William Devlin, Cyril Done, John Evans, **Steven Gerrard,** Dick Johnson, Terry McDermott, Steve McMahon, Malcolm McVean, Fred Pagnam, Henry Race, Robert Robinson, Jimmy Ross, Antonio Rowley, Ian St John, Dean Saunders, Graeme Souness, Paul Walsh

1 Alan Arnell, Alf Arrowsmith, Milan Baros, Peter Beardsley, Patrik Berger, Louis Bimpson, Phil Boersma, Ian Callaghan, Stan Collymore, **Peter Crouch,** Alun Evans, David Fairclough, Gary Gillespie, Bobby Graham, Jimmy Harrower, Emile Heskey, Dave Hickson, 'Sailor' Hunter, David Johnson, Kevin Keegan, Kevin Lewis, Andy McGuigan, William McPherson, Arthur Metcalfe, Jan Molby, Steve Nicol, Ronald Orr, Tom Reid, Michael Robinson, Ronny Rosenthal, Danny Shone, Jimmy Smith, Steve Staunton, James Stewart, James Stott, John Walker, Jimmy Walsh, Mark Walters, Johnny Wheeler, Ronnie Whelan, Jack Whitham, Dave Wright

85 players have scored a total of 218 hat-tricks

MOST GOALS IN A SEASON

SCORED BY LIVERPOOL SUBSTITUTES

GOALS	PLAYER	SEASON	GOALS	PLAYER	SEASON
7	Ryan Babel	2007/08	3	Vladimir Smicer	2001/02
7	Djibril Cisse	2005/06	3	Robbie Fowler	2000/01
6	David Fairclough	1979/80	3	Steve Staunton	1989/90
5	David Fairclough	1975/76	3	Kenny Dalglish	1986/87
3	Luis Garcia	2005/06	3	David Fairclough	1977/78
3	Steven Gerrard	2005/06	3	Phil Boersma	1972/73
3	Milan Baros	2004/05	3	Alun Evans	1969/70
3	Jari Litmanen	2001/02	3	Roger Hunt	1969/70

LANDMARK LIVERPOOL GOALS

GOAL	SCORER	OPPONENT	VENUE	DATE	RESULT
1	Malcolm McVean	Middlesbrough Ironopolis	A	02/09/1893	2-0
500	Charlie Satterthwaite	Wolverhampton Wanderers	H	09/11/1901	4-1
1000	Ronald Orr	Sunderland	H	12/04/1909	3-0
1500	Danny Shone	Middlesbrough	H	19/11/1921	4-0
2000	Gordon Hodgson	Bury	A	29/12/1928	2-2
2500	Vic Wright	Stoke City	H	19/04/1935	5-0
3000	Willie Fagan	Everton	H	24/12/1949	3-1
3500	Billy Liddell	Fulham	A	02/03/1957	2-1
4000	Roger Hunt	Sheffield Wednesday	A	08/12/1962	2-0
4500	Sammy Chapman (o.g.)	Nottingham Forest	H	04/10/1969	1-1
5000	Kenny Dalglish	Wolverhampton Wanderers	A	25/03/1978	3-1
5500	Paul Walsh	Manchester United	A	22/09/1984	1-1
6000	Jan Molby	Derby County	A	23/03/1991	7-1
6500	David Thompson	Southampton	H	16/01/1999	7-1
7000	Mohamed Sissoko	Sunderland	A	25/08/2007	2-0

David Thompson (centre) - Scorer of goal number 6500

BIGGEST-EVER VICTORIES

DATE	OPPONENTS	VENUE	COMPETITION	SCORE
17th Sept 1974	Stromsgodset	Home	European Cup Winners' Cup	11-0
16th Sept 1969	Dundalk	Home	Inter Cities' Fairs Cup	10-0
23rd Sept 1986	Fulham	Home	League Cup	10-0
18th Feb 1896	Rotherham United	Home	League	10-1
1st Oct 1980	Oulu Palloseura	Home	European Cup	10-1
29th Oct 1892	Newtown	Home	FA Cup	9-0
12th Sept 1989	Crystal Palace	Home	League	9-0
26th Dec 1928	Burnley	Home	League	8-0
7th Nov 1967	TSV Munich 1860	Home	Inter Cities' Fairs Cup	8-0
9th Jan 1990	Swansea City	Home	FA Cup	8-0
29th Nov 2000	Stoke City	Away	League Cup	8-0
6th Nov 2008	Besiktas	Home	Champions League	8-0
6th Dec 1902	Grimsby Town	Home	League	9-2
8th Apr 1905	Burslem Port Vale	Home	League	8-1
29th Feb 1896	Burton Swifts	Away	League	7-0
28th Mar 1896	Crewe Alexandra	Away	League	7-0
4th Jan 1902	Stoke City	Home	League	7-0
26th Nov 1955	Fulham	Home	League	7-0
2nd Sept 1978	Tottenham Hotspur	Home	League	7-0
30th Sept 1981	Oulu Palloseura	Home	European Cup	7-0
20th Feb 1985	York City	Home	FA Cup	7-0
6th Jan 1996	Rochdale	Home	FA Cup	7-0
21st Mar 2006	Birmingham City	Away	FA Cup	7-0
1st Oct 1927	Portsmouth	Home	League	8-2
12th Oct 1895	Newton Heath	Home	League	7-1
12th Sept 1936	Grimsby Town	Home	League	7-1
23rd Mar 1991	Derby County	Away	League	7-1
16th Jan 1999	Southampton	Home	League	7-1

BIGGEST-EVER DEFEATS

DATE	OPPONENTS	VENUE	COMPETITION	SCORE
11th Dec 1954	Birmingham City	Away	League	9-1
10th Nov 1934	Huddersfield Town	Away	League	8-0
1st Jan 1934	Newcastle United	Away	League	9-2
7th May 1932	Bolton Wanderers	Away	League	8-1
1st Sept 1934	Arsenal	Away	League	8-1
7th Dec 1912	Sunderland	Away	League	7-0
1st Sept 1930	West Ham United	Away	League	7-0
19th Apr 1930	Sunderland	Home	League	6-0
28th Nov 1931	Arsenal	Away	League	6-0
11th Sept 1935	Manchester City	Away	League	6-0
26th Sept 1953	Charlton Athletic	Away	League	6-0

THE INDIVIDUAL HONOURS

YEAR	PLAYER	HONOURS WON (THAT SEASON)
1974	Ian Callaghan	FA Cup
1976	Kevin Keegan	First Division, UEFA Cup
1977	Emlyn Hughes	First Division, European Cup, FA Charity Shield
1979	Kenny Dalglish	First Division
1980	Terry McDermott	First Division, FA Charity Shield
1983	Kenny Dalglish	First Division, League Cup, FA Charity Shield
1984	Ian Rush	First Division, League Cup, European Cup
1988	John Barnes	First Division
1989	Steve Nicol	FA Cup, FA Charity Shield
1990	John Barnes	First Division, FA Charity Shield

PFA PLAYER OF THE YEAR

1980	Terry McDermott	First Division, FA Charity Shield
1983	Kenny Dalglish	First Division, League Cup, FA Charity Shield
1984	Ian Rush	First Division, League Cup, European Cup
1988	John Barnes	First Division
2006	Steven Gerrard	FA Cup, European Super Cup

PFA YOUNG PLAYER OF THE YEAR

1983	Ian Rush	First Division, League Cup, FA Charity Shield
1995	Robbie Fowler	League Cup
1996	Robbie Fowler	-
1998	Michael Owen	-
2001	Steven Gerrard	FA Cup, League Cup, UEFA Cup

EUROPEAN FOOTBALLER OF THE YEAR

2001	Michael Owen	FA Cup, League Cup, UEFA Cup

MANAGER OF THE YEAR

1973	Bill Shankly	First Division, UEFA Cup
1976	Bob Paisley	First Division, UEFA Cup
1977	Bob Paisley	First Division, European Cup, European Super Cup, FA Charity Shield
1979	Bob Paisley	First Division
1980	Bob Paisley	First Division, FA Charity Shield
1982	Bob Paisley	First Division, League Cup
1983	Bob Paisley	First Division, League Cup, FA Charity Shield
1984	Joe Fagan	First Division, League Cup, European Cup
1986	Kenny Dalglish	First Division, FA Cup
1988	Kenny Dalglish	First Division
1990	Kenny Dalglish	First Division, FA Charity Shield

PLAYER WITH MOST MEDALS

20	Phil Neal (8 League, 1 FA Cup runner-up, 4 League Cup, 1 runner-up, 5 European, 1 runner-up)

MOST GOALS SCORED AT HOME

SCORED BY LIVERPOOL IN A SEASON (ALL COMPETITIONS)

SEASON	TOTAL	GAMES PLAYED
1985/86	87	32
2007/08	**79**	**30**
1980/81	78	31
1982/83	77	31
1895/96	75	18
1967/68	74	29
1983/84	74	31
1961/62	72	23

HOME GOALSCORER

SCORED IN MOST SUCCESSIVE HOME GAMES FOR LIVERPOOL

PLAYER	NO. OF GAMES IN SUCCESSION	YEAR
Fernando Torres	8	2008
Roger Hunt	8	1961/62
Michael Owen	6	1998/99
Ian Rush	6	1983
Roger Hunt	6	1963/64
Fred Pagnam	6	1919

MOST GOALS SCORED BY AN OVERSEAS PLAYER

DEBUT SEASON IN THE PREMIER LEAGUE (FIRST FULL SEASON)

PLAYER	CLUB	SEASON	GAMES	GOALS
Fernando Torres	Liverpool	2007/08	33	24
Ruud van Nistelrooy	Manchester United	2001/02	32	23
Jurgen Klinsmann	Tottenham Hotspur	1994/95	41	20
Roque Santa Cruz	Blackburn Rovers	2007/08	37	19
Ole Gunnar Solskjaer	Manchester United	1996/97	32	18
Benni McCarthy	Blackburn Rovers	2006/07	36	18
Thierry Henry	Arsenal	1999/00	31	17
Mark Viduka	Leeds United	2000/01	34	17
Jimmy Floyd Hasselbaink	Leeds United	1997/98	33	16
Fabrizio Ravanelli	Middlesbrough	1996/97	33	16
Uwe Rosler	Manchester City	1994/95	31	15
Eric Cantona	Leeds United/ Manchester United	1992/93	35	15
Hamilton Ricard	Middlesbrough	1998/99	36	15
Ayegbeni Yakubu	Portsmouth	2004/05	30	13
John Carew	Aston Villa	2007/08	31	13
Paulo Wanchope	Derby County	1997/98	32	13
Marian Pahars	Southampton	1999/00	33	13
Bryan Roy	Nottingham Forest	1994/95	37	13

CLEAN SHEET RECORDS

MOST CLEAN SHEETS IN A SEASON (ALL COMPS)				**HIGHEST % OF CLEAN SHEETS IN SEASON (ALL COMPS)**			
SEASON	**CLEAN SHEETS**	**GAMES PLAYED**		**SEASON**	**%**	**CLEAN SHEETS**	**GAMES PLAYED**
1978/79	34	54		1978/79	62.96	34	54
1970/71	34	62		1970/71	54.84	34	62
1983/84	34	67		1987/88	54.00	27	50
2005/06	33	62		2005/06	53.23	33	62
1977/78	32	62		1971/72	52.83	28	53
1981/82	31	62		1977/78	51.61	32	62
1973/74	30	61		1983/84	50.75	34	67
1975/76	29	59		1893/94	50.00	16	32
1984/85	29	64		1922/23	50.00	23	46
1971/72	28	53		1981/82	50.00	31	62
2006/07	28	58		1973/74	49.18	30	61
2001/02	28	59		1975/76	49.15	29	59
2000/01	28	63		1995/96	49.06	26	53
1987/88	27	50		1968/69	49.02	25	51
1979/80	27	60		2006/07	48.28	28	58
1982/83	27	60		2001/02	47.46	28	59
1976/77	27	62		1984/85	45.31	29	64
1995/96	26	53		1974/75	45.28	24	53
1972/73	26	66		1898/99	45.00	18	40
1968/69	25	51		1979/80	45.00	27	60
1994/95	25	57		1982/83	45.00	27	60
2007/08	**25**	**59**					
1974/75	24	53					
1986/87	24	57					
1980/81	24	63					
1985/86	24	63					

MOST CLEAN SHEETS KEPT BY LIVERPOOL IN A LEAGUE SEASON					
SEASON	**CLEAN SHEETS**	**GAMES**	**SEASON**	**CLEAN SHEETS**	**GAMES**
1978/79	28	42	1968/69	21	42
1975/76	23	42	1987/88	21	40
1977/78	23	42	1981/82	20	42
1970/71	22	42	1983/84	20	42
1971/72	22	42	2006/07	20	38
2005/06	22	38			
1922/23	21	42			

CLEAN SHEET RECORDS

CLEAN SHEETS ACHIEVED BY LIVERPOOL GOALKEEPERS IN FIRST 100 FULL LEAGUE GAMES

Goalkeepers have to play the full game for the clean sheet to be awarded.
However, if injured, substituted or sent-off having conceded in that game the appearance counts.

PLAYER	CLEAN SHEETS	GOALS CONCEDED	DATE OF 100TH START UNDER CRITERIA
Pepe Reina	54	70	30th March 2008
Ray Clemence	53	65	19th August 1972
Bruce Grobbelaar	47	78	3rd December 1983
Jerzy Dudek	43	93	14th December 2004
Harry Storer	37	111	16th December 1899
David James	34	104	2nd December 1995
Cyril Sidlow	34	106	4th May 1949
Elisha Scott	34	112	22nd April 1922
William Perkins	32	115	4th October 1902
Sam Hardy	30	136	12th September 1908
Tommy Younger	28	137	20th December 1958
Tommy Lawrence	25	132	13th March 1965
Kenny Campbell	19	173	27th September 1919
Arthur Riley	19	191	29th November 1930

GOALKEEPERS TO REACH 50 CLEAN SHEETS FOR LIVERPOOL THE QUICKEST

PLAYER	NO. OF GAMES TAKEN	50TH CLEAN SHEET
Pepe Reina	92	2nd February 2008 v Sunderland
Ray Clemence	95	22nd April 1972 v Ipswich Town
Bruce Grobbelaar	109	1st February 1984 v Watford
Elisha Scott	135	24th March 1923 v Manchester City
David James	136	2nd December 1996 v Tottenham H.
Tommy Lawrence	171	3rd December 1966 v Sheffield Utd
Sam Hardy	185	14th April 1911 v Arsenal
Arthur Riley	263	27th November 1937 v Blackpool

GOLDEN GLOVE 2007/08

MOST CLEAN SHEETS KEPT BY A GOALKEEPER IN THE PREMIER LEAGUE

POS.	GOALKEEPER	TEAM	CLEAN SHEET
1	Jose Reina	Liverpool	18
2	David James	Portsmouth	16
3	Petr Cech	Chelsea	14
=	Tim Howard	Everton	14
=	Edwin van der Sar	Manchester United	14
6	Chris Kirkland	Wigan Athletic	12
7	Manuel Almunia	Arsenal	11
8	Scott Carson	Aston Villa	9
9	Brad Friedel	Blackburn Rovers	8
=	Robert Green	West Ham United	8
=	Marcus Hahnemann	Reading	8
=	Jussi Jaaskelainen	Bolton Wanderers	8
=	Mark Schwarzer	Middlesbrough	8

NATIONALITIES

Brazilian goalkeeper Diego Cavalieri, Italian defender Andrea Dossena, French forward David Ngog and Swiss defender Philipp Degen are amongst the 2008 summer signings who are likely to join the growing number of overseas players to represent Liverpool Football Club in competitive first-team action.

Up and coming young players like Mikel San Jose and Krisztian Nemeth are amongst a host of overseas reserve players who could also make their claim for a start this term.

Below is a comprehensive list of those overseas players who have represented the club:

COUNTRIES REPRESENTED	PLAYERS
Argentina	5 - Mauricio Pellegrino, Gabriel Paletta, Javier Mascherano, Emiliano Insua, Sebastian Leto
Australia	1 - Harry Kewell
Brazil	2 - Fabio Aurelio, Lucas Leiva
Cameroon	1 - Rigobert Song
Chile	1 - Mark Gonzalez
Croatia	1 - Igor Biscan
Czech Republic	3 - Patrik Berger, Vladimir Smicer, Milan Baros
Denmark	3 - Jan Molby, Torben Piechnik, Daniel Agger
Finland	2 - Sami Hyypia, Jari Litmanen
France	12 - Jean-Michel Ferri, Pegguy Arphexad, Bernard Diomede, Gregory Vignal, Nicolas Anelka, Bruno Cheyrou, Patrice Luzi, Anthony Le Tallec, Florent Sinama-Pongolle, Djibril Cisse, Charles Itandje, Damien Plessis
Germany	5 - Karlheinz Riedle, Dietmar Hamann, Markus Babbel, Christian Ziege, Sean Dundee
Guinea	1 - Titi Camara
Holland	6 - Erik Meijer, Sander Westerveld, Bolo Zenden, Jan Kromkamp, Dirk Kuyt, Ryan Babel
Hungary	1 - Istvan Kozma
Israel	3 - Avi Cohen, Ronny Rosenthal, Yossi Benayoun
Italy	1 - Daniele Padelli
Mali	2 - Djimi Traore, Mohamed Sissoko
Morocco	1 - Nabil El Zhar
Norway	6 - Stig Inge Bjornebye, Oyvind Leonhardsen, Bjorn Tore Kvarme, Vegard Heggem, Frode Kippe, John Arne Riise
Poland	1 - Jerzy Dudek
Portugal	1 - Abel Xavier
Senegal	2 - El-Hadji Diouf, Salif Diao
Slovakia	1 - Martin Skrtel
South Africa	10 - Lance Carr, Hugh Gerhadi, Gordon Hodgson, Dirk Kemp, Berry Nieuwenhuys, Robert Priday, Arthur Riley, Doug Rudham, Charlie Thompson, Harman Van Den Berg
Spain	10 - Josemi, Luis Garcia, Xabi Alonso, Antonio Nunez, Fernando Morientes, Pepe Reina, Antonio Barragan, Miki Roque, Alvaro Arbeloa, Fernando Torres
Sweden	1 - Glenn Hysen
Switzerland	1 - Stephane Henchoz
Ukraine	1 - Andriy Voronin
USA	2 - Brad Friedel, Zak Whitbread
Zimbabwe	1 - Bruce Grobbelaar

ENGLAND

PLAYER	CAPS WON AT LIVERPOOL	TOTAL CAPS	PLAYER	CAPS WON AT LIVERPOOL	TOTAL CAPS
Steven Gerrard	67	67	Tom Bromilow	5	5
Michael Owen	60	89	David Johnson	5	8
Emlyn Hughes	59	62	Ephraim Longworth	5	5
Ray Clemence	56	61	Mark Wright	5	45
Phil Neal	50	50	Ian Callaghan	4	4
John Barnes	48	79	Chris Lawler	4	4
Phil Thompson	42	42	Alec Lindsay	4	4
Emile Heskey	35	45	Jack Cox	3	3
Peter Beardsley	34	59	Gordon Hodgson	3	3
Jamie Carragher	34	34	Laurie Hughes	3	3
Roger Hunt	34	34	Larry Lloyd	3	4
Kevin Keegan	28	63	Tommy Lucas	3	3
Peter Crouch	27	28	John Scales	3	3
Terry McDermott	25	25	Phil Taylor	3	3
Steve McManaman	24	37	Gerry Byrne	2	2
Robbie Fowler	22	26	Scott Carson	2	2
Ray Kennedy	17	17	Bill Jones	2	2
Steve McMahon	17	17	Alan Kennedy	2	2
Jamie Redknapp	17	17	Jimmy Melia	2	2
Peter Thompson	16	16	Jack Parkinson	2	2
Sam Hardy	14	21	John Bamber	1	1
Sammy Lee	14	14	Frank Becton	1	2
Gordon Milne	14	14	Thomas Bradshaw	1	1
Paul Ince	12	53	Raby Howell	1	2
Danny Murphy	9	9	David James	1	39
Nick Barmby	8	23	Chris Kirkland	1	1
Harry Chambers	8	8	Neil Ruddock	1	1
Rob Jones	8	8	Tommy Smith	1	1
Alan A'Court	5	5			

England and Liverpool (left to right): Tommy Smith, Roger Hunt, Alan A'Court

SCOTLAND

PLAYER	CAPS WON AT LIVERPOOL	TOTAL CAPS	PLAYER	CAPS WON AT LIVERPOOL	TOTAL CAPS
Kenny Dalglish	55	102	John Wark	3	29
Graeme Souness	37	54	Jimmy McDougall	2	2
Billy Liddell	28	28	Frank McGarvey	2	7
Steve Nicol	27	27	Donald MacKinlay	2	2
Alan Hansen	26	26	Ron Yeats	2	2
Tommy Younger	16	24	George Allan	1	1
Ian St John	14	21	Billy Dunlop	1	1
Gary Gillespie	13	13	Jock McNab	1	1
Alex Raisbeck	8	8	Tom Miller	1	3
Ken Campbell	3	8	Hugh Morgan	1	2
Tommy Lawrence	3	3			

WALES

PLAYER	CAPS WON AT LIVERPOOL	TOTAL CAPS	PLAYER	CAPS WON AT LIVERPOOL	TOTAL CAPS
Ian Rush	67	73	Cyril Sidlow	7	7
John Toshack	26	40	Ray Lambert	5	5
Joey Jones	18	72	Richard Morris	5	11
Maurice Parry	16	16	Edward Parry	5	5
Craig Bellamy	11	51	John Hughes	3	3
Ernest Peake	10	11	Lee Jones	1	2
George Lathom	8	10	Robert Matthews	1	3
Dean Saunders	8	75			

IRELAND

PLAYER	CAPS WON AT LIVERPOOL	TOTAL CAPS	PLAYER	CAPS WON AT LIVERPOOL	TOTAL CAPS
Ronnie Whelan	51	53	John Aldridge	19	69
Steve Staunton	38	102	Mark Kennedy	17	34
Ray Houghton	34	73	Jim Beglin	15	15
Steve Heighway	33	34	Jason McAteer	14	52
Steve Finnan	28	50	Billy Lacey (NI)	12	23
Elisha Scott (NI)	27	31	Michael Robinson	5	24
Phil Babb	25	35	David McMullan (NI)	3	3
Mark Lawrenson	24	39	Ken De Mange	1	2

INTERNATIONAL GOALS

PLAYER	COUNTRY	GOALS	PLAYER	COUNTRY	GOALS
Michael Owen	England	26	Terry McDermott	England	3
Ian Rush	Wales	26	Ronnie Whelan	Republic of Ireland	3
Roger Hunt	England	18	Frank Becton	England	2
Peter Crouch	England	14	Billy Lacey	Northern Ireland	2
Kenny Dalglish	Scotland	13	Sammy Lee	England	2
Steven Gerrard	England	13	Tom Miller	Scotland	2
John Barnes	England	8	Dean Saunders	Wales	2
Ian St John	Scotland	8	Steve Staunton	Republic of Ireland	2
John Toshack	Wales	8	Alan A'Court	England	1
Kevin Keegan	England	7	John Aldridge	Republic of Ireland	1
Peter Beardsley	England	6	Nick Barmby	England	1
Billy Liddell	Scotland	6	Steve Finnan	Republic of Ireland	1
Harry Chambers	England	5	Gordon Hodgson	England	1
Robbie Fowler	England	5	Emlyn Hughes	England	1
Emile Heskey	England	5	Chris Lawler	England	1
Phil Neal	England	5	Jason McAteer	Republic of Ireland	1
Craig Bellamy	Wales	4	Jimmy Melia	England	1
Graeme Souness	Scotland	4	Danny Murphy	England	1
Ray Houghton	Republic of Ireland	3	Ernest Peake	Wales	1
David Johnson	England	3	Jamie Redknapp	England	1
Ray Kennedy	England	3	Phil Thompson	England	1
Mark Lawrenson	Republic of Ireland	3			

International goalscorers (left to right): Terry McDermott, Kenny Dalglish and Phil Thompson

EUROPEAN CHAMPIONSHIP FINALS

The following lists Liverpool players who have been called up by their countries for the European Championship finals - and the players' respective record at the tournament (note "games" refers to an apperance made whether from the start, or coming on as a substitute).

1968 - ITALY

Only the third tournament and the first to be held under its current name (changed from the European Nations Cup). Only four teams could qualify for the finals, with world champions England losing to Yugoslavia in the semis - beating USSR in the third-place play-off. Italy were winners.

England - Roger Hunt (2 games), Peter Thompson (did not play)

1980 - ITALY

For the first time the hosts qualified automatically, while Liverpool's England men went out after finishing third in their four-team group which included the hosts and Spain. The top team in the group, Belgium, lost the final 2-1 to West Germany.

England - Phil Thompson (3 games), Ray Clemence (2 games), Ray Kennedy (2 games),
England - Terry McDermott (2 games), Phil Neal (2 games), David Johnson (1 game)

1988 - WEST GERMANY

England and Republic of Ireland were drawn in the same group, with the Irish winning 1-0. The scorer, Ray Houghton, became the first Liverpool player to score in the Euro finals and in what turned out to be a woeful tournament for England (three defeats from three), Eire came within a whisker of the last four. Ronnie Whelan scored in the 1-1 draw with USSR, while Holland, who the Irish lost to in their final group game, were worthy champions.

England - John Barnes (3 games), Peter Beardsley (2 games), Steve McMahon (1 game)
Republic of Ireland - Ray Houghton (3 games, 1 goal), Ronnie Whelan (3 games, 1 goal),
Republic of Ireland - John Aldridge (3 games)

1992 - SWEDEN

Graham Taylor's England again failed to progress to the last four, finishing bottom of their group having failed to win a game. Their group though did include surprise winners Denmark - only participating due to their qualifying group winners Yugoslavia being disqualified due to civil war.

England - Mark Wright (did not play)

1996 - ENGLAND

Steve McManaman was an ever present, being named one of the best midfielders at the tournament as the hosts showed some impressive form to reach the semi-finals, going out on penalties to eventual winners Germany. It was the first time 16 teams played in the finals.

England - Steve McManaman (5 games), Robbie Fowler (2 games), Jamie Redknapp (1 game)

2000 - BELGIUM & HOLLAND

The flood of overseas stars to grace the English game in the modern era can best be reflected by Liverpool's 10-strong contingent at Euro 2000. Vladimir Smicer was top scorer amongst them thanks to his double in the Czech's final group game win over Denmark, while Sander Westerveld's Holland were beaten in the semi-finals by Italy - France going on to win it. Michael Owen was on target in the final group game for England, a decisive 3-2 defeat to Romania.

England - Michael Owen (3 games, 1 goal), Emile Heskey (2 games), Steven Gerrard (1 game),
England - Robbie Fowler (did not play)
Czech Republic - Vladimir Smicer (3 games, 2 goals), Patrik Berger (1 game)
Germany - Dietmar Hamann (3 games)
Holland - Sander Westerveld (2 games)
Norway - Vegard Heggem (2 games) Stig Inge Bjornebye (2 games)

EUROPEAN CHAMPIONSHIP FINALS

2004 - PORTUGAL

Liverpool's players again failed to break their duck at the finals, with the Czech Republic going out to surprise winners Greece in the semi-finals. Milan Baros finished as top scorer, while Michael Owen and Steven Gerrard were amonst the goals in England's run to the last eight.

England - Steven Gerrard (4 games, 1 goal), Michael Owen (4 games, 1 goal),
England - Jamie Carragher (did not play)
Czech Republic - Milan Baros (5 games, 4 goals), Vladimir Smicer (3 games, 1 goal)
Germany - Dietmar Hamann (3 games)
Switzerland - Stephane Henchoz (2 games)

2008 - AUSTRIA & SWITZERLAND

Summer 2008 will long be remembered for Spain's first major football success since 1964, Fernando Torres scoring the winner in the final against Germany. With England's failure to qualify, Liverpool's Spanish quartet were adopted as the team to follow and with the Reds' star striker showing some fine form, they were deserved winners.

Spain - Fernando Torres (5 games, 2 goals), Xabi Alonso (4 games), Pepe Reina (1 game),
Spain - Alvaro Arbeloa (1 game)
Holland - Dirk Kuyt (4 games, 1 goal)

Liverpool and Villarreal's Spanish squad members line-up with the European Championship trophy ahead of the friendly between the sides in August 2008

ARSENAL

2007/08 OVERVIEW

Final position: 3rd, Premier League
Best cup runs: SF, League Cup, QF, Ch. Lge
Player of season: Cesc Fabregas
Top scorer (all): 30, Emmanuel Adebayor

ALL-TIME RECORD

(League matches only)

	PL	W	D	L
Home:	84	48	15	21
Away:	84	20	27	37
Overall:	168	68	42	58

LAST 2 MEETINGS (LEAGUE)

05/04/2008

Arsenal	1-1	Liverpool
Bendtner 54		Crouch 42

28/10/2007

Liverpool	1-1	Arsenal
Gerrard 7		Fabregas 80

CLUB DETAILS

Nickname: The Gunners
Ground: Emirates Stadium, capacity 60,432 (away allocation 3,000)
Manager: Arsene Wenger (app. 01/10/96)
Ex Red: Jermaine Pennant
Year formed: 1886

USEFUL INFORMATION

Website: www.arsenal.com
Address: Emirates Stadium, Highbury House, 75 Drayton Park N5 1BU
Switchboard: 0207 704 4000

TRAVEL INFORMATION

By Tube: The nearest station is Arsenal (Piccadilly Line), around three minutes walk from the ground. Finsbury Park and Highbury & Islington are also within a 10-minute walking distance.
By Bus: Main bus stops are located on Holloway Road, Nag's Head, Seven Sisters Road, Blackstock Road and Highbury Corner. Regular services will take you to within 10 minutes walk of the ground.

ASTON VILLA

2007/08 STATISTICS

Final position: 6th, Premier League
Best cup runs: R3, League Cup, FA Cup
Player of season: Ashley Young
Top scorer (all): 13, John Carew

ALL-TIME RECORD

(League matches only)

	PL	W	D	L
Home:	83	52	17	14
Away:	83	26	20	37
Overall:	166	78	37	51

LAST 2 MEETINGS

21/01/2008

Liverpool	2-2	Aston Villa
Benayoun 19, Crouch 88		Harewood 69, Aurelio 72 (o.g.)

11/08/2007

Aston Villa	1-2	Liverpool
Barry 85 (p)		Laursen 31 (o.g.), Gerrard 87

CLUB DETAILS

Nickname: The Villans
Ground: Villa Park, capacity 42,573 (away allocation 3,000)
Manager: Martin O'Neill (app. 04/08/06)
Ex Reds: Patrik Berger, Scott Carson
Year formed: 1874

USEFUL INFORMATION

Website: www.avfc.co.uk
Address: Villa Park, Trinity Road, Birmingham B6 6HE
Switchboard: 0871 423 8100

TRAVEL INFORMATION

By Train: Witton station is a 5-minute walk from the ground, while Aston is 15 minutes away. From New Street Station, a taxi should take 15 minutes.
By Bus: The number 7 West Midlands Travel Bus runs from Birmingham City Centre directly to the ground (Witton). To check services check at: www.travelwm.co.uk .

BLACKBURN ROVERS

2007/08 STATISTICS

Final position: 7th, Premier League
Best cup runs: QF, League Cup, R3, FA Cup
Player of season: Roque Santa Cruz
Top scorer (all): 23, Roque Santa Cruz

ALL-TIME RECORD

(League matches only)

	PL	W	D	L
Home:	60	35	16	9
Away:	60	14	21	25
Overall:	120	49	37	34

LAST 2 MEETINGS

13/04/2008

Liverpool 3-1 Blackburn Rovers
Gerrard 60, Torres 82   Santa Cruz 90
Voronin 90

03/11/2007

Blackburn Rovers 0-0   Liverpool

CLUB DETAILS

Nickname: Rovers
Ground: Ewood Park, capacity 31,367 (away allocation 4,000)
Manager: Paul Ince (app. 24/06/08)
Ex Reds: Brad Friedel, Stephen Warnock
Year formed: 1875

USEFUL INFORMATION

Website: www.rovers.co.uk
Address: Ewood Park, Bolton Road, Blackburn, Lancashire BB2 4JF
Switchboard: 08701 113232

TRAVEL INFORMATION

By Train: Blackburn station is a mile and a half away, while Mill Hill is 1 mile from the stadium. Direct trains run from Manchester Victoria, Salford Crescent and Preston.
By Bus: The central bus station is next to the railway station. Services 3, 3A, 3B, 46, and 346 all go from Blackburn to Darwen. Ewood Park is a mile and a half along the journey.

BOLTON WANDERERS

2007/08 STATISTICS

Final position: 16th, Premier League
Best cup runs: L16, UEFA Cup, R4, League Cup
Player of season: Kevin Davies
Top scorer (all): 11, Nicolas Anelka

ALL-TIME RECORD

(League matches only)

	PL	W	D	L
Home:	55	29	16	10
Away:	55	17	13	25
Overall:	110	46	29	35

LAST 2 MEETINGS

02/03/2008

Bolton Wanderers 1-3   Liverpool
Cohen 79   Jaaskelainen 12 (o.g.),
             Babel 60, Aurelio 75

02/12/2007

Liverpool 4-0 Bolton Wanderers
Hyypia 17, Torres 45,
Gerrard 56 (p), Babel 86

CLUB DETAILS

Nickname: The Trotters
Ground: Reebok Stadium, capacity 28,000 (away allocation 3-5,000)
Manager: Gary Megson (app. 26/10/07)
Ex Red: El Hadji Diouf
Year formed: 1874

USEFUL INFORMATION

Website: www.bwfc.co.uk
Address: Reebok Stadium, Burnden Way, Lostock, Bolton BL6 6JW
Switchboard: 01204 673673

TRAVEL INFORMATION

By Train: Horwich Parkway station is 100 yards from the stadium, which is on the Manchester Airport to Preston and Blackpool North/Blackpool North and Preston to Manchester Airport line.
By Bus: The club operate regular buses to and from Bolton town centre.

CHELSEA

2007/08 STATISTICS

Final position: 2nd, Premier League
Best cup runs: RU, Ch. League, League Cup
Player of season: Ricardo Carvalho
Top scorer (all): 20, Frank Lampard

ALL-TIME RECORD

(League matches only)

	PL	W	D	L
Home:	65	43	14	8
Away:	65	15	14	36
Overall:	130	58	28	44

LAST 2 MEETINGS (LEAGUE)

10/02/2008
Chelsea   0-0   Liverpool

19/08/2007
Liverpool   1-1   Chelsea
Torres 16   Lampard 62 (p)

CLUB DETAILS

Nickname: The Blues
Ground: Stamford Bridge, capacity 42,360 (away allocation 3,000)
Manager: Luiz Felipe Scolari (app. 01/07/08)
Ex Red: Nicolas Anelka
Year formed: 1905

USEFUL INFORMATION

Website: www.chelseafc.com
Address: Stamford Bridge, Fulham Road, London SW6 1HS
Switchboard: 0870 300 2322

TRAVEL INFORMATION

By Tube: Fulham Broadway is on the District Line, around 5 minutes walk. Take a train to Earl's Court and change for Wimbledon-bound trains. West Brompton is a new railway station accessible from Clapham Junction.
By Bus: Numbers 14, 211 and 414 go along Fulham Road from central London via West Brompton train station.

EVERTON

2007/08 STATISTICS

Final position: 5th, Premier League
Best cup runs: SF, League Cup, L16, UEFA Cup
Player of season: Joleon Lescott
Top scorer (all): 21, Ayegbeni Yakubu

ALL-TIME RECORD

(League matches only)

	PL	W	D	L
Home:	89	38	28	23
Away:	89	29	27	33
Overall:	178	67	55	56

LAST 2 MEETINGS

30/03/2008
Liverpool   1-0   Everton
Torres 7

20/10/2007
Everton   1-2   Liverpool
Hyypia 38 (o.g.)   Kuyt 54, 90 (2 pens)

CLUB DETAILS

Nickname: The Toffees
Ground: Goodison Park, capacity 40,260 (away allocation 3,000)
Manager: David Moyes (app. 14/03/02)
Ex Reds: Nick Barmby, Peter Beardsley
Year formed: 1878

USEFUL INFORMATION

Website: www.evertonfc.com
Address: Goodison Park, Goodison Road, Liverpool L4 4EL
Switchboard: 0151 330 2200

TRAVEL INFORMATION

By Train: From Liverpool Central, take any train heading for Ormskirk or Kirkby and get off at Kirkdale - from there it is a 10-minute walk.
By Bus: From Queen's Square Bus Station in Liverpool city centre, numbers 1, 2, 19, 20, 311, 345 and 350 go past the stadium.

FULHAM

2007/08 STATISTICS

Final position: 17th, Premier League
Best cup runs: R3, League Cup, FA Cup
Player of season: Simon Davies
Top scorers (all): 6, Clint Dempsey, David Healy, Diomansy Kamara, Danny Murphy

ALL-TIME RECORD

(League matches only)

	PL	W	D	L
Home:	21	16	5	0
Away:	21	8	6	7
Overall:	42	24	11	7

LAST 2 MEETINGS

19/04/2008

Fulham	0-2	Liverpool
		Pennant 17, Crouch 70

10/11/2007

Liverpool	2-0	Fulham
Torres 81, Gerrard 85 (p)		

CLUB DETAILS

Nickname: Cottagers
Ground: Craven Cottage, capacity 22,000 (away allocation 3,000)
Manager: Roy Hodgson (app. 30/12/07)
Ex Red: Danny Murphy
Year formed: 1879

USEFUL INFORMATION

Website: www.fulhamfc.com
Address: Craven Cottage, Stevenage Road, Fulham, London SW6 6HH
Switchboard: 0870 442 1222

TRAVEL INFORMATION

By Tube: Alight at Putney Bridge (District line) from Central London. Turn left out of station and right down Ranleigh Gardens. At the end of the road (before the Eight Bells pub) turn left into Willow Bank and right through the underpass into Bishops Park. Walk along river to ground (note park is closed after night games).
By Bus: The numbers 74 and 220 both run along Fulham Palace Road.

HULL CITY

2007/08 STATISTICS

Final position: 3rd, Championship
Best cup runs: R3, League Cup, FA Cup
Player of season: Michael Turner
Top scorers (all): 15, Fraizer Campbell, Dean Windass

ALL-TIME RECORD

(League matches only)

	PL	W	D	L
Home:	3	3	0	0
Away:	3	2	1	0
Overall:	6	5	1	0

LAST 2 MEETINGS (LEAGUE)

02/01/1960

Hull City	0-1	Liverpool
		Melia 31

29/08/1959

Liverpool	5-3	Hull City
Harrower 52, Melia 58, Moran 65, A'Court 80, Liddell 85		Coates 2 (F-H, S-H) Metcalfe (F-H)

CLUB DETAILS

Nickname: The Tigers
Ground: The KC Stadium, capacity 25,404 (away allocation 4,000)
Manager: Phil Brown (app. 04/12/06)
Ex Reds: Nick Barmby, John Welsh
Year formed: 1904

USEFUL INFORMATION

Website: www.hullcityafc.premiumtv.co.uk
Address: The Circle, Walton Street, Hull HU3 6HU
Switchboard: 08708 370 003

TRAVEL INFORMATION

By Train: Leave Hull Paragon on the south side and turn right onto Anlaby Road. Stadium is 15 minutes away.
By Road: Leave M62 at junction 38 and join the A63, towards Hull. Stay on A63 and the stadium is signposted (KC Stadium). One mile from the centre of Hull leave A63 (signposted Hull Royal Infirmary) and take the 2nd exit at the roundabout. Turn left at the lights and then over the flyover, right at the next lights and the ground is down on the right.

MANCHESTER CITY

2007/08 STANDINGS

Final position: 9th, Premier League
Best cup runs: QF, League Cup, R4 FA Cup
Player of season: Joe Hart
Top scorer (all): 10, Elano

ALL-TIME RECORD

(League matches only)

	PL	W	D	L
Home:	72	45	14	13
Away:	72	28	20	24
Overall:	144	73	34	37

LAST 2 MEETINGS

04/05/2008

Liverpool	1-0	Manchester City

Torres 58

30/12/2007

Manchester City	0-0	Liverpool

CLUB DETAILS

Nickname: Blues/The Citizens
Ground: City of Manchester Stadium, capacity 48,000 (away allocation 4,800)
Manager: Mark Hughes (app. 05/06/08)
Ex Red: Dietmar Hamann
Year formed: 1887

USEFUL INFORMATION

Website: www.mcfc.co.uk
Address: City of Manchester Stadium, SportCity, Rowsley Street, Manchester M11 3FF
Switchboard: 0870 062 1894

TRAVEL INFORMATION

By Train: The nearest station is Ashburys (a 10-minute walk), which is a five-minute train ride from Piccadilly (which itself is a 20-25 minute walk).
By Bus: Numbers 216 and 217 are the main services from the city centre, but 53, 54, 185, 186, 230, 231, 232, 233, 234, 235, 236, 237, X36 and X37 also run to SportCity.

MANCHESTER UNITED

2007/08 STATISTICS

Final position: 1st, Premier League
Best cup runs: W, Ch. League, QF, FA Cup
Player of season: Cristiano Ronaldo
Top scorer (all): 42, Cristiano Ronaldo

ALL-TIME RECORD

(League matches only)

	PL	W	D	L
Home:	75	35	18	22
Away:	75	14	25	36
Overall:	150	49	43	58

LAST 2 MEETINGS

23/03/2008

Manchester Utd	3-0	Liverpool

Brown 34, Ronaldo 79, Nani 81

16/12/2007

Liverpool	0-1	Manchester Utd

Tevez 43

CLUB DETAILS

Nickname: Red Devils
Ground: Old Trafford, capacity 76,312 (away allocation 3,000)
Manager: Sir Alex Ferguson (app. 06/11/86)
Ex Red: Paul Ince
Year formed: 1878

USEFUL INFORMATION

Website: www.manutd.com
Address: Old Trafford, Manchester M16 0RA
Switchboard: 0870 442 1994

TRAVEL INFORMATION

By Train: Special services run from Manchester Piccadilly to the clubs own railway station. There is also a Metrolink service, with the station located next to Lancashire County Cricket Club on Warwick Road, which leads up to Sir Matt Busby Way.
By Bus: Numbers 114, 230, 252 and 253 all run from the city centre to the ground.

MIDDLESBROUGH

2007/08 STATISTICS

Final position: 13th, Premier League
Best cup runs: QF, FA Cup, R3, League Cup
Player of season: David Wheater
Top scorer (all): 10, Stuart Downing

ALL-TIME RECORD

(League matches only)

	PL	W	D	L
Home:	66	36	17	13
Away:	66	20	22	24
Overall:	132	56	39	37

LAST 2 MEETINGS

23/02/2008

Liverpool	3-2	Middlesbrough
Torres 28, 29, 61		Tuncay 9, Downing 83

12/01/2008

Middlesbrough	1-1	Liverpool
Boateng 26		Torres 71

CLUB DETAILS

Nickname: Boro
Ground: Riverside Stadium, capacity 35,100 (away allocation 4,000)
Manager: Gareth Southgate (app. 07/06/06)
Ex Reds: Abel Xavier, Bolo Zenden
Year formed: 1876

USEFUL INFORMATION

Website: www.mfc.co.uk
Address: Riverside Stadium, Middlesbrough, Cleveland TS3 6RS
Switchboard: 0844 499 6789

TRAVEL INFORMATION

By Train: Middlesbrough station is about 15 minutes walk from the stadium, served by trains from Darlington. Take the back exit from the station, turn right then after a couple of minutes right again into Wynward Way for the ground.
By Bus: Numbers 36, 37 and 38 go from the town centre close to the ground.

NEWCASTLE UNITED

2007/08 STATISTICS

Final position: 12th, Premier League
Best cup runs: R4, FA Cup, R3, League Cup
Player of season: Habib Beye
Top scorer (all): 13, Michael Owen

ALL-TIME RECORD

(League matches only)

	PL	W	D	L
Home:	73	48	14	11
Away:	73	21	23	29
Overall:	146	69	37	40

LAST 2 MEETINGS

08/03/2008

Liverpool	3-0	Newcastle United
Pennant 43, Torres 45, Gerrard 51		

24/11/2007

Newcastle United	0-3	Liverpool
		Gerrard 28, Kuyt 46, Babel 66

CLUB DETAILS

Nickname: Magpies
Ground: St James' Park, capacity 52,387 (away allocation 3,000)
Manager: TBA
Ex Reds: Michael Owen, Terry McDermott
Year formed: 1881

USEFUL INFORMATION

Website: www.nufc.co.uk
Address: St. James' Park, Newcastle-upon-Tyne NE1 4ST
Switchboard: 0191 201 8400

TRAVEL INFORMATION

By Train: St James' Park is a 10-minute walk from Newcastle Central Station. The stadium is also served by its own Metro station (St James' Metro).
By Bus: Any bus from the town centre heading towards Gallowgate takes you past the stadium.

PORTSMOUTH

2007/08 STATISTICS

Final position: 8th, Premier League
Best cup runs: W, FA Cup, R4, League Cup
Player of season: David James
Top scorer (all): 12, Benjani

ALL-TIME RECORD

(League matches only)

	PL	W	D	L
Home:	28	14	10	4
Away:	28	8	5	15
Overall:	56	22	15	19

LAST 2 MEETINGS

22/12/2007

Liverpool	4-1	Portsmouth

Benayoun 13,
Distin 16 (o.g.),
Torres 67, 85

Benjani 57

15/09/2007

Portsmouth	0-0	Liverpool

CLUB DETAILS

Nickname: Pompey
Ground: Fratton Park, capacity 20,200
(away allocation 2,000)
Manager: Harry Redknapp (app. 07/12/05)
Ex Reds: David James, Djimi Traore
Year formed: 1898

USEFUL INFORMATION

Website: www.pompeyfc.co.uk
Address: Fratton Park,
Frogmore Road,
Portsmouth,
Hants PO4 8RA
Switchboard: 0239 273 1204

TRAVEL INFORMATION

By Train: Fratton Bridge Station is a 10-minute walk from the ground - on arrival by train you pass the ground on your left. Portsmouth mainline station is at least a 25-minute walk.
By Bus: 13, 17 and 18 all run to the ground, while other services that stop close to Fratton Park are the 3, 16, 16A, 24, 27 (all Fratton Bridge); 4, 4A, 6 (all

STOKE CITY

2007/08 STATISTICS

Final position: 2nd, Championship
Best cup runs: R3, FA Cup, R1, League Cup
Player of season: Liam Lawrence
Top scorers (all): 15, Ricardo Fuller,
Liam Lawrence

ALL-TIME RECORD

(League matches only)

	PL	W	D	L
Home:	53	41	9	3
Away:	53	12	18	23
Overall:	106	53	27	26

LAST 2 MEETINGS (LEAGUE)

23/02/1985

Liverpool	2-0	Stoke City

Nicol 14, Dalglish 28

03/11/1984

Stoke City	0-1	Liverpool

Whelan 86

CLUB DETAILS

Nickname: The Potters
Ground: Britannia Stadium, capacity 28,384 (away allocation 4,800)
Manager: Tony Pulis (app. 13/06/06)
Ex Reds: Salif Diao, Dominic Matteo
Year formed: 1863

USEFUL INFORMATION

Website: www.stokecityfc.premiumtv.co.uk
Address: Stanley Matthews Way,
Stoke-on-Trent
ST4 4EG
Switchboard: 01782 592 222

TRAVEL INFORMATION

By Train: Stoke-on-Trent station is two minutes from Glebe Street, where buses to the stadium run. Turn right out of the station and then next right. Follow the road to the end then turn left, down a bank into Glebe Street. Buses depart on the left by the church.
By Bus: From Hanley Bus Station taken the 23 to Glebe Street where shuttle bus services to the stadium depart. Service is at 15-minute intervals until 15 minutes before kick-off.

SUNDERLAND

2007/08 STATISTICS

Final position: 15th, Premier League
Best cup runs: R3, FA Cup, R2, League Cup
Player of season: Kenwyne Jones
Top scorer (all): 7, Kenwyne Jones

ALL-TIME RECORD

(League matches only)

	PL	W	D	L
Home:	71	35	18	18
Away:	71	27	13	31
Overall:	142	62	31	49

LAST 2 MEETINGS

02/02/2008
Liverpool   3-0   Sunderland
Crouch 57, Torres 69,
Gerrard 89 (p)

25/08/2007
Sunderland   0-2   Liverpool
                                  Sissoko 37, Voronin 87

CLUB DETAILS

Nickname: The Black Cats
Ground: Stadium of Light, capacity 49,000 (away allocation 3,600)
Manager: Roy Keane (app. 28/08/06)
Ex Red: Stephen Wright
Year formed: 1879

USEFUL INFORMATION

Website: www.safc.com
Address: The Sunderland Stadium of Light, Sunderland SR5 1SU
Switchboard: 0191 551 5000

TRAVEL INFORMATION

By Train: Sunderland mainline station is a 10-15 minute walk. The Metro service also runs from here, with St. Peter's or the Stadium of Light stations nearest the stadium.
By Bus: Numbers 2, 3, 4, 12, 13, 15 and 16 all stop within a few minutes walk of the ground. All routes connect to the central bus station, Park Lane Interchange.

TOTTENHAM HOTSPUR

2007/08 STATISTICS

Final position: 11th, Premier League
Best cup runs: W, League Cup, L16, UEFA Cup
Player of season: Robbie Keane
Top scorers (all): 23, Dimitar Berbatov, Robbie Keane

ALL-TIME RECORD

(League matches only)

	PL	W	D	L
Home:	65	41	19	5
Away:	65	20	15	30
Overall:	130	61	34	35

LAST 2 MEETINGS

11/05/2008
Tottenham H.   0-2   Liverpool
                                  Voronin 69, Torres 74

07/10/2007
Liverpool   2-2   Tottenham H.
Voronin 12, Torres 90   Keane 45, 47

CLUB DETAILS

Nickname: Spurs
Ground: White Hart Lane, capacity 36,240 (away allocation 3,500)
Manager: Juande Ramos (app. 27/10/07)
Ex Reds: Jamie Redknapp, John Scales
Year formed: 1882

USEFUL INFORMATION

Website: www.spurs.co.uk
Address: 748 High Road, Tottenham, London N17 0AP
Switchboard: 0208 365 5000

TRAVEL INFORMATION

By Tube: The nearest tube station is Seven Sisters (Victoria - a 25-minute walk), with trains running to Liverpool Street. The nearest mainline station is White Hart Lane, approx 5 minutes walk, on the Liverpool Street-Enfield Town line.
By Bus: A regular service runs from Seven Sisters past the stadium entrance (numbers 259, 279, 149).

WEST BROMWICH ALBION

2007/08 STATISTICS

Final position: 1st, Championship
Best cup runs: SF, FA Cup, R3, League Cup
Player of season: Kevin Phillips
Top scorer (all): 24, Kevin Phillips

ALL-TIME RECORD

(League matches only)

	PL	W	D	L
Home:	57	31	17	9
Away:	57	22	16	19
Overall:	114	53	33	28

LAST 2 MEETINGS

01/04/2006
West Brom	0-2	Liverpool
		Fowler 7, Cisse 38

31/12/2005
Liverpool	1-0	West Brom
Crouch 51		

CLUB DETAILS

Nickname: Baggies/Albion
Ground: The Hawthorns, capacity 27,877 (away allocation 3,000)
Manager: Tony Mowbray (app. 13/10/06)
Ex Red: Chris Kirkland
Year formed: 1878

USEFUL INFORMATION

Website: www.wba.premiumtv.co.uk
Address: Halfords Lane, West Bromwich, West Midlands B71 4LF
Switchboard: 08700 668 888

TRAVEL INFORMATION

By Train: The Hawthorns Metro stop is 10 minutes away from the ground, served by a service from Birmingham Snow Hill station.Smethwick Rolf Street is 15 minutes away, served by local trains from Birmingham New Street.
By Bus: 74 (between Birmingham and Dudley), 79 (Birmingham and Wolverhampton) and 450 (Bearwood and West Bromwich) all stop at Birmingham Road.

WEST HAM UNITED

2007/08 STATISTICS

Final position: 10th, Premier League
Best cup runs: QF, League Cup, R3, FA Cup
Player of season: Robert Green
Top scorer (all): 11, Dean Ashton

ALL-TIME RECORD

(League matches only)

	PL	W	D	L
Home:	51	35	13	3
Away:	51	18	15	18
Overall:	102	53	28	21

LAST 2 MEETINGS

05/03/2008
Liverpool	4-0	West Ham
Torres 8, 61, 81,		
Gerrard 83		

30/01/2008
West Ham	1-0	Liverpool
Noble 90 (p)		

CLUB DETAILS

Nickname: The Hammers
Ground: Upton Park, capacity 35,647 (away allocation 2,000)
Manager: TBA
Ex Red: Craig Bellamy
Year formed: 1895

USEFUL INFORMATION

Website: www.whufc.com
Address: Boleyn Ground, Green Street, Upton Park, London E13 9AZ
Switchboard: 0208 548 2748

TRAVEL INFORMATION

By Tube: Upton Park is the closest tube station, around 45 minutes from Central London on the District (and also Hammersmith & City) line. When you exit the station turn right, the stadium is then a two-minute walk. East Ham and Plaistow Stations, which are further away, may also be worth using to avoid congestion after the match.
By Bus: Routes 5, 15, 58, 104, 115, 147, 330 and 376 all serve The Boleyn Ground.

WIGAN ATHLETIC

2007/08 STATISTICS

Final position: 14th, Premier League
Best cup runs: R4, FA Cup, R2, League Cup
Player of season: Paul Scharner
Top scorer (all): 7, Marcus Bent

ALL-TIME RECORD

(League matches only)

	PL	W	D	L
Home:	3	2	1	0
Away:	3	3	0	0
Overall:	6	5	1	0

LAST 2 MEETINGS

02/01/2008

Liverpool	1-1	Wigan
Torres 49		Bramble 80

29/09/2007

Wigan	0-1	Liverpool
		Benayoun 75

CLUB DETAILS

Nickname: The Latics
Ground: JJB Stadium,
capacity 25,023
(away allocation 5,000+)
Manager: Steve Bruce (app. 26/11/07)
Ex Reds: Emile Heskey, Chris Kirkland
Year formed: 1932

USEFUL INFORMATION

Website: www.wiganlatics.co.uk
Address: JJB Stadium, Robin Park,
Newtown, Wigan WN5 0UZ
Switchboard: 01942 774000

TRAVEL INFORMATION

By Train: Wigan Wallgate and Wigan North Western are a 15-minute walk from the stadium. From either station head under the railway bridge and keep to the right - following the road (A49) for 10 minutes. The complex should soon be visible.
By Bus: No particular route, as the venue is within easy distance of the station.

Robbie Keane in action against Liverpool's first European opponents of 2008/09, Standard Liege

LFC IN THE COMMUNITY

TICKETS

Address

Ticket Office,
PO Box 204,
Liverpool
L69 4PQ

Telephone Number

0844 844 0844 (24-Hour Ticket Information Line)
0844 844 2005 (Customer Services)

Ticket Office Hours

Monday-Friday 8.15am-5.30pm
Matchdays 9.15am to kick-off, then 15 minutes after end of game
Non Match Saturdays/Sundays 9.15am-1.00pm

Prices

	Category A	Category B
Kop		
Adult	£37	£35
Over 65	£28	£26
Disabled and Visually Impaired	£28	£26
Main Stand		
Adult	£39	£37
Over 65	£29.50	£28
Centenary		
Adult	£39	£37
Over 65	£29.50	£28
Paddock		
Adult	£39	£37
Over 65	£29.50	£28
Disabled and Visually Impaired	£29.50	£28
Anfield Road		
Adult	£39	£37
Over 65	£29.50	£28
Combined 1 Adult/1 Child (16 or under)	£58.50	£55.50
Disabled and Visually Impaired	£29.50	£28

Category A matches

Arsenal, Aston Villa, Blackburn Rovers, Chelsea, Everton, Manchester City, Manchester United, Newcastle United and Tottenham Hotspur.

Family tickets

For adult/child combined tickets a ratio of two adults to one child, or two children to one adult is allowed. In the event that the number of children exceeds the ratio of 2:1 the additional tickets will be charged at the adult rate.

Buying tickets

General sales begin 18 days before a home fixture and are available through the credit card hotline (Monday-Friday 8.30am-5.30pm - a maximum of four tickets, minimum booking fee of 50p per ticket applies), postal application and for Fan Card holders, online (subject to a booking fee of £2.50 per ticket). A small number are often made available online on the date of general sale.

TICKETS

By post

State the match and number of tickets you require, with the correct remittance and a stamped addressed envelope, to LFC Ticket Office, PO Box 204, Liverpool L69 4PQ. You can pay by cheque, postal order, credit or debit card. Cheques must be made payable to Liverpool FC. If you want to pay by credit or debit card, include card number and expiry date, plus debit card issue number where applicable. If applications exceed the number of tickets, they will be allocated through a ballot.

By phone

You can apply for a maximum of four tickets, by calling the credit card hotline, quoting your credit or debit card number and expiry date. A minimum booking fee of 50p per ticket will be charged. Tickets booked more than three days before the match will be sent out by post, those booked after this must be collected from the credit card collections window at the ticket office, and you must produce the card used to book the tickets.

In person

Any remaining tickets will go on sale at the ticket office 11 days in advance. A maximum of four tickets may be purcased in one transaction (subject to change). However, tickets usually sell out through phone and postal bookings.

Away matches (Barclays Premier League)

Tickets go on sale first based on a priority system (i.e. to supporters who have attended the most away fixtures in the Premiership during season 2007/08 - and subsequently 2008/09). The number of matches attended will be determined from the information held on the ticket office database.

Cup matches

Ticket information concerning European and domestic Cup match allocations are made as soon as possible after each draw has taken place. Supporters are advised that they should quote their Fan Card number for all ticket purcahses, and to retain their ticket stubs for potential use for any additional fixtures allocated on a voucher system or in the ven of a home match being abandoned.

THE LFC FAN CARD

Buying tickets

When purchasing tickets you must provide your Members/Fan Card customer number either by handing your Members/Fan Card to the ticket office, quoting it via the telephone booking line or by post, or using it to log in online. Further information may be requested for security reasons. Purchases made online will require your Members/Fan Card customer number and password.

Only one ticket per match will be recorded on your Members/Fan Card. If applying for tickets as a group it will be necessary for you to disclose each Card customer number and the customer name.

What happens if I lose my Fan Card?

Please let the ticket office know immediately in writing. Your Members/Fan Card will then be deactivated and a new card will be issued for a fee of £10. The data held on your lost or stolen card will be transferred onto your new card. Should you change address, please inform the ticket office in writing, quoting your old address and enclosing a copy of a utility bill (gas, electric, water or telephone) to the ticket office.

OFFICIAL WEBSITE

WWW.LIVERPOOLFC.TV

About

Despite being the last Premiership club to launch an official website in 1999, when the club transformed the independent fans' site 'Mighty Reds' into liverpoolfc.net, the launch of **www.liverpoolfc.tv** in April 2001 propelled the club into the Champions League of football websites, where it has remained as the forerunner ever since.

Within a year, the site was firmly established as the most popular football club website in the world. With up to 2.9 million people visiting up to 64 million pages every month, the website is the first-stop shop for everything LFC... and here are some of the reasons why:

News	24/7 news from Anfield, Melwood and The Academy.
Match	Fixtures, results, match reports, teamsheets, previews and analysis.
Interactive	Communicate with fellow fans on the forums, play LFC games and more!
Mobile	Get Anfield on your phone! Videos, pictures, chants and SMS alerts.
Tickets	Latest availability and selling arrangements, season-ticket renewals, online ticket sales, directions and travel planning.
Team	Player profiles, exclusive interviews, statistics - it's all here.
History	The LFC story – and what a lot there is to tell! Including honours, records, quotes, profiles and pictures.
Shop	The official club online store with a full range of kits and merchandise.

With a new site launching towards the end of 2008 (offering improved content, a new User Generated Content platform for fans to share their own pictures, videos and thoughts), the site is set to build further on it's reputation as being THE place for Liverpool FC supporters from round the globe to stay in touch with the club.

Premium Content

NOW TAKE YOUR SEAT!

The Liverpool FC e-Season Ticket takes you to the heart of the club you love:

- Watch LFC TV, the club's TV channel LIVE or catch up with the best bits, at your leisure
- Watch selected pre-season matches LIVE
- LIVE match commentary & picture slideshow of every LFC game
- Goal clips & video highlights of all our Premier League and Champions League matches
- See the future! Every reserve match exclusively LIVE, plus interviews with future stars
- Exclusive video interviews with players, managers and legends
- The only place to watch every Reds' press conference - IN FULL
- Relive KOP classics – live and breathe Liverpool's history
- Enter our exclusive match ticket ballot

... all from your computer and all from as little as 13 pence per day!

e-Season Ticket is available to fans the world over.
For a FREE PREVIEW, visit **www.liverpoolfc.tv/preview**

OFFICIAL CLUB TV CHANNEL

About

LFC TV is the dedicated channel for Britain's most successful football club. Bringing you unrivalled access to Liverpool FC on and off the pitch, past and present, and is the place to follow the team you love from the comfort of your home.
The exciting programming includes:

- Every minute of every game the Reds play in the Barclays Premier League, Champions League and Carling Cup (TBC), followed by in-depth reaction and analysis.
- Every reserve match – exclusively LIVE. A unique opportunity to cast an eye over the emerging talent knocking on the first-team dressing room door.
- No less than 50% of all friendlies on a live and exclusive basis.
- This is Anfield - The expert and, sometimes controversial, views of former heroes who form the backbone of this live and interactive studio-based chat show. Special guests, presenters and fans debate the big issues, demonstrating why Liverpool followers are rightly considered by many to be the most passionate and knowledgeable in the world.
- LFC Now – The channel's flagship news programme has every angle covered – including exclusive interviews with the manager, former stars and, of course, the current players themselves. Broadcast nightly from our studio complex, the show brings fans all the latest from Anfield, Melwood and the Academy.
- Kop 10 – Who are the 10 greatest Reds to have worn the famous number 7? Who have been our top 10 greatest captains? The "Kop 10" series presents a countdown from 10 to 1 on a variety of Anfield topics. Every Red has an opinion, does yours match ours?
- Sixty Minutes – From Gerrard to Collymore, Torres to Aldridge, Sixty Minutes is the show where we put players past and present in the studio hot-seat and ask them questions set by the supporters. Hear us quiz the legends and hear their stories of this great club.

Join us for all of this plus much, much more!
Available in the UK and Ireland (Sky Channel 434, Virgin Media Channel 544)
as part of the Setanta Sports Pack.

LFC TV is also available to watch worldwide on **www.liverpoolfc.tv** as part of e-Season Ticket, the official website's premium content service. Plus selected programmes are available on demand – watch your favourite programmes as and when you want (previous seven days archive available in full plus selected classic available indefinitely)! All this and more for as little as 13 pence a day!

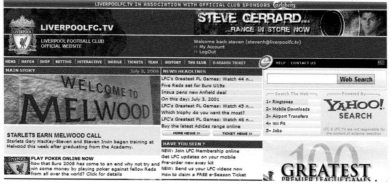

www.liverpoolfc.tv homepage, July 2008

MUSEUM & STADIUM TOUR

"The very word Anfield means more to me than I can describe."
Bill Shankly

Anfield - the name alone conjures up a million memories; be they good or bad, tragic or triumphant. It is one of the oldest and most famous football grounds in the world. Originally the home of Everton Football Club between 1884 and 1892, Anfield has long since become synonymous with Liverpool Football Club and the amazing success achieved by the Reds.

Over the years some of football's greatest names have graced the hallowed turf (which is actually grown from seed) and contributed to some of the most memorable matches ever played. Just think Inter Milan 1965, St Etienne 1976, Chelsea 2005 and 2007, to name but four!

The legendary Anfield atmosphere, associated with the Spion Kop Stand but actually made by the 45,000 squeezed into this intimate cauldron of a ground, is renowned throughout the world. The flags, banners, wit and singing have even been celebrated on television, radio, film, CD and DVD.

"It's the atmosphere that I love. It's unbelievable. I've played in a lot of stadia, but for me there is nothing like playing at Liverpool."
Thierry Henry

With plans to create a new LFC Stadium close by in Stanley Park, you will want to see Anfield Stadium before it finally becomes history itself, and there is an excellent Stadium Tour, which runs on most (non-match) days.

About

The stadium tour will take you on a walk from the players' tunnel down into the dressing rooms (the home dressing room has been extensively re-furbished in 2008), view the referee's room, imagine standing in front of the cameras in the interview areas, and then touch the famous "This is Anfield" sign as you walk down the players' tunnel to the sound of 45,000 cheering fans!

Sit in the dug out, and then visit the Kop - the largest single-tier stand in Europe – accompanied the whole time by two knowledgeable and enthusiastic guides who will tell you all about the club and give you behind-the-scenes insights into match day!

You can then explore the museum, packed with history – see a blue and white player's shirt as first worn by Liverpool in 1892 – right up to Xabi Alonso's boots and the match ball from the 2005 Champions League Final, and now, the 2008 Premier League Reserve Trophy.

See the five European Cups that make Liverpool FC one of only three clubs to have ever won this great prize five times or more. See also the FA Cup, League Cup, UEFA Cup, Super Cup and of course, the First Division League trophy – won a record-breaking 18 times – and many other trophies, medals, shirts, programmes, banners and other unique memorabilia.

The museum and stadium tour has been breaking all previous attendance records in recent years; now in the region of 160,000 visits a year, and Anfield is truly a "must-see destination" for any visitor to the City of Liverpool.

Whether you support LFC or not – everyone is welcome to Anfield, but beware – you might just go away a Red!

MUSEUM & STADIUM TOUR

Opening times:	Every day of the week from 10am until 5pm.
	Last admission to museum 4pm.
	On match days last admission is 1 hour before kick-off.
	NO STADIUM TOURS ON MATCH DAYS.
	Tours on day before a match will be MINI TOURS, at reduced prices.
Museum & Tour Prices:	Adults £10.00, Children/Student/OAPS £6.00, Family £25.00
Museum Prices:	Adults £5.00, Children/OAPS £3.00 Families, £13.00
	WE RECOMMEND BOOKING IN ADVANCE FOR STADIUM TOURS.
	THERE IS NO NEED TO PRE-BOOK A MUSEUM-ONLY VISIT.
	All times and prices subject to change at short notice.
	Due to operational reasons, tours can be cancelled at very short notice.
Booking hotline:	0151 260 6677

Important Security Information

We regret that we cannot accept suitcases and other large and bulky items into either the Museum or Stadium. There is no place to store such items in the ground.

European souvenirs adorn the LFC Museum at Anfield

THE ANFIELD EXPERIENCE

Liverpool Football Club offers you the perfect opportunity to treat yourself or anybody else to a choice of two exclusive VIP days. These can be purchased either as an open voucher giving you the flexibility to redeem the day over the next nine months (subject to availability) or on a specific date. As they come in a stylish presentation pack which can be personalised for the lucky recipient, they make the perfect gift for any Liverpool fan.

The stadium tour takes you behind the scenes at Anfield, visiting the dressing rooms, down the tunnel to the sound of the crowd, a chance to touch the famous "This Is Anfield" sign and sit in the team dug-out. Informative tour guides will tell you about the historic Anfield Stadium and escort you on to The Kop - the most famous terrace in world football. Bring your cameras and hand-held video recorders to take those precious pictures of the stadium and museum.

You'll enjoy a luxurious "Heathcotes at Anfield" three-course lunch in one of our executive boxes overlooking the pitch - expect one of our Legends to drop in and make a special personal appearance. Before you leave with your limited edition gift, join the rest of the guests for a fun question and answer session with your Liverpool Legend. A great day out for all Liverpool fans!

THE ULTIMATE ANFIELD EXPERIENCE

What if you could live a life in the day of a Liverpool Legend? Take a nostalgic tour around Anfield Stadium and Museum, and revel in the club's great history. Then play with Reds' Legends at the Liverpool Academy in a unique training session before dining with them in one of our luxury suites. The Ultimate Anfield Experience is truly unique.
You'll be spending a day at the club you love...meeting past greats, collecting autographs and accessing areas of Liverpool FC that few fans are privileged to see. It's a real once-in-a-lifetime VIP experience.
For more information please call **0151 263 7744** or visit **www.theanfieldexperience.com**

GETTING TO ANFIELD

How to get there - by car
Follow the M62 until you reach the end of the motorway. Then follow the A5058 towards Liverpool for 3 miles, then turn left at the traffic lights into Utting Avenue (there is a McDonalds on the corner of this junction). Proceed for one mile and then turn right at The Arkles pub for the ground. It is recommended that you arrive at least two hours before kick-off in order to secure your parking spec. Otherwise, you can park in the streets around Goodison Park and walk across Stanley Park to Anfield, or you can park in a secure parking area at Goodison.

How to get there - by train
Kirkdale Station is the closest to Anfield (about a mile away), although Sandhills Station the stop before has the benefit of a bus service to the ground (Soccerbus). Both stations can be reached by first getting a train from Liverpool Lime Street (which is over 3 miles from the ground) to Liverpool Central (Merseyrail Northern Line), and then changing there for trains to Sandhills (2 stops away) or Kirkdale (3 stops). Note: only trains to Ormskirk or Kirkby go to Kirkdale station. A taxi from Liverpool Lime Street should cost between £5 and £7.

How to get there - Soccerbus
There are frequent shuttle buses from Sandhills Station, to Anfield for all Liverpool home Premiership and Cup matches. Soccerbus will run for two hours before each match (last bus from Sandhills Station is approximately 15 minutes before kick-off) and for 50 minutes after the final whistle (subject to availability). You can pay as you board the bus. Soccerbus is FREE for those who hold a valid TRIO, SOLO or SAVEAWAY ticket or Merseytravel Free Travel Pass.

How to get there - by bus
Take a 26 (or 27) from Paradise Street Bus Station or a 17B, 17C, 17D, or 217 from Queen Square bus station directly to the ground. The 68 and 168 which operate between Bootle and Aigburth and the 14 (from Queen Square) and 19 stop a short walk away.

How to get there - by air
Liverpool John Lennon Airport is around 10 miles from the ground, and taxis should be easily obtainable. Alternatively, you can catch the 80A bus to Garston Station and change at Sandhills for the Soccerbus service.

How to get there - on foot
From Kirkdale Station, turn right and then cross the railway bridge, where you will see the Melrose Abbey pub. Walk past up Westminster Road for around 1/3 of a mile before you arrive at the Elm Tree pub. Follow the road around the right-hand bend and then turn left into Bradwell Street. At the end of the road you will come to County Road (A59). Cross over at the traffic lights and then go down the road to the left of the Aldi superstore. At the end of this road you will reach Walton Lane (A580). You should be able to see Goodison Park on your left and Stanley Park in front of you. Cross Walton Lane and either enter Stanley Park, following the footpath through the park (keeping to the right) which will exit into Anfield Road. As an alternative to going through Stanley Park, bear right down Walton Lane and then turn left down the road at the end of Stanley Park to the ground.

To check bus and train times (8am-8pm, 7 days a week):

Traveline Merseyside   0870 608 2 608
Soccerbus   0151 330 1066

CLUB STORES

Selling everything from the new replica kits to the latest toys and games, the club stores provide Reds fans with a wealth of souvenirs. With the new adidas range having been unveiled, there remains a wealth of choice for the new season.
Addresses and contact details are as follows:

Williamson Square Official Club Store

11 Williamson Square, Liverpool, L1 1EQ
United Kingdom
Tel +44 (0)151 330 3077
Opening times: Mon-Sat 9.00am - 5.30pm
Sundays 10.00am - 4.00pm

Liverpool One Superstore

7 South John Street, Liverpool, L1 8BU
United Kingdom
Tel +44 (0)151 709 4345
Opening times: Mon-Fri 9.30am - 8.00pm
Saturdays 9.00am - 7.00pm
Sundays 11.00am - 5.00pm

Anfield Official Club Store

Telephone +44 (0)151 263 1760
Fax +44 (0)151 264 9088
Opening times Mon - Fri 9.00am - 5.00pm
Saturdays 9.00am - 5.00pm
Sundays 10.00am - 4.00pm
Match Saturdays 9.00am - 45 mins after game
Match Sundays 10.00am - 45 mins after game
Match Evenings 9.00am - 45 mins after game

Chester Official Club Store

48 Eastgate Street, Chester, CH1 1LE
United Kingdom
Tel +44 (0)1244 344 608
Opening times: Mon-Sat 9.00am - 5.30pm
Sundays 10.00am - 4.00pm

Online Store

liverpoolfc.tv

Ordering by phone

0844 800 4239
(International calls) +44 138 684 8247
(Lines open 8am-9pm Monday-Sunday)

New layout at the Liverpool One Superstore

MATCHDAY PROGRAMME AND OFFICIAL MAGAZINE

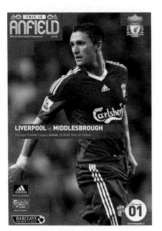

Official Matchday Programme

Liverpool's award-winning official matchday programme is written and produced in Liverpool by Sport Media on behalf of the club. The 84-page publication includes new features such as The Pool, The Annie Road Corner, 78/79 relived, exclusive Anfield news, features, a message from the manager plus captain's notes while for the new campaign there will be a column with one of six different personalities, including John Bishop and Peter Hooton.

How to subscribe

Phone: 0845 143 0001 (Monday-Friday 9am-5pm)
Website: **liverpoolfc.tv/match/magazine**
(Also available in braille and other formats - contact community department on 0151 264 2316 for details)

LFC Magazine

Liverpool are the only club boasting an official weekly magazine in the Premiership. The Sport Media-produced glossy *LFC Magazine*, priced £2.10, provides up-to-date news and views on all aspects of the club, from exclusive player interviews, match previews and reports to features on former players and famous Reds - plus the most accurate, up-to-date statistics. Regular features include LFCCTV, while the mag will keep an eye on the fortune of AFC Liverpool. Legendary duo Kenny Dalglish and Alan Hansen also remain as star columnists.

How to subscribe

Phone: 0845 143 0001 (Monday-Friday 9am-5pm)
Website: **liverpoolfc.tv/match/magazine**

LFC Family Album

This new publication is an up-to-date keepsake for all Liverpool supporters who have revelled in the modern-day glory years while still keeping an eye on the past triumphs that continue to inspire future generations Heroes like Steven Gerrard, Jamie Carragher, Sami Hyypia and Fernando Torres are among the many who give us their personal take on unique moments captured in time by the camera lens. Former players and celebrities also contribute as do the legendary fans that make the club so special.

How to order

Phone: 0845 143 0001 (Monday-Friday 9am-5pm)
Website: **merseyshop.com/**

ASSOCIATION OF INTERNATIONAL BRANCHES

About

There are almost 200 Association of International Branches, and several new ones are being formed each season. Benefits of affiliating include the chance to attend an exclusive Q&A session with a Reds legend, as well as meeting like-minded supporters in your area.

However, please note that new branches have restricted access to tickets.

If there isn't an AIB near you, why not form one. You'll need 25 supporters and will have to pay a small fee and sign up to AIB regulations.

Contact Details

For further details or information on your nearest branch, please call:
0844 499 3000 or fax **0151 264 7213**.

LIVERPOOL DISABLED SUPPORTERS' ASSOCIATION

Aims and Objectives

To act in partnership with Liverpool Football Club to promote inclusiveness for the disabled fans of the club, the disabled fans of visiting clubs as well as those individuals who support disabled people and those with impairments.

This association recognises that all fans should have an equal opportunity to participate in an enjoyable matchday experience and that people with disabilities and/or impairments must have their interests recognised and promoted by LFC with equal status to that of all other Liverpool fans.

Contact Details

Disability liaison officer Colin McCall continues to develop the LDSA, acting as a link between the club and its supporters. The LDSA committee is made up of 10 members who are all Liverpool supporters and they meet once a month with the liaison officer to discuss disability issues at LFC.

If you would like any more information about the LDSA then please email **LDSA@liverpoolfc.tv** or write to **LDSA, Liverpool Football Club, Anfield Road, Liverpool, L4 0TH**.

REDUC@TE

About

The Liverpool FC Study Support Centre has been open for eight years and almost 30,000 children have benefitted from the fun and enjoyable educational activities on offer. The main aim is to help children improve their skills in literacy, numeracy and ICT.

New

Software, equipment and special 'Spanish Learning Days', with children attending sessions chauffeured to and from Reduc@te in our brand new Reduc@te minibus, the keys of which were handed over by Liverpool manager Rafael Benitez (right).

Contact Details

Centre manager, Keith White.
Telephone: **0151 263 1313**
Email: **krwhite.lfc.study@talk21.com** or **keith.white@liverpoolfc.tv**

LIVERPOOL FC OFFICIAL MEMBERSHIP

About

Feel part of your club with the Liverpool FC Official Membership.

For 2008/09 Liverpool Football Club is pleased to announce a new and improved membership scheme with a whole host of new benefits for members. Join today and you'll enjoy discounts, free gifts, exclusive offers and more access to match tickets!

Membership Benefits

- Access to Liverpool Ticket Exchange.
- 10% off merchandise in all official club stores.
- Exclusive Stevie G DVD.
- Discounted e-Season Ticket.
- Free SMS ticket alerts.
- Executive pen, key ring and notepad.
- Members' monthly prize draws.
- LFC Reserves home games discount.
- Museum and Stadium Tour discount.
- Discount on LFC Weekly Magazine.
- Christmas card and gift.
- Exclusive offers from LFC partners.

Junior Membership Benefits (recommended for ages 5-11)

- Access to Liverpool Ticket Exchange.
- 10% off merchandise in all official club stores.
- Exclusive Stevie G DVD.
- LFC Reserves home games discount.
- Free SMS ticket alerts.
- Museum and Stadium Tour discount.
- Members' monthly prize draws.
- Discount on LFC weekly magazine.
- Junior member magazine.
- Mascot draw.
- Christmas Soccer School draw.
- Personalised certificate.
- Football fun book and LFC stopwatch.
- Referee pack.
- Christmas card and gift.
- Exclusive offers from LFC partners.

Prices

Adult Members: £29 (Inc P&P)
Junior Members: £20 (Inc P&P)

How to Join

Visit **www.liverpoolfc.tv/membership** or telephone **0844 499 3000**.

LIVERPOOL PR DEPARTMENT

About

Headed by former player Brian Hall, the Public Relations department plays an important role in communicating with the huge national and international fan base that support our club.

Thousands of letters are received and answered, with requests concerning just about every aspect of life at Liverpool Football Club.

Please Note: THE PR DEPARTMENT DO NOT DEAL WITH REQUESTS FOR MATCH DAY TICKETS

The sheer volume of mail, especially for autographs, requires us to answer most in a standard format with pre-printed signed photos of the team and individual players. The PR department produce an information pack which covers many aspects of club activities.

The demand for players to sign autographs is enormous, so the club have to prioritise and focus on special needs and terminally ill youngsters/adults. Charities are also given priority for help with fundraising activities.

The PR department also organise visits to our training ground, Melwood, to meet staff and players for photos and autographs, again they prioritise as above. At the end of each season, the redundant matchday and training kits are distributed around the world to help support the wonderful work of the many Relief Agencies.

The national anti-racism campaigns, "Show Racism the Red Card" and "Kick it Out", are supported each year through this department. Other strong and important social messages are backed by the club through the PR department. For example, art competitions in schools are promoted using the influential images of our players, supporting "Kick Drugs into Touch", "Give Smoking the Boot"and other social messages.

2007/08

The club have supported the charity "Football Aid" for many years and the calendar year 2008 was the most successful to date with £61,000 being raised. This is the largest amount raised by one club for Football Aid.

If you have ever dreamed of playing at Anfield then visit their website **www.footballaid.com** where dreams do come true.

Alder Hey

The highlight of the year is the annual visit to Alder Hey Children's Hospital in Liverpool. The department organise the visit by the first-team squad who see every child in the hospital and give them all a Christmas present from Liverpool Football Club. The visit is emotional but very rewarding for everyone concerned.

Right: Ryan Babel and pupils from Shorefields Community School "Kick Out Racism"

Contact details

Telephone:	0151 260 1433
Fax:	0151 264 2918
E-mail:	**pr.department@liverpoolfc.tv**

LFC IN THE COMMUNITY

About

Liverpool Football Club's community department is a vibrant and multi-functional area of the club. The department has a close and wide-ranging involvement with local schools, sports centres, community organisations and resident groups.

Truth 4 Youth Assemblies
We visit schools with important messages of: Give Bullying the Boot, Show Racism the Red Card, Kick Drugs into Touch, More important than being a Good Footballer is being a Good Person, Health is Wealth, Before you Please think Disease, We is better than Me, Shoot Goals not Guns and You'll Never Walk Alone. These assemblies are enjoyable but sometimes hard-hitting and greatly appreciated by teachers and pupils alike.

Coaching 4 All
We provide free football coaching in schools, after schools clubs and community centres. Coaching is also provided in school half terms and summer holidays.

Respect 4 All
Providing free football coaching in special needs schools and adult day centres. The department also has five disabled football teams. In 2008 we began running an after schools academy for young people who are blind, deaf, wheelchair bound or with severe learning difficulties.

SweeperZone
Now in its sixth year, this project has 15 groups and gives away, over the season, 750 free matchday tickets.

Tactics 4 Families
An initiative aimed specifically at supporting positive family relationships. The project is aimed at parents as well as children.

Kickz
A football-based community project that aims to engage with young people aged 12-18 years using local ball parks and facilities.

Football 4 All
A social diversity project to deliver grass-roots football coaching to young people from ethnic and low social income backgrounds.

Care 4 All
A project to provide care and support to all children, regardless of their age, race, background or ability.

Young Person of the Year Award
A prestigious evening, attended by a first-team player, to commend local young people for either their courage, bravery, caring and commitment to others, or the community.

Charity 4 All
Sending old and unused kit to the poor and needy in third-world countries.

For detailed information on the above please see our website **liverpoolfc.tv/community**
To get involved in any of the above schemes email us at **community.department@liverpoolfc.tv**

Liverpool FC : The Official Guide 2009

2009	Jan	Feb	March	April	May	June
Monday						1
Tuesday						2
Wednesday				1		3
Thursday	1			2		4
Friday	2			3	1	5
Saturday	3			4	2	6
Sunday	4	1	1	5	3	7
Monday	5	2	2	6	4	8
Tuesday	6	3	3	7	5	9
Wednesday	7	4	4	8	6	10
Thursday	8	5	5	9	7	11
Friday	9	6	6	10	8	12
Saturday	10	7	7	11	9	13
Sunday	11	8	8	12	10	14
Monday	12	9	9	13	11	15
Tuesday	13	10	10	14	12	16
Wednesday	14	11	11	15	13	17
Thursday	15	12	12	16	14	18
Friday	16	13	13	17	15	18
Saturday	17	14	14	18	16	20
Sunday	18	15	15	18	17	21
Monday	18	16	16	20	18	22
Tuesday	20	17	17	21	18	23
Wednesday	21	18	18	22	20	24
Thursday	22	18	18	23	21	25
Friday	23	20	20	24	22	26
Saturday	24	21	21	25	23	27
Sunday	25	22	22	26	24	28
Monday	26	23	23	27	25	29
Tuesday	27	24	24	28	26	30
Wednesday	28	25	25	29	27	
Thursday	29	26	26	30	28	
Friday	30	27	27		29	
Saturday	31	28	28		30	
Sunday			29		31	
Monday			30			
Tuesday			31			

July	Aug	Sept	Oct	Nov	Dec	
						Monday
		1			1	Tuesday
		2			2	Wednesday
		3	1		3	Thursday
		4	2		4	Friday
1		5	3		5	Saturday
2		6	4	1	6	Sunday
3		7	5	2	7	Monday
4		8	6	3	8	Tuesday
5		9	7	4	9	Wednesday
6		10	8	5	10	Thursday
7		11	9	6	11	Friday
8		12	10	7	12	Saturday
9		13	11	8	13	Sunday
10		14	12	9	14	Monday
11		15	13	10	15	Tuesday
12		16	14	11	16	Wednesday
13		17	15	12	17	Thursday
14		18	16	13	18	Friday
15		18	17	14	18	Saturday
16		20	18	15	20	Sunday
17		21	18	16	21	Monday
18		22	20	17	22	Tuesday
18		23	21	18	23	Wednesday
20		24	22	18	24	Thursday
21		25	23	20	25	Friday
22		26	24	21	26	Saturday
23		27	25	22	27	Sunday
24		28	26	23	28	Monday
25		29	27	24	29	Tuesday
26		30	28	25	30	Wednesday
27			29	26	31	Thursday
28			30	27		Friday
29			31	28		Saturday
30				29		Sunday
31				30		Monday
						Tuesday

OTHER USEFUL CONTACTS

The Premier League
30, Gloucester Place, London W1U 8PL
Phone: 0207 864 9000
Email: **info@premierleague.com**

The Football Association
25 Soho Square, London W1D 4FA
Phone: 0207 745 4545

The Football League
Edward VII Quay, Navigation Way,
Preston, Lancashire
PR2 2YF
Email: **fl@football-league.co.uk**

Professional Footballers' Association
2, Oxford Court,
Bishopsgate,
Off Lower Mosley Street,
Manchester
M2 3WQ
Phone: 0161 236 0575
Email: **info@thepfa.co.uk**

Hillsborough Family
Support Group
69, Anfield Road,
Liverpool
L4 0TH
Phone: 0151 264 2931
Email: **hfsg@liverpoolfc.tv**

LFC logo and crest are registered trade marks of
The Liverpool Football Club and Athletics Grounds.
Published in Great Britain in 2008 by: Trinity Mirror Sport Media, PO Box 48, Old Hall Street, Liverpool L69 3EB

ISBN: 1 9052 6665 4
978 1 9052 6665 4

Printed and finished by Scotprint, Haddington, Scotland